The Debate in
the United States
over Immigration

The Hoover Institution
gratefully acknowledges generous support from

TAD TAUBE
TAUBE FAMILY FOUNDATION
KORET FOUNDATION

Founders of the Program on
American Institutions and Economic Performance

and Cornerstone gifts from

JOANNE AND JOHAN BLOKKER
SARAH SCAIFE FOUNDATION

The Debate in the United States over Immigration

Edited by
Peter Duignan
and
L. H. Gann

Hoover Institution Press
Stanford University
Stanford, California

Hoover Institution Press Publication No. 444

Copyright © 1998 by the Board of Trustees of the
  Leland Stanford Junior University

First printing, 1998
04   03   02   01   00   99   98   9   8   7   6   5   4   3   2   1

Manufactured in the United States of America

The paper used in this publication meets the minimum requirements
of American National Standard for Information Sciences—Permanence
of Paper for Printed Library Materials, ANSI Z39.48–1984. ⊗

Library of Congress Cataloging-in-Publication Data
The debate in the United States over immigration / edited by
Peter Duignan and L. H. Gann
        p.   cm.
   Includes bibliographical references and index.
   ISBN 0-8179-9522-6
   1. United States—Emigration and immigration—Government policy.
I. Duignan, Peter.   II. Gann, Lewis H., 1924–1997.
JV6483.D42   1997
325.73—dc21   97-39555
                                               CIP

CONTENTS

PREFACE

This volume follows from a Hoover Institution conference on U.S. immigration held October 17–18, 1996; a conference agenda is contained in an appendix to this volume. The conference was conceived by Hoover fellows Peter Duignan and Lewis Gann and Hoover associate director and senior fellow Gerald Dorfman. Unfortunately, Lewis Gann passed away before this volume could be published.

Following an introduction into the salient issues in the immigration debate by coeditors Duignan and Gann, this collection of essays begins with articles on the perceived costs and benefits of immigration into the United States along with an examination of current rules and regulations associated with immigration. Concluding essays examine specific welfare, education, and employment issues.

Continuing analysis of the impact of legal and illegal immigration into the United States is part of the Hoover Institution's Program on American Institutions and Economic Performance. This program addresses two overarching questions: (1) How can the U.S. economy provide an ever-higher quality of life, increased economic opportunity, and greater economic freedom for all? and (2) Why do U.S. government institutions, despite enormous expenditures of financial and human resources, seem incapable of, or at least have great difficulty in, solving persistent economic and social problems?

Convening scholars and managing a scholarly project requires both talent and efficiency. The Hoover Institution is fortunate to have able administrative assistance, at the direction of Associate Director Richard Sousa, to undertake these projects. I am pleased to acknowledge Joanne Fraser-Thompson and Teresa Terry Judd for their assistance in putting on the conference and Patricia Baker, executive editor of the Hoover Press, and the staff at the Hoover Press for their efforts in publishing this volume.

John Raisian
Director, Hoover Institution

CONTRIBUTORS

STUART ANDERSON was formerly director of trade and immigration studies at the Cato Institute

ROY BECK is the author of two books on the effects of immigration on the American people: *The Case against Immigration: The Moral, Economic, Social and Environmental Reasons for Reducing Immigration Back to Traditional Levels* (Norton, 1996) and *Re-Charting America's Future: Responses to Arguments against Stabilizing U.S. Population and Limiting Immigration* (Social Contract Press, 1994). He has written about the subject for dozens of publications including the *Atlantic Monthly*, *National Review*, and *Washington Post* and is Washington editor of the *Social Contract*, a quarterly journal.

GEORGE J. BORJAS is a professor of public policy at the John F. Kennedy School of Government at Harvard University and a research associate at the National Bureau of Economic Research. His teaching and research interests focus on the impact of government regulations on labor markets, with an emphasis on the economic impact of immigration. He is the author of *Wage Policy in the Federal Bureaucracy*; *Friends or Strangers: The Impact of Immigrants on the U.S. Economy*;

and the textbook *Labor Economics* and is the coeditor of *Immigration and the Work Force*. He has been a consultant to various government agencies and is an economic adviser to California governor Pete Wilson. Borjas received his Ph.D. in economics from Columbia.

PETER BRIMELOW is a senior editor of *Forbes* and *National Review* magazines. He was educated at the University of Sussex in England and at Stanford University's Graduate School of Business and is the author of *Alien Nation: Common Sense about America's Immigration Disaster* (1994).

JOSEPH B. COSTELLO is the president and CEO of Cadence Design Systems in San Jose, California.

PETER DUIGNAN took his M.A. and Ph.D. degrees at Stanford University and lectured there for three years before joining the Hoover Institution in 1960. He is now a senior fellow emeritus at Hoover. He has been awarded Ford, Guggenheim, and Rockefeller Fellowships, was a visiting scholar at Saint Antony's College, Oxford, at Jesus College, Cambridge, and the Institute for Advanced Study, Princeton. He was elected a member of the Royal Historical Society of Great Britain in 1995. He has written, with Lewis H. Gann, *The Hispanics in the United States: A History* (1986), *The Rebirth of the West: The Americanization of the Democratic World, 1945–1958* (1991), *The United States and the New Europe, 1945–1993* (Blackwell, 1994), and *Contemporary Europe and the Atlantic Alliance* (1997).

LEWIS H. GANN, who died suddenly in early 1997, was a senior fellow at the Hoover Institution. He was a historian, author, coauthor, or coeditor of some thirty-eight published works and monographs dealing with modern African history and the history of Western Europe. Gann was a Domus Scholar of Balliol College, Oxford, was elected a fellow of the Royal Historical Society, and was awarded the Officer's Cross of the Order of Merit of the German Federal Republic in 1995. His past posts include visiting appointments at Saint Antony's College, Oxford, the Historische Kommission zu Berlin, and the Institute for Advanced Study, Princeton.

NICHOLAS IMPARATO is a research fellow at the Hoover Institution and a professor of marketing and management at the University of San Francisco.

STEPHEN H. LEGOMSKY is the Charles Nagel Professor of International and Comparative Law at Washington University in Saint Louis, Missouri. He is the author of *Immigration Law and Policy,* which has been adopted as the required text for immigration courses at eighty-four American law schools. His other books include *Immigration and the Judiciary: Law and Politics in Britain and America* and *Specialised Justice.* Legomsky has chaired the immigration law section of the Association of American Law Schools and the Law Professors Committee of the American Immigration Lawyers Association. He has testified before Congress and has advised President Clinton's transition team, President Bush's commission of immigration, the Administrative Conference of the United States, and the immigration ministers of Russia and Ukraine on migration, refugee, and citizenship issues. He is an elected member of the American Law Institute. Legomsky has taught or researched these subjects in England, Mexico, New Zealand, Switzerland, Germany, Italy, Austria, and Australia.

PHILIP L. MARTIN is a professor of agricultural economics at the University of California at Davis. He earned a joint Ph.D. in economics and agricultural economics at the University of Wisconsin at Madison in 1975. He is the author of books and articles on European guest-worker programs, U.S. farmworkers, and the relationship between migration and development in Turkey, Mexico, and Egypt and edits the monthly *Migration News* and the quarterly *Rural Migration News* (both available on the Internet). He was a member of the Commission on Agricultural Workers (1989–1993).

KEVIN F. MCCARTHY is the coordinator of California Research and research group manager for International Studies. He is the former director of RAND's Institute for Civil Justice.

LANCE DIRECTOR NAGEL is an attorney with Cooley, Godward, Castro, Huddleston and Tatum.

JEFFREY S. PASSEL is director of the Urban Institute's Program for Research on Immigration Policy, a program aimed at providing analysis and research to inform the nation's immigration and immigrant policies. Before joining the Urban Institute in 1989, Passel directed the Census Bureau's program of population estimates and projections. His research at the Urban Institute has focused on the demography of immigration, particularly the measurement of illegal immigration and the impacts of integration of immigrants into American society. Most recently, Passel and his colleagues have been investigating the fiscal impacts of immigrants, including taxes paid and social services used. Recent publications include *Immigration and Immigrants: Setting the Record Straight* (with Michael Fix), *Immigration and Ethnicity: The Integration of America's Newest Immigrants* (edited with Barry Edmonston), and *Undocumented Migration to the United States: IRCA and the Experience of the 1980s* (edited with Frank D. Bean and Barry Edmonston).

PETER SKERRY teaches political science and public policy at Claremont McKenna College. He is also a nonresident senior fellow in the Government Studies Program at the Brookings Institution, where he is doing research on the politics of the U.S. census and on U.S. immigration policy. Skerry has been a fellow at the Woodrow Wilson International Center for Scholars in Washington and served as director of Washington Programs for the University of California at Los Angeles's Center for American Politics and Public Policy, where he also taught political science. His writings on politics, racial and ethnic issues, and social policy have appeared in a variety of scholarly and general-interest publications. His book *Mexican Americans: The Ambivalent Minority* was awarded the 1993 Los Angeles Times Book Prize. Skerry received his Ph.D. in political science from Harvard University.

GEORGES VERNEZ is director of RAND's Center for Research on Immigration Policy. He is founder and former director of RAND's Institute on Education and Training. He writes extensively on immigration, human resources, and education.

Peter Duignan and
L. H. Gann

INTRODUCTION

From the United States' very beginnings, Americans have vigorously debated the merits of immigration. (Although the colonists wanted more immigrants to come, George III called for fewer. One of the crimes imputed to George III by the Declaration of Independence was "Obstructing the Laws for the Naturalization of Foreigners" and "Refusing to encourage their Migration hither.") Since the beginning of the nineteenth century hostility to immigration has been common in the United States, but it has increased of late, finding expression, for instance, in California's 1994 Proposition 187 denying welfare benefits to illegal immigrants. Thereafter, a Commission on Immigration Reform (1994) called for fewer immigrants and for a registration system against employment of illegal aliens. By 1996, four laws were working their way through Congress. One passed the Senate, another passed the House, and a reconciliation bill cleared Congress in late 1996. Immigration has steadily increased since 1986, as have welfare costs for these new immigrants. Many critics worry that this increase will change the United States ethnically, culturally, and politically because many of the immigrants are Asian or Hispanic and thus supposedly threaten the United States' European traditions.

All too many immigrants, the argument continues, come to the United States just to get welfare; the newcomers allegedly contribute disproportionately to the crime rate; they also are accused of taking jobs from unskilled whites, women, and blacks. The yearly number of immigrants is at an all-time high in absolute numbers but not in relative numbers. The immigrants, moreover, are concentrated in five states (California, Texas, New York, Illinois, Florida) and are therefore highly visible. The presence of so many newcomers supposedly entails high costs for local government services such as schooling, medical care, and welfare. Many of the new immigrants (mainly Hispanics) have little education, lack specialized skills or knowledge of English. Overall, recent immigrants are less well educated than are the native born. Indeed, the proportion of skilled immigrants may have declined since the 1986 reforms because of amnestied illegals (2.6 million) who on average had less than nine years schooling and who, once legalized, brought in millions of family members. The economic crisis in Mexico since 1994 has also pushed hundreds of thousands more into the United States. Illegal immigration has especially upset Americans, and some politicians, like Pat Buchanan, have called for closing the border and stopping all immigration.

The immigration debate has thus become a personal issue for millions of Americans and perhaps one of economic survival for some high-tech firms. The immigration controversy covers many contentious issues. The United States, for instance, provides generous welfare benefits. How far should immigrants, including refugees and elderly people, be permitted to benefit from them? What are the political, as well as the social, costs of immigration? Do immigrants take jobs from Americans or cause crime? What of the burden thrown on state and local governments? What is the extent and what are the costs of illegal immigration? Are there too many immigrants altogether? How many should there be? Does the United States, in fact, need only skilled newcomers? Now that the cold war has ended, does the United States still need a large refugee program? How can the United States control immigration?[1] These are hard questions to answer.

Historical Background

Public opinion polls taken since the end of World War II indicate a striking decline of ethnic and religious prejudice in the United States. But now a new specter has come to haunt the land, fear of foreigners—the "new immigrants." Earlier immigrants had overwhelmingly come from Europe. In 1965, however, U.S. policy changed decisively. The preference for Europeans was abandoned; henceforth, the great majority of newcomers would be Asians and, above all, Hispanic people from Mexico and other Spanish-speaking countries. Equally important in effecting this shift was the postwar recovery of Europe. Highly industrialized countries such as Germany and Britain, France, and later Italy and Spain ceased to send abroad large numbers of emigrants but themselves attracted newcomers from Europe's rural or semirural periphery, from as far afield as Turkey and Algeria.

As regards the United States, the pace of immigration likewise grew in a striking fashion. (Between 1940 and 1990 alone, more than eighteen million foreigners entered the United States legally and millions more illegally.) Each decade saw more newcomers than had arrived in the previous ten years. By 1993, the annual intake amounted to more than 900,000.[2] (In addition to the newcomers who were born abroad, the United States also has a substantial number from Puerto Rico who

---

1. See Joe Cobb, *Issues: The Candidate's Briefing Book*, chapter 11, "Immigration" (Washington, D.C.: Heritage Foundation, 1996).

2. The numbers were 1941–1950: 100,035; 1951–1960: 200,515; 1961–1970: 300,322; 1971–1980: 400,493; 1981–1990: 700,338; 1991–1993: 300,705; (see Cobb, "Immigration," p. 10).

are not counted as immigrants because the islanders are U.S. citizens who can come and go freely.)

Since 1965, the great majority of newcomers have been Hispanics or Asians. (In 1993, 904,292 foreigners legally entered the United States. Of these, 301,380 derived from the Americas and 358,049 from Asia.) As a result, the ethnic composition of the foreign-born population shifted radically (see table 1).

In a certain sense, the United States has become truly a world nation. Asians include newcomers from countries as diverse as China, India, Korea, Japan, Pakistan, Vietnam, Cambodia, Laos—an extraordinary mix. Roughly 9,000,000 people who live in the United States are of Asian descent; those of Chinese ancestry make up 23 percent of the total; Filipino, 20 percent; Asian Indian, 12 percent; and Japanese, Korean, and Vietnamese, each about 10 percent. Asians are America's fastest-growing ethnic group, but only in Hawaii do they constitute a majority. The highest concentration on the mainland—more than 35 percent—is in San Francisco. Mexicans form the largest Latin American group, but Latins too have become more diverse—with Cubans, Guatemalans, Dominicans, Chileans, El Salvadorans, and a host of others.[3] The newcomers are equally mixed in terms of culture and education.

Traditionally, Americans used to think of immigrants as poor people who would naturally start at the bottom of the ladder. To some extent, this pattern continues, as many newcomers lack education and specialized skills and therefore eke out a living in the clothing, meat, and poultry industries; as domestics, janitors, servers; or as farmworkers doing "stoop labor." But many other immigrants now speak excellent English and have college degrees or postgraduate qualifications.

---

3. According to the Bureau of the Census, the Hispanic population exceeded 20,000,000 by 1990. Six out of ten Hispanics (12,600,000) were of Mexican origin, 2,300,000 were of Puerto Rican descent, 1,100,000 of Cuban provenance, 2,500,000 of Central or South American origin, and 1,600,000 reported other Hispanic origins. Two-thirds of all Hispanics live in three states—California, Texas, and New York.

Table 1   Percentage of Foreign-Born by Region of Birth

	1900	*1990*
Europe	84.9%	22.0%
Latin America	1.3	42.5
Asia	1.2	25.2
All other	12.6%	10.3%

NOTE: The regional categories shown above encompass many ethnicities. In 1990, for example, more than eighty ethnic divisions comprised "Europe."
SOURCE: Susan J. Lapham, *We the American-: Foreign Born* (Washington, D.C.: U.S. Department of Commerce, Bureau of the Census, September 1993).

According to the 1990 census, foreign-born Americans had as high a percentage of degrees and postgraduate degrees as native-born Americans. Certain ethnic groups, in particular East Indians, had overall much higher educational and income levels than the average U.S. citizen. Not surprisingly, East Indians do extremely well in the United States, as do many other Asians who excel in business and academia.

The immigrants also include a substantial body of political refugees (about 10 percent of the immigrant population). Contrary to public expectations, the end of the cold war did not reduce the number of people wishing to come to the United States, and in fact the global reservoir of people seeking new homes appears to be getting ever larger. Recurrent crises in Mexico, Africa, the Balkans, and Asia have added to the number of displaced people in the world. Many more wish to leave their present homes in the successor states of the Soviet Union and the former Warsaw Pact countries.

In addition to legal immigrants, a great number of undocumented aliens have come to the United States, evading alike the scrutiny of immigration inspectors, census takers, and tax collectors. The United States is unique among highly industrialized nations in that it shares a 2,000-mile-long border with a relatively underdeveloped country, Mexico, which, with a population of 91,000,000, has a substantial surplus of people who cannot find enough work at home and look for jobs in the United States. The great majority of undocumented aliens come, therefore, from Mexico and from Central America (which in turn also sends illegal immigrants into and through Mexico). Mexico's economic position may further deteriorate, as Mexico still has to cope with an extensive peasantry whose small holdings are becoming less competitive now that the North American Free Trade Agreement (NAFTA) assures free trade throughout North America. (Illegal immigrants from Mexico since 1994 include well-educated people—clerks, teachers, doctors, and others—who either can earn more in the states or can no longer find jobs at home.) Undocumented aliens also come from East Asia and Southeast Asia (particularly from China); a much smaller number come from Europe, especially Ireland.

Estimates concerning the total number of undocumented aliens differ widely and are apt to reflect the ideological orientation of those responsible for these assessments. In 1976 the Immigration and Naturalization Service (INS) guessed that between four and twelve million undocumenteds lived in the United States. Later the figure was changed to between six and eight million. A more realistic estimate amounts to some 4,500,000, possibly 5,000,000, aliens residing in the United States without proper papers.[4] (For many reasons, even remotely accurate figures are impossible to provide. No one knows, for

---

4. Jeffrey S. Passel, "Illegal Immigration to the United States," in Wayne A. Cornelius et al., eds., *Controlling Immigration: A Global Perspective* (Stanford: Stanford University Press, 1994), p. 114. Also see Frank D. Bean, Barry Edmonton, Jeffrey S. Passel, eds., *Undocumented Migration to the United States: IRCA and the Experience of the 1980s* (Santa Monica, Calif.: Rand Corporation, 1990); Michael Fix, ed., *The Paper Curtain: Employer Sanctions: Implementation, Impact, and Reform* (Santa Monica, Calif.: Rand Corporation, 1991); Edwin Harwood, *In Liberty's Shadow: Illegal Aliens and Immigration Law Enforcement* (Stanford: Hoover Institution Press, 1986); Barry Edmonton and Jeffrey S. Passel, eds., *Immigration and Ethnicity: The Integration of America's Newest Arrivals* (Washington, D.C.: Urban Institute, 1995); L. H. Gann and Peter Duignan, *The Hispanics in the United States: A History* (Boulder, Colo.: Westview Press, 1986); Maldwyn Allen Jones, *American Immigration* (Chicago, Ill.: University of Chicago Press, 1992); Julian L. Simon, *The Economic Consequences of Immigration* (Oxford, Eng.: Basil Blackwell, 1989).

instance, the size of the U.S. underground economy. No one can be sure of the illegal residents' collective income. No one can count their numbers, particularly as a great number keep shifting their domicile — from Mexico and Central America to the United States, then home again — as jobs get scarce in the United States or as a migrant gets homesick or as he or she has saved enough money.) In the past, if migrants could not find work or were laid off, they went "home." But the availability of welfare and unemployment benefits now keeps workers here. Recently it has become more difficult to get in *or* out of the United States because of the strengthened border patrols and fencing; hence more illegals stay in "el Norte" rather than risk being caught leaving or entering. Furthermore, the 1996 reforms pushed legal migrants to become citizens — to avoid losing welfare benefits, 1.3 million were naturalized. These new citizens will now have to stay, whereas many would normally have returned to their homelands.

Diversity, then, is the keynote of the U.S. immigrant population. This diversity is concealed in part by stereotypes concerning the newcomers. These misconceptions are fostered by the crude classification scheme employed by the U.S. Census Bureau and other agencies, who use six separate categories for pigeonholing U.S. citizens and newcomers to the United States: "Native Americans," "Asian or Pacific Islanders," "blacks not of Hispanic origin," "Hispanics," "whites not of Hispanic origin," and "others." These definitions follow no recognizable system; they were created by bureaucratic fiat. ("Asian" refers to geographic origins; "white" and "black," to skin color; "Hispanic," to cultural tradition.) Nor do these categories take account of broader cultural definitions. An Indian Hindu is classed as "Asian," as is a Malaysian, an Indonesian, a Pakistani Muslim, a Chinese Buddhist, or a Japanese adherent of Shinto. Culturally, these people differ more than, say, a Catholic from Mexico on the one hand, and one from Sicily on the other, even though the Mexican is classed as "Hispanic" and the Sicilian as "white."

The Hispanic category (created in 1980) is as arbitrary as any. (In the 1980 census, 52 percent of Hispanics also described themselves as "white.") Hispanics are people of diverse national backgrounds—Cubans, Puerto Ricans, Argentineans, Salvadoreans, Dominicans, Mexicans, Spaniards, and so on. There are striking variations even within the same family, say, between a person who grew up in the United States and habitually speaks English and a relative, a newcomer, who can hardly talk in English. As Carlos Hamann, a freelance reporter based in El Paso, puts it: "Don't mix up your categories. The average Mexican-American resident here considers himself a Hispanic from Texas (a Tex-Mex). Call them Latinos, and you will be slapped; call them Chicanos, and you might get a broken nose."[5]

Americans are ambiguous with regard to the immigration issue—more perhaps than any other people. According to recent opinion polls, a great majority wants to cut down on immigration. But Americans, unlike the great bulk of Germans, British, French, or Italians, know that they themselves derive from immigrant stock (except Native Americans). Polls therefore are strikingly contradictory: 64 percent of respondents want immigration to be decreased; 78 percent agree that many immigrants work hard and often take jobs that Americans do not want; 55 percent say that the diversity brought by immigrants to the United States threatens American culture; 60 percent insist that immigrants improve the United States with their different talents and backgrounds.[6]

Americans differ from Europeans in a more fundamental respect. In Britain, for example, a naturalized foreigner may achieve high honors as a "British subject." But he or she will never be regarded as "English" (or, for that matter, as Scottish or Welsh)—not because British people are more xenophobic than others but because they define ethnicity by descent, as do Germans. A Volga German, speaking bro-

---

5. Carlos Hamann, "Tex-Mex," *New Republic*, 15 April 1996, pp. 14–18.
6. "Immigration," *American Enterprise*, January–February 1994, pp. 97–100.

ken German, is legally entitled to German nationality. But the German-born and German-speaking son of a Turk, resident in Germany for many years, remains a Turk. By contrast, once a foreigner takes the oath of allegiance in the United States, he or she is accepted as an American, even if the new citizen speaks English with an accent as did Henry Kissinger (former secretary of state) and Zbigniew Brzezinski (former national security adviser). No country in the world is as generous with regard to its new citizens as the United States.

American ambiguity with regard to immigration is reflected in constant vacillations over legislation affecting immigrants. Periods marked by a massive influx of foreigners have traditionally been followed by an anti-immigration backlash. The arguments pro and con cut across traditional party lines and traditional distinctions between liberals and conservatives. This has always been the case. During the nineteenth century, the Know-Nothings, a third party, bitterly opposed immigrants, especially Catholics, who supposedly plotted with the pope to subvert Protestant liberties, spread drink, and entrapped innocent maidens for servitude in nunneries. Yet the Know-Nothings also strove for social reform and Negro emancipation. For good economic reasons, employers of labor, libertarians, humanists, and ethnic spokespeople are united in favoring immigration. They are opposed by an equally heterogeneous alliance made up of old-style barroom patriots, environmentalists, cultural conservatives, trade unionists, and Zero Population Growth activists who want to keep out or restrict the influx of newcomers. The Carrying Capacity Network puts the case against immigration on ecological grounds. By contrast, Molly Ivins, a liberal columnist, will have nothing to do with such arguments: "It's not Irish secretaries or French restaurateurs who are about to cut down the last great stands of redwood on private property in California."[7] Senator

---

7. *The Immigration Briefing Book* (Washington, D.C.: Carrying Capacity Network,

Diane Feinstein, a liberals' liberal, wants to cut down on immigration, including legal immigration. By contrast, Senator Phil Gramm, a conservatives' conservative, censures Feinstein for abandoning the United States' liberal heritage in welcoming strangers.

But anti-immigration sentiments may now predominate, deriving from profound cultural apprehension. The new immigrants, critics say, will transform traditional U.S. culture; some time in the next century they may reduce whites to minority status. Look at Miami! In 1960 non-Hispanic whites formed some 80 percent of the population; by 1996 they had become a minority. Cubans and other Latins had revived and expanded Miami's economy—but no comfort that to, say, an elderly Anglo pensioner who complained of Spanish on the school grounds, Spanish in the hospital wards, Spanish on the bus, Spanish on the freeways, Spanish in the store and bank. Middle class flight and corruption to boot! Let the last American haul down the flag!

Immigrants also incur blame for rising crime. (Immigrants, on the average, are more youthful and have more children than the settled population. And crime is predominantly a young man's occupation.) Immigrants, it is said, benefit unfairly from affirmative action programs; immigrants are a charge on the welfare system. (Elderly immigrants in fact make up one of the fastest-growing groups of people receiving welfare, even though most were admitted to the United States on the promise by their children that they would not become "public charges.") The presence of so many new immigrants upsets the customary ethnic balance—(an argument heard most often in Texas, Florida, New York, and particularly California, where the majority of newcomers have settled). Immigrants, the argument continues, contribute to U.S. population growth at a time when natural resources are supposedly diminishing and getting more expensive (in fact they are increas-

---

1994); Molly Ivins, "Our Problems Aren't Caused by Immigrants," *San Francisco Chronicle*, 26 April 1996.

ing and getting cheaper). Undesirable immigrants include asylum seekers who abuse the U.S. laws designed to benefit legitimate refugees from political persecution. (Applicants for asylum in 1996 included a homosexual fleeing "oppression" and an African woman from Togo who claims she fled her native village in Africa so that she would not be subjected to the tribal rite of female genital mutilation.)[8]

Hostility is greatest against illegal immigrants. Indeed, many people drawn from the racial minorities have joined the anti-immigration lobbies. The Californian taxpayer must spend huge sums to educate immigrant children, to pay for welfare and medical services, and to house illegals in prison. The National Research Council released on May 17, 1997, a 500-page report that estimated that California taxpayers pay about $1,178 each year in state and local taxes to cover services used by immigrants that immigants' state and local taxes do not cover. In time the flood will become unmanageable, write Yeh Ling-Ling and Gil Wong, both board members of the Diversity Coalition for an Immigration Moratorium.[9] Many Hispanics feel the same way. (According to a 1996 poll, Hispanics favor reduced immigration by a margin of 53 percent to 35 percent in Texas; 48 percent to 40 percent in New York; 47 percent to 39 percent in Florida; and 47 percent to 37 percent in California.)[10]

Critics of immigration thus fear the United States will lose its traditional character and culture. According to the pessimists, the United States has already lost control of its own borders. Optimists deny all such complaints; immigrants add value to the United States; they create jobs and wealth and keep the population growing and youthful.

---

8. Celia W. Dugger, "A Woman's Plea for Asylum Puts Tribal Ritual on Trial," *New York Times*, 15 April 1996, p. 1.

9. Yeh Ling-Ling and Gil Wong, "Why It's Time to Limit Immigration," *San Francisco Chronicle*, 27 March 1996.

10. Jonathan Tilove, "Poll of 4 States: Hispanic-Americans Yield Surprises," *Jersey Journal*, 4 March 1996, p. 12.

Immigration and the Law

When the United States attained independence, no restrictions were placed on the arrival of newcomers. Newcomers came and left as they pleased. The state made no provision either to hinder or help. For assistance they would call on kinfolk, friends, neighbors, their respective churches, or welfare societies (commonly made up from persons born in the same region of the old country, *Landsmannschaften*, in German and Yiddish). Immigrants were generally welcomed to offset what Alexander Hamilton called "the scarcity of hands" and the "dearness of labor."

It was only from the end of the last and the beginning of the present century that the United States enacted restrictive measures. (Chinese were excluded altogether in addition to newcomers considered criminal, diseased, insane, or politically subversive.) Massive immigration continued, all the more so since transatlantic communications had undergone enormous improvements. (Steam vessels replaced sailing ships, and emigrants no longer risked their lives crossing the ocean to reach the New World.) But whereas the earlier immigrants had largely come from northwestern Europe, the new immigrants primarily derived from eastern and southern Europe. The new immigrants mainly settled in the big cities and found employment in mining, building, and manufacturing—so much so that by 1909 immigrants formed the majority of workers in the biggest U.S. mining and manufacturing enterprises.

After the end of World War I the United States retreated into isolationism. There was a new dread of crime and of political subversion supposedly instigated or supported by foreigners; there were new fears aroused by racist and eugenicist theoreticians who maintained that Slavs and Latins (not to speak of brown-, yellow-, and black-skinned people) would fail to come up to the genetic standards set by British, German, and Scandinavian immigrants. After World War I, the United States therefore set up national quotas, a system retained by the 1952 Immigration and Nationality Act (INA) passed over the veto of President Truman. Known also as the McCarran-Walter Act, it once more allotted to each foreign country an annual quota for immigrants based on the proportion of people from that country present in the United States in 1920. The INA thereby continued the national origins system, which decisively favored Europe. But in deference to agricultural interests of the Southwest, no restrictions were placed on migrants from the Western Hemisphere, especially Mexico. The INA also established a preference system, to assist family reunification, giving first preference to immediate kin, a system that remains in force to this day.

More fundamental still was the change made in 1965 during the heady days of President Lyndon Johnson's Great Society. Since the 1920s, the United States had favored northern Europeans—British, German, Scandinavian, and Dutch, most of them Protestants. This policy kept out many Catholics (except those who could enter under the Irish and German quotas). There were equally severe restrictions on countries such as Poland, Lithuania, and Russia from which most Jewish immigrants came. The coalition calling for immigration reform thus consisted of the traditional New Deal supporters—liberals, Catholics, and Jews.

In a message to a predominantly liberal Congress, Johnson thus vowed to abolish the national origins quota system, which he considered "incompatible with our best American traditions" and which also conflicted with the assumed solidarity of the nations in the Western Hemisphere. Instead, the new legislation would give preferential admissions "based upon the advantage to our nation of the skills of the immigrant, and the existence of a close family relationship between immigrants and people who are already citizens or permanent residents."[11] Subsequent amendments established a ceiling of 20,000 im-

---

11. "President Johnson's Message to Congress," *Keesing's Contemporary Archives,* 20–27 September 1995, p. 21083.

migrants per country and a ceiling of 290,000 persons to be admitted every year. (The 1980 Refugee Act took refugees out of the preference system, giving new powers to the president to establish the annual limits of the refugees to be accepted.)

It was a major policy reversal whose importance was not fully understood when it was made. The traditional preference given to Europe disappeared—this at a time when the member states of the European Community (EC) were themselves experiencing a new prosperity. (Henceforth, Spaniards, Greeks, Portuguese, and Sicilians looked for jobs in Germany, France, and Britain rather than in the United States. In due course, the Mediterranean states of the EC would in turn attract newcomers—mainly from North Africa and the Near East.)

Although the 1965 immigration law was debated, its consequences were unforeseen. Senator Edward Kennedy (Dem.-Mass.) was totally wrong in saying what the bill would not do:

> First, our cities will not be flooded with a million immigrants annually. Under the proposed bill, the present level of immigration remains substantially the same. . . . Secondly, the ethnic mix of this country will not be upset. . . . Contrary to the charges in some quarters, [the bill] will not inundate America with immigrants from any one country or area, or the most populated and deprived nations of Africa and Asia. . . . In the final analysis, the ethnic pattern of immigration under the proposed measure is not expected to change as sharply as the critics seem to think.

In fact, immigration levels rose to over one million a year, not counting undocumenteds; immigrants overwhelmingly came from three areas, Asia, the Caribbean, and Latin America (85 percent), and the ethnic pattern changed dramatically away from Europe to Asia and Latin America.

These immigrants came to a country that had developed extensive welfare provisions administered by the federal, state, and local authorities. Newcomers became more welfare-wise, as civic organizations and also private legal firms increasingly apprised immigrants of their rights under U.S. law. Illegal immigrants also kept coming in growing numbers, as did political refugees—to an extent that few U.S. legislators had foreseen. By 1986 the United States housed, in addition to more than one million Cubans, an estimated 600,000 refugees, mainly from strife-torn Guatemala, Nicaragua, San Salvador, and Vietnam. Their arrival was supported by a church-supported sanctuary movement that persuaded some twenty cities (including San Francisco and Seattle) to declare themselves "sanctuary cities."

The radical 1960s also saw other changes. Since the early part of the present century, immigrants seeking citizenship had been required to demonstrate an adequate understanding of English and of American history and government. The 1965 Voting Rights Act, as amended in 1975 and thereafter, for the first time made a striking inroad in the official position of the English language. New legislation required multilingual ballots in jurisdictions with certain demographic characteristics pertaining to linguistic minorities.[12]

The program of affirmative action, initially popular in the 1960s, later proved unpopular and not only among white males. In 1995, in a *Washington Post* survey, 75 percent of respondents—81 percent of whites and 47 percent of blacks—opposed preferences on the basis of past discrimination. Also, as Michael Tomasky, a committed liberal, put it, "a policy of affirmative action for diversity's sake cannot for long coexist with a policy of open immigration."[13] For why should, say, a wealthy brown-skinned contractor from Mexico City or a prosperous black college professor from Kingston, Jamaica, become beneficiaries of affirmative action as opposed to an unemployed and disabled white steelworker from Pittsburgh or an unemployed white professor? Multi-

---

12. Cited by George Will, "Discomforting Truths about Bilingual Ballots," *San Francisco Chronicle*, 2 May 1996.

13. Michael Tomasky, "Reaffirming Our Actions," *Nation*, 13 May 1996, pp. 21–23.

cultural ideals proclaimed by progressive churchmen and academi-
cians were greeted with equal hostility. Traditional notions concerning
America as a "melting pot" seemed passé to the elites—but not to the
mass of voters who expressed their hostility to bilingualism and multiculturalism in various state initiatives calling for English to be recognized as the "official language."

Serious objections also arose to provisions in the law that allowed
certain kinds of undocumented immigrants to adjust their status to
legal permanent residents and eventually to citizenship. A new program permitted adjustment of the status of undocumented immigrants
who could demonstrate continuous residence in the United States as
of 1 January 1982. Another clause allowed for the adjustment of certain
undocumented farmworkers through the so-called Special Agricultural
Worker (SAW) and Replenishment Agricultural Worker (RAW) program.

The Seasonal Agricultural Workers' provision of IRCA (1986)
granted legal status to more than 1.1 million workers nationwide; it has
been a failure.[14] It did not stop undocumented immigrants; it merely
replaced them with those once legalized under IRCA who had left the
fields for higher-paying jobs in town. Some 35 to 70 percent of agricultural workers, it is estimated, now have fake papers to evade the border
patrol and to fool employers.

SAW did not slow the rate of illegal immigration. Instead it spread
undocumented workers to other parts of the country. Once in, the
farmworkers departed the fields for better jobs and were then replaced
by other illegals. As a result of SAW, many illegals no longer only work
in California or other border states. (Michoacan tomato workers left
the California fields for jobs in the meatpacking industry in the Mid-
west and doubled their wages, to $9.50 an hour.) Since 1986 the SAWs
have set up an efficient networking system that sends friends and family
in Mexico to jobs first in California, then Nebraska, Wyoming, Min-

---

14. Alfredo Corchado's article in the *Dallas Morning News*, 29 October 1996.

nesota, even to Maine, where Mexicans, who had been rare, now pick strawberries, blueberries, potatoes, and broccoli. The pattern is now well established: undocumented workers have replaced those legalized under IRCA (more than 1,000,000) not only in California but throughout the United States.

Amnesty programs further reduced the authority of the United States and respect for its laws. Once granted, amnesty was bound to arouse expectations of further amnesties to come. Having attained citizenship, naturalized aliens would in turn bring more relatives, including elderly folk who might become a charge on the U.S. taxpayer. The family preference policy also had a built-in bias in favor of newcomers from Asia, Latin America, and the Caribbean, as against Europeans. The most recent immigrants enjoy the advantages of family preference, advantages not available to those European immigrants who had come at an earlier time. In earlier times, immigrants had in the main been unmarried young men. But as time went on, the family structure of illegal immigrants increasingly resembled that of the settled population. Men brought in their families; hence there was increased pressure on educational, health, and welfare facilities. This was true especially in California, above all in Los Angeles, the new Ellis Island, a huge, multiethnic conurbation and now the country's largest port of entry.

The 1980s saw additional legislation that further transformed immigration into the United States. These were the Refugee Act of 1980, the Immigration Reform and Control Act of 1986 (IRCA), and the Immigration Act of 1990. The Refugee Act of 1980 modernized refugee policy and allowed aliens to declare themselves refugees. The purpose of IRCA was to decrease the numbers of illegal immigrants by limiting their flow and legalizing those who were already living in the United States. The border patrol was strengthened, and employers were penalized for knowingly hiring illegals. As noted previously, IRCA also set up a program to admit agricultural workers when native farmworkers were not available. IRCA legalized 2.6 million people previously regarded as illegals. The new legal aliens in 1990 then requested visas to bring in their relatives, another 2 million or so. (Employer sanctions and a strengthened border patrol did not diminish the flow of illegal immigrants according to Frank D. Bean, a U.S. scholar.) The Immigration Act of 1990 further revised the 1965 immigration law. The 1990 act aimed to reunite families for immediate relatives of U.S. citizens, restrict visas for the unskilled, increase the number of visas (to 140,000) for priority workers and professionals if they had job offers, and provide eleven thousand visas for investors with $1 million or more in order to create jobs for at least ten U.S. residents. The 1990 act also gave more visas to underrepresented countries, especially Ireland.

Nevertheless, public dissatisfaction continued to grow with regard to immigration. These fears found expression in California's Proposition 187, passed in 1994 by a vote of 59 percent as against 41 percent. The proposition denied California's estimated 1,600,000 undocumented aliens access to schools, hospitals, and other welfare services. The proposition was struck down in federal court. But the size of the yes vote reflected the growing anti-immigration sentiment. As Ezola Foster, president of Americans for Family Values, put it: "In my more than 30 years as a public school teacher with the Los Angeles Unified School District, I've seen the devastating effect illegal immigration has on our schools. American children are being treated as second-class citizens, and they know it. In many schools you would be hard pressed to find a class-room with an American flag. American children are not taught pride in American culture, while school districts are promoting cultures of foreign countries."[15] Other states passed propositions resembling 187.

The case against immigration was also pleaded by groups such as Federation for American Immigration Reform (FAIR), whose opposition to immigration could in no wise be stigmatized as racist. (John Tanton, FAIR's founder and chairman, had previously been a senior

---

15. *San Francisco Chronicle*, 16 July 1996, p. A18.

officeholder in bodies such as Zero Population Growth, Planned Parenthood, and the Sierra Club.) FAIR's conviction that the country faced an emergency came to be shared more widely than before, especially in states such as California, New York, and Florida. In 1993 alone, more than 900,000 newcomers were legally admitted to the United States, not to mention an unspecified number of undocumented aliens.

Nevertheless, congressional opinion for a time continued to favor immigration, especially in the late 1980s, when jobs were created at a rapid rate in California and nationwide and when influential studies such as *Workforce, 2000* warned of impending labor shortages. Congress thus overwhelmingly approved a new bill, signed by President George Bush in 1990. The act raised the then current limit on immigration from 490,000 to 645,000 in each fiscal year until 1994 and to 675,000 annually thereafter. These quotas, moreover, did not include refugees who could show "a well founded fear of persecution" in their homelands, an easy claim to make in a world where so many governments rule their respective subjects with a rod of iron. More skilled people would be admitted. Ideological restrictions imposed by previous legislation disappeared. In response to the now powerful gay and lesbian lobbies, the act thus removed a ban on homosexual immigrants, while the health secretary received authority to remove AIDS and other diseases from the medical list for which a person might be denied entry.

In the end, however, Congress bent to increasing public fears concerning immigration. In 1996, after long and contentious debate, President Bill Clinton signed a new law, the Illegal Immigration Reform and Immigrant Responsibility Act. The new law disappointed those who wanted considerable cuts in legal immigration. The lawmakers, nevertheless, made great changes. This new immigration act took a hard line against illegal immigrants. Border enforcement was strengthened: additional officers (a thousand a year for five years) would be appointed to the INS, and funds were set aside for a new border fence.

The act introduced a pilot telephone verification program, which enabled employers to verify the status of newly hired workers and social service agencies to determine the legal status of applicants for benefits. In addition, the law expanded restrictions on the access of *legal* immigrants to welfare benefits. The legislators also prevented immigrants from requesting taxpayer-funded assistance after the immigrant's arrival in the United States; henceforth, U.S. sponsors of immigrants would have to prove a higher income than before so that they would not default on their obligation to the newcomers whom they had sponsored.

The 1996 immigration bill also added six hundred new investigators to arrest criminal aliens, employers who hired illegals, and visitors who overstayed their visas; increased penalties for alien smuggling and document fraud; made it easier to expel foreigners who enter illegally, even those who apply for political asylum; and provided full reimbursement by the federal government to hospitals for emergency medical services for illegals.[16]

Equally important was the Personal Responsibility and Work Opportunity Reconciliation Act (1996). The new law vastly restricted the eligibility of most legal and illegal immigrants for federal welfare assistance. The bill grouped foreigners into three major categories for determining their access to welfare aid. The first was made up of legal immigrants who had worked in the United States for at least ten years, were veterans, or had been admitted as refugees. The second group, which consisted of "qualified aliens" (most legal immigrants), was not eligible for specific means-tested benefit programs until five years after their entry to the United States. "Nonqualified aliens" as well as illegal aliens and some categories of nonimmigrants with INS permission to

---

16. William Branigin, "Congress Finishes Major Legislation Immigration, Focus on Borders Not Benefits," *Washington Post*, 1 October 1996. For details of the left-right coalition that prevented true immigration reform in 1996, see John B. Judes, "Huddled Elites," *New Republic*, 23 December 1996.

remain in the United States were not qualified for most federal public benefits or for many state and local benefits.[17]

At the time of writing, experts had failed to agree on the presumed effect of this legislation. Liberals feared that family reunification would be possible only for the middle income, that poor people would suffer, especially children and the elderly. Conservatives and liberal environmentalists complained that the new legislation would simply encourage aliens of whatever nationality to seek naturalization, thereby enabling them to go on receiving benefits such as supplemental security income. Conservatives in particular censured the legislators for not restricting legal immigration. This was a fundamental mistake, according to experts such as Mark Krikorian, director of the Center for Immigration Studies in Washington, D.C. Legal and illegal immigration were inextricably linked; one reinforced the other, as the same immigrant family might include both documented and undocumented aliens, the latter relying on support and encouragement from the former. And the major issues in the immigration debate—how many and who—were not addressed.

Whatever the pros and cons of the arguments, the country's political atmosphere had changed. There was less confidence in politics and politicians than in the olden days, less faith in experts and their presumed expertise, less certainty that the United States' resources could sustain an ever-growing population, less belief that the United States could cope with a multicultural future. The rightward shift also led to action within individual states. In 1996 Governor Pete Wilson of California signed an executive order cutting off numerous state services, including welfare, food stamps, prenatal care, and higher education, to illegal immigrants and to legals who were not citizens. By doing so, Wilson put into force numerous provisions of California Proposition 187, approved by California voters in 1994 but thereafter held up in the courts. In this, as in many other respects, the United States became

---

17. *Immigration News* 3, no. 10 (October 1996): 1–3.

more like the member states of the European Union, where hostility to foreigners had grown.[18] In the United States, pro-immigration advocates henceforth stood on the defensive.

The Pro-Immigration Case

The United States is a nation made up of immigrants and their off-spring. From its beginnings, the United States stood indebted to the newcomers' skills. Pro-immigration advocates thus display traditional U.S. optimism. As they see it, Americans need not worry about immigration.

Natural resources and the environment are not at risk from immigration, thus the conviction of notable scholars such as Milton Friedman and Julian L. Simon. They point to past forecasts predicting ecological disasters and show that these were either exaggerated or mistaken altogether. Take, for example, a report known as *Global 2000*, prepared in 1980 by a group of leading scholars at President Jimmy Carter's initiative. The report predicted global crises: famine and disease would spread; the plagues of Egypt would be as nothing compared with the wrath to come. But, in fact, the world is getting richer, not poorer.[19] Ecological disaster does not necessarily stand

18. German authorities estimate 500,000 illegals work there and may cost Germany about $65 billion in lost taxes and social welfare contributions every year. Undocumented jobs are most often in construction, sanitation, and the food industry. Claims for political asylum have shot up all over Western Europe. Germany has been hardest hit, but so has Great Britain—in 1989, 2,900 people applied for asylum; in 1995 the number was 50,000. Germany and Britain have had to tighten up the process and to deny political asylum to more people—Britain denied 94 percent of applications for political asylum last year. Germany had 86,000 applications through September, 6.3 percent fewer than in the same period in 1995.

19. Interview with Herman Kahn, *Conservative Digest*, September 1983, pp. 36–38. "False Bad News vs. Truly Bad News," *Public Interest*, no. 65 (fall 1981): 71–89. For a detailed discussion of *Global 2000 Report to the President*, see "The Global 2000 Juggernaut," Washington, D.C., Institutional Analysis, the Heritage Foundation, 1983.

round the corner. There is no necessary correlation between poverty and a high population density. (Singapore and Hong Kong, two densely crowded urban communities, are far more prosperous than, say, Angola or Mozambique, both of them huge countries with plenty of acres to spare.) The world is not running out of food; urban sprawl does not wipe out prime agricultural land; the world's resources are not "finite." There is indeed "a funding incentive for scholars and institutions to produce bad news about population, resources and the environment." But the world is, in fact, much better off than the doomsday sayers prophesy.[20]

The U.S. population and income have increased, yet natural resources have not declined; the environment has improved rather than deteriorated, despite massive immigration. In fact, immigration keeps the population growing and the economy developing, which accelerate the positive trends in the availability of natural resources and cleaner air and water.[21]

The Zero Population Growth movement dreads immigrants lest the newcomers have too many children, consume too many resources, and pollute the land. But modern industry, while causing new ecological problems, also creates the means for dealing with them. (The British, for example, have done away with the London pea soup fogs familiar to Sherlock Holmes; they have also cleaned up the once-polluted Thames, all at a time when new settlers were coming to the United Kingdom from the Commonwealth.)

In any case, argue the optimists, demographers have a bad record in forecasting anything—be it the future size of specific populations, the long-term availability of natural resources, or whatever. Demographers have made egregious errors by extrapolating existing data into

---

20. Julian L. Simon, "Resources, Population, Environment: An Oversupply of Bad False News," *Science* 208 (27 June 1980): 1421–37. See also Simon, *Economic Consequences of Immigration.*

21. Julian L. Simon, *Immigration and Economic Facts* (Washington, D.C.: Cato Institute, 1995).

the distant future. Economists have done no better. In the 1970s, for instance, West German chancellor Willy Brandt put together a distinguished commission to study the future of global resources and world-wide development in decades to come. The commissioners published a pessimistic report. The report was brilliant, but the forecasts were all wrong.

The fact is that the free market, if allowed to operate, will take care of all these concerns. Immigrants tend to be more motivated and therefore more apt to succeed than their stay-at-home counterparts or even native-born Americans. Thomas Sowell, a U.S. economist, has found that blacks who migrate to the United States from the West Indies have higher average earnings than native-born black Americans. European immigrants do equally well. Barry Chiswick, another economist, has ascertained that, despite language and cultural barriers, European immigrants on the average earn more than white native-born Americans within fifteen years after arriving in the United States.[22] Asian immigrants also do well. For example, Chinese and Koreans have helped to revive the economy of Los Angeles.

Immigration in economic terms represents a transfer of skills to the receiving country without cost at the expense of the immigrant's country of origin, which developed the immigrant's mind and muscle. Newcomers create work both for themselves and others as immigrants need housing, shoes to wear, cars to get to work, bread to eat, books to read. Furthermore, in many cases the immigrants do jobs that Americans will not or cannot do. How many Americans want to do housekeeping chores or restaurant work? Without immigrant labor Americans could not so readily afford the grapes, oranges, lettuce they buy in the supermarkets, although the savings here to farm wages held down by immigrants are minuscule. And prices in service industries and restaurants

---

22. Thomas Sowell, *Ethnic America: A History* (New York: Basic Books, 1981), p. 220; and Barry Chiswick, "The Effects of Americanization on the Earnings of Foreign Born," *Journal of Political Economy* 11 (October 1978): 879–922.

are kept lower than they otherwise would be because of low-paid labor, most of which is done by new immigrants.

Immigrants may, in some cases, increase the rate of unemployment among native Americans with low skills, especially minority and female workers. But, if cheap immigrant labor were not available, some jobs would likely move offshore or there would be technological or other changes to get work done, from self-service gasoline to mechanical grape harvesters. The effect of immigration on wages, Simon concludes, is negative for some special groups but positive for most, and the overall effects are small.

Some unskilled Americans (mostly blacks and women but also Mexican Americans) do suffer from the competition of foreigners because they work for less. (Nevertheless, according to the researches of Stephen Moore, a Cato Institute expert on immigration, U.S. cities with a high proportion of immigrants do not suffer from higher rates of unemployment, crime, poverty, or high taxation than do cities with low rates of immigration. Cities with high rates of immigration in fact gain wealth faster and increase their respective per capita incomes more quickly than cities with few immigrants. (Ironically, cities with the most immigrants — New York, Houston, Los Angeles — are the least anti-immigrant.) Some native-born workers do suffer from foreign-born competitors. But native-born workers in the United States should not complain too much; they enjoy a competitive advantage over newcomers because they already know the language, the culture, and the job. Nor are American workers simply helpless victims of circumstances. Faced with competition, they have new incentives to find better employment or acquire further training. To the extent that the wages of unskilled men and women fall, the benefits of additional training grow. Consequently, immigration may lead to greater self-investment in education.

Ron Unz, an economist and Silicon Valley entrepreneur, concedes that job competition from foreigners can hurt native borns and lead to unemployment but that that is true for all economic policies in

American society. But overall Unz (and free market economists) argues that foreign workers benefit Americans and the economy, and even those hurt temporarily, by lowering consumer costs, which raises productivity and in turn increases the number of jobs.

As for those who would restrict foreigners' access to U.S. graduate schools, Simon argues that they benefit us, their native countries and are one of our best exports. In addition, the melting pot concept helps American high-tech industries by bringing talented people here who were educated elsewhere at someone else's expense. The United States should not therefore make it difficult for talented people to come here as it does now.

Whereas skilled people add significantly to gross domestic product (GDP), unskilled ones add less than 1 percent, according to George Borjas of the Kennedy School of Government at Harvard. Borjas notes that, with regard to immigration, two primary questions we have yet "to address are how many and who?" Efforts in the Senate to reduce the number of skilled immigrants were defeated, and no efforts were made to limit the total number of legal immigrants other than skilled ones. That debate did not come up again after the presidential election because the Republicans feared being seen as anti-immigrant.

Immigrants do not merely perform menial jobs. They also play an important part in those new industries—computers, biotechnicals, pharmaceuticals, information, and entertainment—where the United States is the world leader. Thus T. J. Rodgers, president and CEO of Cypress Semiconductors, a major firm in San Jose, California, notes that the major *Fortune* 500 companies have reduced employment. By contrast smaller, innovative, and more-flexible firms have expanded and hired more staff. Indeed, firms such as Cypress cannot find enough qualified people. Cypress is not alone in its predicament. The eleven semiconductor companies that make up the Sematech chip consortium have seventeen thousand open requisitions that they are unable to fill. Cypress itself is so short of skilled engineers that the company has started to move design centers abroad. Critics such as Norman

Matloff of the University of California at Davis accuse the high-tech industries of hiring foreigners to keep down the wages of native-born experts. But this is not so. Recruiting a person from overseas may itself be a costly undertaking when it involves relocating to the United States both the foreign expert and his or her family. Keeping out skilled newcomers may have the perverse effect of forcing U.S. high-tech firms to export jobs. (Senator Alan Simpson's [Rep.-Wyo.] efforts to reduce the number of skilled immigrants admitted into the United States were defeated in the 1996 legislation.)

As old industries decay, new forms of enterprise such as American Express, MCI, Sun Microsystems have created new work. Rodgers also observes that "our $600,000,000 Silicon Valley company [Cypress] is run by ten officers. Four of them are immigrants."[23] Far from taking work from Americans, they have made the industry stronger. In any case, the U.S. population is aging. The United States thus needs a constant influx of young, new, skilled workers. Without them, there will not be enough young people to pay for the social benefits destined for an ever-growing army of elderly or to help Americans remain competitive in high-tech industries.

From economic issues, we pass to questions of social concern. Do immigrants contribute to U.S. crime? The United States' underworld has expanded, with new Vietnamese, Russian, Israeli, Mexican, Dominican, Chinese, Korean, and other mobsters terrorizing their fellow citizens. Inner-city gangs have changed their ethnic composition (as have the law-abiding segments of the population in the inner cities). But according to Joe Cobb, an expert at the Heritage Foundation, the number of noncitizens in prison is about the same proportion as the number in the general population. Of the states with the largest proportion of alien prisoners in 1992 (California, New York, Florida, Illi-

---

23. Letter from T. J. Rodgers, president and CEO of Cypress Semiconductor, to Senator Spencer Abraham (Rep.-Mich.), 26 February 1996, communicated to us by the author.

nois), only New York had a greater share of aliens in jail than in the general population. There is no reason to think that crime would necessarily diminish if immigration were stopped. Big-time crime has become globalized; some of the most formidable rackets in the United States are run from places such as Hong Kong or Lima.

The bulk of immigrants are law abiding, and more than 80 percent are employed; in fact they do remarkably well in meeting American family values. Some 40 percent of immigrant households consist of four or more people, compared with 25 percent of native American ones. Immigrants are more likely to be married than natives (60 percent, as against 55 percent) and less likely to be divorced or separated (8 percent, as against 11 percent). (Figures for Mexicans are even higher—73 percent of families consist of married couples.) A typical immigrant is less likely to have finished high school, but if she or he does succeed, he or she is twice as likely to have a doctorate. The immigrant is a little more likely to do paid work than a native but less likely to work for the government.[24] Contrary to widespread stereotypes, the bulk of the "new immigrants" learn English with as much dedication as did the "old immigrants." (English self-study courses, massively advertised by private enterprise on Hispanic TV stations, do a flourishing business.) Immigrants are, in fact, remarkably well attuned to the American tradition of self-help and enterprise. They relish consumer goods; they have an even greater interest than native Americans in quality products and brand names. They like to keep up with modern lifestyles and fashions. The majority do not feel alienated from their work. The immigrants like to make their own decisions without reference to what their neighbors prefer.[25]

Some restrictionists believe that immigrants should be specially selected so that the United States will attract only winners. Peter Bri-

---

24. "The Best Americans?" *The Economist*, 26 November 1994, reporting on "The Index of Leading Immigration Indicators," Manhattan Institute, 1994.

25. Cited in Gann and Duignan, *Hispanics in the United States*, pp. 320–22.

melow, in contrast, argues that the United States does not need *any* immigrants. But who can predict with certainty any newcomer's economic future? Take the case of Cecil Rhodes, one of the greatest empire builders of the nineteenth century, founder of Rhodesia (now Zimbabwe), which went on to set up Immigrant Selection Boards to recruit suitable people. But none of these boards would have admitted Rhodes when he first came to southern Africa as a sickly young man without special skills or academic qualifications and no capital. Neither would Rhodes have won one of his own Rhodes Scholarships (which require from applicants proven aptitude in "manly sports" as well as academic work). Forecasting of this kind, say the skeptics, is a trade for fools. Furthermore, no one knows how many low-skilled immigrants we may need in agriculture, meatpacking, the poultry industry, and so on to do jobs Americans do not want to do for low wages.

What of the costs inflicted on the United States by immigrants? According to popular opinion, they are horrendous. True enough, welfare expenditure, narrowly defined, is greater for immigrants (21 percent) compared with 14 percent for native Americans. Aid to Families with Dependent Children (AFDC) and supplemental security income (SSI) pay out more to immigrants than natives (on the average $404 per immigrant as opposed to $260 for the average native). Refugees in particular obtain more welfare than natives, as evidenced by table 2.

Immigrants also get more, on average, in the way of food stamps or Medicaid because they are poorer. By contrast, costs of schooling and

Table 2   Native- and Foreign-Born Population, Fifteen Years and
           Older, Receiving Welfare Payments (in percent)

	1979	1989	Entered 1970–1979	Entered 1980–1990
Natives	4.3	4.2		
Foreign born	4.8	4.7	4.7	4.5
Refugees				15.6

SOURCE: *Population and Development Review*, March 1996, p. 106.

unemployment compensation are about the same for native born and immigrants. But immigrants, on average, are younger than the native born. Immigrants usually arrive healthy; hence they get less than the native born in the way of Social Security and Medicare—by far the most expensive government programs. It is the native born who are the principal beneficiaries. The welfare expenditure on immigrants, narrowly defined, is but a "red herring."[26] Overall, economist Simon concludes, immigrants contribute more to the public coffers than they receive. In fact, the immigrants' relative contribution of late may have increased rather than diminished.

In any case, welfare expenditures are only a small fraction of total government outlays on immigrants and natives. Schooling costs and payments to the elderly represent the bulk of government expenditures, Simon argues, and natives use more of these programs, especially Social Security and Medicare. Education is a long-term expense but a necessary one if the United States is to remain competitive in the global economy.

Nicholas Imparato, a management professor, and Joseph Costello, a Silicon Valley entrepreneur, argue that traditional notions concerning immigration may have to be revised altogether in considering a new character on the high-tech scene, the "electronic immigrant." Imagine an East Indian programmer, a resident of Bombay, who jointly works as a programmer with a team in California; his work centers on California; his wages derive from California. He communicates electronically with his California colleagues on personal as well as professional matters; indeed he knows his California associates better than his Indian neighbors. He is not an immigrant in the physical or legal sense. But in many ways he resembles an immigrant to the United States as concerns both his economic function and his mind-set. He lives in a world where visas, quotas, and their like have ceased to count.

---

26. Julian L. Simon, "Public Expenditure on Immigrants to the United States: Past and Present," *Population and Development Review* 22, no. 1 (March 1996): 99–110.

Pro-immigrationist groups include the National Immigration Forum, the National Council of La Raza, the American Immigration Lawyers Association. They conclude that the U.S. immigration policy should not hinge solely on a cost-benefit analysis. Politics should also have a moral dimension. Claiming to be the world's bastion of liberty, the United States has a general obligation to admit political refugees from tyrannies wherever these exist. In particular, the United States has close relations with Mexico and should place few obstacles on legal immigration from that country. These obstacles are particularly strong in the light of NAFTA. The creation of the North Atlantic Free Trade Area is of great benefit to the United States, but the initial costs to Mexico may be high. Mexican peasants cannot compete against some agricultural imports from the United States and Canada but are able to produce fruits and vegetables at a lower price and thus increase their trade with the United States. Mexican village traders may be unable to hold their own against great trading corporations such as Walmart. Hence more and more rural people may have to look for jobs in towns—in the United States as well as Mexico. Emigration to the United States therefore is a social safety valve; some argue that the United States cannot afford to shut it too tightly, lest the Mexican boiler explode.[27]

The Case against Immigration

Whereas the advocates of immigration are optimists, their opponents incline to pessimism. Massive population growth, in their opinion, will confront the United States with a wide range of insoluble problems. In 1930, the population of the United States amounted to just under 123,000,000 people; by 1990 this number had risen to nearly

---

27. Paul Rich, "Mexican Neoliberal Nightmares: Tampico Is Not Taiwan," *Journal of Interamerican Studies* 37, no. 4 (winter 1995): 173–90.

249,000,000. Census Bureau projections for the future vary; but they keep rising. (In 1989 statisticians calculated that, by the year 2050, the United States would have 300,000,000 people; in 1992 the estimate increased to 383,000,000, and in 1993, to 392,000,000 because of increased immigration and amnestied illegals who, in turn, brought in relatives.) Whatever the value of such projections, the United States will continue to face enormous pressures. The United States shares a 2,000-mile border with poor, backward Mexico and a maritime frontier with the Caribbean, whose people exist on a much lower living standard than that of the United States. A growing number of Haitians, Jamaicans, Dominicans, Cubans, Mexicans, Central Americans, and others will therefore wish to come to the United States for jobs they cannot find at home. Immigration is a response to trade restrictions; freer trade would reduce the desire to immigrate. If the United States were to open up trade in sugar and clothing, the Caribbean economies would benefit and many would stay at home. These pressures will increase as travel further cheapens and as would-be immigrants increasingly can count on help from friends and kinfolk already established in the United States. And the presence of an unlimited supply of cheap, unskilled labor keeps wages low, takes jobs from native-born people, and curtails the modernization of industry.

The most important source of newcomers is Mexico. No other Western country borders on a state as economically backward as Mexico. To job seekers from Mexico (and also from Central American countries) the United States offers enormous attractions, including political stability, constitutional government, and relative freedom from corruption. The United States affords a greater number and variety of jobs, new opportunities of economic advancement. In addition to these "pull" factors, there are also "push" factors. Mexico faces a long-term demographic crisis. The Mexican population (more than 91,000,000) continues to grow at a substantial rate; it is also much more youthful than the U.S. population. At the same time, well-educated people are being replaced in offices by new forms of high technology. Unemployment and underemployment both remain high. The difference in the growth rate per capita between the United States and Mexico is striking. Conditions similar to those in Mexico exist throughout much of Latin America. (Mexico itself has to cope with numerous illegal immigrants who are much more harshly treated in Mexico than they are in the United States.) "Obviously, enormous pressures are building throughout the less developed world for emigration, legal or illegal."[28]

Striking also are the number of immigrants from Asia. (Between 1971 and 1990, the Hispanic population of the United States increased by 141 percent, the Asian population, by 385 percent.) Asians in the United States now consist of many nationalities: Filipinos, Japanese, East Indians, Koreans, and Vietnamese, with the largest group the Chinese (22.6 percent of the Asian population in 1990). A gigantic additional reservoir of emigrants would open up if the U.S. drive for a democratic world order were even partially successful. Imagine a world in which the dictatorships that now run the People's Republic of China, Vietnam, and North Korea were to liberalize and permit free emigration. Untold more millions would wish to come to the United States. Africa is a strife-torn continent from which many might wish to escape. Additional claimants for refuge in the United States might include Russians, Ukrainians, Slovaks, Croats, Serbs, and Bosnian Muslims whose respective homelands are or could again be stricken by economic slumps, political turmoil, or war.

Zero population advocate Paul Ehrlich does not want to close the "golden door" of immigration but desires to limit population growth by having Americans have (on average) fewer than one child per couple. Immigration, according to Ehrlich, should be limited to less than the sum of deaths plus outmigrants. But for most restrictionists, the solution is simpler: limit immigration. Polls show that the majority of the public consider there are too many immigrants, especially the citi-

---

28. John Tanton, "Rethinking Immigration Policy," Washington, D.C., FAIR, 1980, p. 13.

zens of California, Florida, Texas, and New York, who mostly think the gates should be closed for at least a few years.[29]

For ecological reasons alone, the United States will not be able to cope unless it can radically restrict immigration. No matter whether the newcomers arrive with or without proper papers, their mere presence in the United States erodes the quality of life by increasing the pressure on U.S. natural wealth—water, soil, timber, energy. The immigrants likewise make new demands on public services—housing, schools, hospitals, and welfare agencies. Such pressure will grow all the more since the United States consumes natural resources at a much greater rate than any other country. Do Americans want to live in a country with 400,000,000 or 500,000,000 people, with even greater traffic snarls, more urban congestion, and more nationwide pollution than at present?

Restrictionists further blame massive immigration for destroying agricultural lands, degrading natural settings, and polluting the environment. Continual immigration will exceed the carrying capacity of the environment, while access to rural and wilderness areas is declining. Do American taxpayers want to pay for huge additional outlays on schools, hospitals, freeways, bridges? Surely not, say politicians such as Richard Lamm, a former governor of Colorado and a presidential nominee of the Reform Party in the U.S. presidential campaign of 1996. Time to call a halt, the restrictionists shout!

Only the elites want large-scale immigration—the masses do not. Such is the argument put forth by anti-immigrationist Peter Brimelow in his book *Alien Nation*.[30] Economic elites need immigrants for cheap labor—house cleaners, nursemaids, busboys, grape pickers, laborers, gardeners. Roy Beck also argues, in *The Case against Immigration*, that

29. B. Meredith Burke, "An Environmental Impact Statement for Immigration," *Wall Street Journal*, 1 April 1993, p. A15.

30. Peter Brimelow, *Alien Nation: Common Sense about America's Immigration Disaster* (New York: Random House, 1995).

immigration is against the interests of working people, especially those with low or outmoded skills. But immigrants also hurt the middle class by lowering wages. An increase in the labor supply tends to lower wages, but a shortage of workers raises wages, states a 1988 General Accounting Office report. The presence of cheap labor from Mexico has kept wages low in California agriculture, for example. Immigrants are responsible for most of the population growth in the United States. If immigration continues at current levels, by 2050 there will be some 400–500 million people. To slow population growth, almost all immigration should be stopped, Beck asserts.

Borjas, the Harvard economist, agrees with Beck that immigration does lower wages in some sectors of the economy, such as agriculture, service industries, and construction. Both argue that low-priced migrant labor has been largely responsible for the growing economic inequality in the United States. Economist Robert Dunn of George Washington University states that a large supply of labor from Mexico willing to work for less has hurt the incomes of less-skilled Americans even as economic growth has increased. Borjas thus rejects the economic argument for immigration, which, according to him, can only be defended on political grounds.

Restrictionists such as Beck and Brimelow also contend that the United States does not need foreign investors or entrepreneurs. The United States has enough American workers, professionals, and graduate students in the sciences and in high-tech industries. Nor are large numbers of immigrants necessary to keep the Social Security system solvent, as some argue. In the United States, the rich are getting richer, the poor are getting poorer and growing in number because of massive legal and illegal immigration.

According to Brimelow, imported labor of any skill level is not necessary for economic development or technological innovation. He points to Japan as having achieved economic prosperity without immigration (only 1.4 million or so resident foreigners live in Japan; the United States has 25 million). Brimelow forcefully argues the political case for a much regulated and reduced immigration. In *Alien Nation,* Brimelow makes numerous recommendations, some of which came to pass in 1996: double the size of the border patrol and increase the size of the INS. But most of his recommendations have not yet been accepted, and many—a national identity card, a new "operation wetback" to expel illegal aliens—are not likely ever to be accepted. In 1997, however, Congress may well follow Brimelow's suggestions and limit family reunification to members of a nuclear family, cut legal immigration from its current one million or so annually to 400,000–500,000, reduce the number of refugees, and lengthen the time of legal residence for naturalization to ten years. (Congress in 1997 failed to address any of these major problems or whether a literacy and skill level would be imposed. But Congress did revise the welfare reform bill to restore rights to legal immigrants, especially the elderly and disabled on SSI.)

Ethnic leaders, organized in bodies such as the National Council of La Raza, favor immigration because it will strengthen their respective ethnic constituencies. Liberal elites—pastors, entertainers, journalists, academics—derive pleasure from the cultural diversity allegedly created by exotic foreigners. These liberal elites equally enjoy a sense of moral superiority derived from their claimed status as spokespersons for the underprivileged and as moral role models for the nation at large. But these cultural preferences are not shared by most ordinary Americans.

Immigration has numerous unintended consequences. The old-style immigrant was usually a European. The new-style immigrant mostly comes from Asia, Latin America, the Caribbean, countries whose political and social traditions greatly differ from those of the United States. The new immigrants (much like previous immigrants), moreover, have higher birthrates than the natives. Hence immigrants have a disproportionately powerful impact on the United States' demographic composition. The post-1970 population growth, according to demographer Leon F. Bouvier, is nearly all due to immigration. (Immigrants now account for 37.1 percent of all new population growth, compared with 27 percent at the peak immigration years between 1900 and 1910.) The old immigrants, however diverse, all derived from the Judeo-Christian tradition. The new immigrants include Muslims, Confucians, Buddhists, adherents of Shinto, votaries of voodoo. Given such cultural multiplicity—anti-immigrationists argue—the United States may split linguistically and spiritually in future.

Does this matter? Did not the United States, in the olden days, successfully absorb Irish, Germans, Poles, and many other nationalities? True enough, argue the anti-immigrationists. But the position has now changed. In the late nineteenth and early twentieth centuries, the United States had a confident core culture. The United States insisted that newcomers should assimilate and learn English—and so they did; there was no bilingual education. By contrast, the new immigrants come at a time when the United States' cultural self-reliance has eroded. Mexican and Asian activists have learned from the civil rights struggles conducted by black Americans and thus demand bilingual education and seek "brown pride" and restoration of "brown dignity," while rejecting assimilation and Western culture. The new immigrants, or rather their self-appointed spokespeople, now desire official recognition as groups and proportional representation—requirements incompatible with the operation of a free market. Group rights are demanded in the makeup of electoral districts, in employment, in the award of official contracts, in education, in every sphere of public life. Opposition to such programs is seen as yet one more proof of white America's inherent racism.[31]

Multiculturists want to preserve immigrant cultures and languages, not absorb or assimilate the American culture. (The melting pot met-

---

31. Lawrence Auster, "Massive Immigration Will Destroy America," *Insight*, 3 October 1994, p. 18.

aphor is rejected by multiculturists.) The United States, the anti-immigration argument continues, therefore must restrict immigration and at the same time promote cultural assimilation. Otherwise multiculturalism will lead to political fragmentation and fragmentation to disaster. Imagine the United States as a Bosnia of continental proportions—without a sense of common nationhood, a common culture, a common political heritage, with dozens of contending ethnic groups and a population of half a billion! These problems will be even harder to face as immigration has exacerbated income inequalities within the United States, worsened the economic prospects of black Americans and recent immigrants, disrupted local communities, and—through sheer force of numbers—further injured the environment. The United States, argue critics such as Brimelow, will in the long run cease to be a mainly white nation; its ethnic character will be transformed—this without proper policy discussion and against the declared will of America's overwhelming majority. Nativists are accused of hysteria when they talk about a threatened Mexican *reconquista* of California. Nativists incur equal censure when they charge foreign-born activists with holding in contempt the *anglo-sajones* and their values. But nativist fears merely reflect the ethnic propaganda common in campus rallies held by ethnic militants.

In a more specialized sense, scholars such as Beck and Matloff do not merely want to protect the United States underclass from foreign competition. They also criticize U.S. employers for importing highly skilled people. Business lobbyists now call for at least 140,000 skilled newcomers a year from other countries. But the United States already has thousands of unemployed engineers, scientists, computer programmers, and other highly skilled people, insist Beck and Matloff. Surely, there must be sufficient Americans to step into those highly skilled positions that industry wants to fill. (Silicon Valley executives say not true; we need skilled foreigners or else we shall have to ship jobs offshore.) From the industrialists' viewpoint, Beck and Matloff argue, it is certainly cheaper to pick foreigners. But why should the

United States aim for "a high-tech workforce . . . that will accept Third World wages and working conditions?"[32]

For the anti-immigrationists, there are also good political reasons for cutting down immigration. Latin immigrants today cluster in large neighborhoods to a greater extent than those foreigners who came here a century ago. Such clustering slows down assimilation and the learning of English, according to Hoover Institution economist Edward P. Lazear, as does the provision of welfare. (Poor people who receive welfare benefits have fewer incentives to learn English and adjust to the demands of the new society.) Latino immigrants in particular now also make political demands of a kind not made by Sicilian or Greek immigrants a century earlier. As Peter Skerry, a U.S. political scientist, puts it, Mexican Americans "are being seduced by the new American political systems into adopting the not entirely appropriate, divisive, and counterproductive stance of a racial minority group."[33] Mexican Americans, Central Americans, and other Latins are now classed as part of a new "Hispanic" minority. The leaders who claim to speak on their behalf demand privileges similar to those claimed for the black minority by bodies such as the National Association for the Advancement of Colored People (NAACP) and by white liberals. The 1996 presidential election showed new Hispanic voting power strengthened by the hurried massive granting of citizenship to Latinos and Asians (critics claim thousands of criminals were naturalized without proper FBI background checks). The "new citizens" were actively registered to vote by Democratic Party activists. (Florida went Democratic for the

---

32. Roy Beck, *The Case against Immigration: The Moral, Economic, Social and Environmental Reasons for Reducing U.S. Immigration Back to Traditional Levels* (New York: W. W. Norton, 1996), p. 246; Nathan Glazer, ed., *Clamor at the Gates: The New American Immigration* (San Francisco, Calif.: Institute for Contemporary Studies, 1985); Chilton Williamson Jr., *The Immigration Mystique: America's False Conscience* (New York: Basic Books, 1996).

33. Peter Skerry, *Mexican-Americans: The Ambivalent Minority* (New York: Free Press, 1993), p. 367. See also Skerry essay in this volume.

first time in recent history, and in California Latinos helped Democrats win the presidency and House and state legislature seats.)

In the November 1996 election Latino voters did go to the polls in record numbers, assisting President Clinton to an overwhelming victory in California and tipping tight races in favor of some Democratic candidates for Congress and the legislature, according to exit polls and analysts.[34] Bloc voting, especially by Mexicans, appeared to push Democrats to victory in California and cost the Republicans Florida for the first time in twenty years. The Latino vote for the Democrats was a backlash for the GOP's perceived anti-immigrant agenda and has huge implications for the future. The Latino share of the vote is increasing rapidly in several key states, helped in part by the 1986 amnesty of 1–2 million illegals and their bringing in another million or so relatives subsequently. Between 1992 and 1996 the Hispanic population grew from 7 to 10 percent in Califronia, from 10 to 16 percent in Texas. Hispanics have tended to vote as a bloc (80–85 percent) for the Democratic Party.

These changes have all contributed to a new sense of anxiety in the United States. This unease is not confined to angry white males. Take, for instance, East Palo Alto, a Bay Area township near Stanford University. East Palo Alto was once as solidly black as Harlem. Now East Palo Alto is undergoing a transformation from black to Latino. (Between 1980 and 1990 alone, the black population dropped from 60 percent to 41.5 percent. The Hispanic population increased from 14 percent to 36 percent.) Blacks leave East Palo Alto for a variety of reasons. Some feel that they must unfairly compete with Hispanics for affordable housing; the black purchaser stands on his own, whereas several extended Latino families may pool their resources to rent or purchase a residence. Whatever the cause, says Gertrude Wilks, a former mayor of East Palo Alto, East Palo Alto now feels much more

---

34. Patrick J. McDonnell et al., "Latinos Make Strong Showing at the Polls," *Los Angeles Times*, 8 November 1996.

Hispanic. "You almost feel that if you don't understand Spanish, you better learn it."[35] The same sentiment can be heard in and around Miami, Los Angeles, and San Francisco.

Troubling to many Americans are the political shifts occasioned by mass immigration. Generalizations, of course, are dangerous. Cubans (who occupy a powerful position, especially in New Jersey and Florida) tend to vote Republican, as do Koreans and Chinese. Mexicans, Puerto Ricans (also Arab Americans and others), by contrast, more often support the Democrats. Vice-President Gore, therefore, organized a group, the Citizenship USA Program, to speed up the naturalization of legal immigrants in time for the presidential election in 1996. The White House even pressured the INS to lower standards for the language and history tests for naturalization before the November election. (The Welfare Act of 1996 also had the unintended effect of encouraging many more legal immigrants to apply for naturalization so as not to lose accustomed benefits. The new citizens [ca. 1.2 million], in all probability, mainly voted [85 percent] for Democrats, with striking effects on the politics of states such as California and Florida.)

Republicans charged massive voter fraud in the 1996 presidential election, claiming Democrats rushed people through the naturalization process in order to get them to vote Democratic in November 1996. For example, frauds were discovered in a training program to teach English and American history and speeding up or ignoring criminal background checks. Governor Pete Wilson charged that the Citizenship USA Program naturalized 1.3 million people of whom 180,000 were not checked for criminal records. The controversy continued well into 1997, and Republican congressman Dornan of California sued to have his seat returned to him, claiming his Latino opponent had won by use of the votes of fraudulently naturalized Latinos and Asians.

---

35. Reported in Michael McCabe, "Historically Black East Palo Alto Now Moving toward a Latino Majority," *San Francisco Chronicle*, 14 May 1996, p. A4.

Should this matter to ordinary Americans who want to preserve their country's existing institutions? Not as far as the mass of new voters are concerned. Few of them are radicals; most of them like their adopted country. These generalizations, however, do not apply to Latino and Chicano activists. Ordinary Americans are offended when Chicano militants deny the United States' right to control its borders or when activists call for the mythical nation of Aztlán (covering the Southwest). Most Americans equally dislike the sight of Mexican demonstrators waving the Mexican flag on U.S. soil. Others complained when the INS in 1996 allegedly devalued standards for citizenship "to the point where naturalization is no longer a meaningful experience."[36]

What of the economic burdens of immigrants? The question remains contentious because investigators lack basic data. Estimates concerning the size of the immigrant population vary by as much as 50 percent. There are equal disparities in estimates concerning the immigrants' respective incomes, the tax rates applied to them, the range of services included in the estimates, and the range of public revenues. No prophet, moreover, can forecast the future long-term impact that any group of immigrants may make on the economic and political fortunes of the United States. (The emigration of many brilliant Jewish scientists from Central Europe during the 1930s enormously reduced Germany's and vastly enhanced the United States' capability to make, in the future, an atomic bomb. But no one understood this at the time, not even the émigrés themselves.)

Nevertheless, immigration also entails costs—this especially in states with heavy immigration: California, Florida, Texas, Arizona, Illinois, New York, and New Jersey. In the early 1990s, 20.7 percent of immigrant households received cash benefits, Medicaid, vouchers (mainly food stamps), or housing subsidies, as compared to 14.1 percent of native households (10.5 percent of white non-Hispanic native households). Second, immigrant households made up of refugees and

---

36. John Miller, "The Naturalizers," *Policy Review*, July–August 1996, p. 31.

older relatives experience both more and longer welfare spells. Immigrant households, especially refugees and older relatives, therefore, spend a relatively large fraction of their time participating in some means-tested program.[37]

These figures are subject to debate. But in general, there seems to be widespread agreement that illegal aliens (and those without a high school diploma) now contribute less to public revenue than those who first came to the United States as undocumented aliens but were later amnestied under the Immigration and Reform Act of 1986. The beneficiaries of amnesty in turn pay less into the public coffers than the native born. Costs are high for the young. To give an example, a family of four that makes $12,000 a year will pay little or no federal and state income tax; they will contribute only a modest amount of sales taxes, property taxes, and, possibly, Social Security payments. But to educate their two children will cost more than $10,000 a year—not to speak of other services.[38] Yet overall immigration is considered a net economic plus for the United States because of the high contributions of those with high school and college degrees. Whereas the poorly educated cost about $13,000 in a lifetime, the educated add $198,000 in net value in taxes paid and welfare benefits deferred.

Immigrants also use welfare at a higher rate than the native born. According to the March 1994 Current Population Survey (CPS), 6.6 percent of the foreign born use Aid to Families with Dependent Children (AFDC), supplemental security income, or general assistance, compared to 4.9 percent of the natives. Welfare is most concentrated

---

37. George J. Borjas and Lynette Hilton, *Immigration and the Welfare State: Immigrant Participation in Means-Tested Entitlement Programs* (Cambridge, Mass.: National Bureau of Economic Research, 1995), pp. 2–3; George J. Borjas, *Immigration and Welfare 1970–1990* (Cambridge, Mass.: National Bureau of Economic Research, 1994).

38. Georges Vernez and Kevin McCarthy, "Public Costs of Immigration. Testimony before the Subcommittee on Immigration and Claims," U.S. House of Representatives, Rand Corporation, CT 133, April 1995.

among two special groups—the elderly and refugees. Taken together, refugees and the elderly make up 21 percent of immigrants but account for 40 percent of all immigrant welfare users. (As of 1995, some 785,400 aliens received SSI.) The number of foreign-born elderly (over sixty-five) immigrants is moreover projected to rise from 2.7 million in 1990 to more than 4.5 million in 2010. The main beneficiaries of SSI are Asians, but immigrants from Mexico, Cuba, and the former Soviet Union also use SSI.

To most Americans this seems absurd. As Senator Rick Santorum (Rep.-Penn.) argued in an ongoing debate concerning a new immigration bill, the United States should not become the world's retirement home. The sponsors of elderly immigrants all signed documents promising that the newcomers would not become public charges. These promises should be honored. Refugees (numbering about one-tenth of the immigrant population), as noted earlier, make extensive use of welfare services. Political refugees tend to be older and less equipped to make a living in the United States than immigrants who came purely for economic reasons, and many older refugees don't learn English.[39] Not all self-described refugees, moreover, have in fact suffered persecution. (Allegedly, members of the Russian Mafia managed to make their way to this country masquerading as victims.)

What of the general burdens imposed by immigrants on the native born? To begin with, we must point out that some 80 percent of immigrants receive no welfare benefits. Even illegal immigrants have their champions. A high proportion of illegal immigrants find employment in agriculture, clothing industries, poultry and meat plants, and service industries. Their presence keeps down the price of food but also keeps wages low for janitors, restaurant workers, farm laborers, and other unskilled workers. Proponents of agricultural guest-worker pro-

---

39. Michael Fix, Jeffrey S. Passel, and Wendy Zimmerman, *The Use of SSI and Other Welfare Programs by Immigrants. Testimony before the US Senate Subcommittee on Immigration. 6 February 1996* (Washington, D.C.: Urban Institute, 1996).

grams claim they cannot find enough legal workers and that raising wages would not bring out more workers but would increase food prices greatly. A 1996 report of the Center for Immigration Studies (CIS, Washington, D.C.)—"How Much Is That Tomato in the Window? Retail Produce Prices Without Illegal Farm-Workers"—refutes that claim. The report found that a transition to an all-legal workforce—doubling wages and without guest workers—would only increase supermarket prices for fresh produce by about 6 percent and then for only a one- or two-year transition period. After that, prices would be only 3 percent higher.

A federal commission on agricultural workers found in 1992 that there was an oversupply of agricultural workers, widespread unemployment and underemployment, and deteriorating wages and working conditions for seasonal workers. Yet Congress, pushed by agro-business interests, is considering a new guest-worker program of one million farmworkers. The proposal is a response to congressional efforts to reduce illegal immigration, which provides approximately 17 percent of seasonal labor in the United States. Growers claim they will not have enough workers to pick their crops if illegals or guest workers are shut out. CIS scholars deny this claim and insist that higher wages will bring out legal laborers and that growers could adjust to labor shortfalls by mechanization and more efficient use of labor. The California tomato industry provides a classic example of mechanization leading to greater productivity with a greatly diminished workforce (4,000 to 175) and higher profits, according to Philip Martin, in this volume.

Even undocumented farm workers in the United States experience upward mobility. According to U.S. economist Philip L. Martin, the average seasonal worker's career as a farm laborer is less than ten years. Hence farmworkers find it easier to better their lot by shifting, in due course, to a nonfarming job than by fighting for change within the farm labor market.

Nevertheless, there are costs to mass immigration, especially illegal immigration. The availability of cheap labor discourages employers from rationalizing labor practices and mechanization. Low wages force some workers, for example, those in agriculture, in poultry, and in restaurant work, to seek welfare benefits such as food stamps. The great majority of illegal immigrants' only offense consists in residing here without proper papers. All the same, their very presence breeds defiance of U.S. laws. Illegal aliens, moreover, include a minority of criminals guilty of drug smuggling and other offenses. Whether aliens come here legally or illegally, the charge sheet continues, they form new ghettos and change the character of entire cities. The presence of illegal aliens in this country discriminates against those waiting abroad for visas and those immigrants who have come here legally and played by the rules.

Conventional wisdom claims that immigrants take jobs that natives do not want. This statement, however, argues Matloff,[40] does not always square with reality. In those parts of the United States where there are few immigrants, natives do the low-level jobs but at a decent wage. The United States should not therefore import foreign workers at lower wages at a time when job opportunities for unskilled and semiskilled workers are diminishing and the income gap between rich and poor Americans is widening. The constant influx of poorly paid workers may also discourage employers from capitalizing their operations and thereby impede technological progress.

Low wages paid to immigrants, moreover, do not tell the whole story. Another factor is network hiring, whereby news of job openings is spread by tight social networks among immigrants of a particular ethnic group. These alleviate the employer's need to advertise and work in the employer's favor. Once an extended network is established, it stays in place. The chief sufferers are the native poor who lack the immigrants' extended ties of kinship, provincial origin, and ethnicity.

---

40. Norman Matloff, "The Adverse Impacts of Immigration on Minorities," testimony to House Judiciary Committee, Subcommittee on Immigration, 5 April 1995 (updated 19 November 1995).

The adverse impact of immigration on the American poor is not limited to wage employment. Legal and illegal aliens alike require space for their children at school. Schools, especially schools in poorer districts, have to adjust to the presence of numerous foreign-born children who have trouble with English and who require bilingual teachers in the most diverse languages. Immigrants receiving low wages compete with the native born for welfare, public housing, and health care. Immigrants also bring in diseases such as tuberculosis and AIDS. Illegal aliens receive welfare benefits via their U.S.-born children who are U.S. citizens and thus eligible for all services. As noted previously, welfare use among elderly immigrants has gone up by 400 percent in the last ten years. Indeed, a new class of permanent welfare users has come into being—elderly immigrants. (Despite their model minority image, about 55 percent of elderly Chinese immigrants were on welfare, mostly SSI, in 1996, as opposed to 9 percent of natives.)[41]

Immigrant advocates claim that immigrants create new jobs. But it is not that simple, Matloff argues. Although participating at the same level in the workforce as natives, immigrants have a lower per capita income and therefore consume less. Immigrants, moreover, create enclave economies, shopping at immigrant-owned stores. Their purchases thus benefit other immigrants more than the native born. Some immigrants do build new businesses. But, as an Urban Institute study found, these also have a lower tax compliance level than native-owned businesses.

What of foreign engineers, computer scientists, and other experts? Matloff points to Softpac of Austin, Texas, which claimed that the software industry needed approximately forty thousand new workers in 1994. This figure is less than the fifty-one thousand new computer science graduates produced every year by U.S. universities. Although

---

41. Norman Matloff, "Welfare Use among Elderly Chinese Immigrants," testimony to the Senate Judiciary Committee, Subcommittee on Immigration, 6 February 1996 (updated 11 March 1996).

Softpac cautions against taking its estimates too precisely, these figures certainly call into question the thirty thousand work visas granted to foreign computer programmers every year. Softpac also found that between 1990 and 1993 U.S. colleges and universities awarded two bachelor degrees in engineering for every engineering job opening created through net replacement. The vast majority of technological advances in the U.S. computer field have been made by natives (as documented by the number of awards for industrial innovation given respectively to natives and immigrants). Moreover, what counts in the programming field is general programming talent, not those highly specific skills for which foreigners are often hired. The United States, Matloff concludes, has plenty of suitably qualified men and women already. It is just that foreigners, on the average, are more tractable and come more cheaply.[42] Given these objections, anti-immigration sentiment has become widespread and not just among Anglo-Saxon whites. For instance, the Latino National Political Survey of 1992 found that 84 percent of Mexican Americans agreed with the statement "there are too many immigrants." Time, say the anti-immigrationists, to heed the people's will.[43] "Wanted: Leaders to say 'Enough,'" wrote demographer B. Meredith Burke.

Restrictionists stress that immigrants cluster in four states (California, Florida, Texas, New York). The resultant ethnic aggregations greatly worsen existing social problems and put an unfair burden on the states most affected. (Asians now make up 30 percent of San Francisco County. Latinos now amount to 40 percent or so of the population in the Los Angeles megalopolis.) In general foreign-born migrants are strongly drawn to large immigrant populations from the same country. Only highly educated migrants move within the United States

---

42. Norman Matloff, "A Critical Look at Immigration's Role in the US Computer Industry," paper submitted to the Hoover Institution Workshop on Immigration, 22 March 1996.

43. Cited by Matloff, "Adverse Impacts of Immigration on Minorities," p. 13.

more in response to the availability of jobs than to the presence of other immigrants from the same stock.[44] Time for a change, conclude the restrictionists. But the final word in the debate may be the 1997 National Science Foundation report, which states that immigration benefits the U.S. economy overall and has little negative effect on the income and job opportunities of most U.S. citizens. Only in a few states (California, Texas) with a high concentration of low-skilled, low-paid immigrants with families are state and local taxpayers paying more on average to support education, health, and welfare services that immigrants use.

Mistaken Solutions

Immigration has become a subject of bitter debate all over the Western world, not just in the United States but also in Canada, Australia, and Western Europe. (By dint of immigration, for instance, Islam has become a major religion in Western Europe; in Britain more people now regularly attend a mosque than an Anglican church.) But in the United States the immigration problem is complicated by policies determined by the courts and administrative agencies to create a level playing field and speed up progress for people of African descent. Affirmative action was originally practiced to speed up black advancement but was extended to other minorities, including Hispanics and Asians; in time affirmative action was increasingly defended as an instrument for assuring "diversity."

Affirmative action, however, had unexpected results. Hostility grew among whites toward Mexican and other immigrants on the grounds that they not only competed with the native born for housing and social

---

44. June Marie Nagle, "Immigrants on the Move: How Internal Migration Increases the Concentration of the Foreign Born," *Backgrounder* (Center for Immigration Studies), January 1996.

benefits but obtained unfair advantages in the allocation of jobs, contracts, and college admission. Affirmative action raised other questions.
How valid were the categories used in dividing the U.S. population?
Why not a special category for Arab Americans or for Afro-Europeans?
Should skin color constitute a legitimate criterion for assuring diversity
on a college campus. (An admissions officer would surely be in trouble
if she were to pursue diversity by giving special advantages to underrepresented groups such as Pentecostals, Hasidic Jews, or Scientologists.)

Affirmative action also has had the unintended effect of promoting
corruption, as some white firms used black or Hispanic front men to
gain contracts. On an individual basis, how could cheating be avoided
when racial identity became a valued asset in the marketplace? The
temptation would grow for a job applicant or a student seeking admission to a college to invent or find a Native American grandmother or a
Hispanic grandmother—easy enough to do as long as racial identity
depended on self-identification. To avoid such cheating, the United
States would, in future, surely require racial identity papers of the kind
once used in Nazi Germany or apartheid South Africa.[45] This is not a
prospect that appeals to the bulk of U.S. voters, who harbor no sense of
historical guilt.

In the field of public education the "Americanizing" of immigrant
children fell into disrepute. The method of teaching English by "immersion" was widely replaced by bilingual education (now required by
nine states in all school districts with a designated number of limited-
English-proficient [LEP] students). In Massachusetts twenty LEP students in one language group in a district will trigger native-language
instruction in a separate classroom taught by a certified bilingual
teacher, even if there are only two students in each grade. As a result,
forty thousand students in fifty-one Massachusetts school districts received bilingual education in 1993–1994. Spanish-speaking students,

---

45. L. H. Gann and Alvin Rabushka, "Racial Classification: Politics of the Future,"
Policy Review, summer 1981; Hoover Institution Reprint series, no. 45.

who represent more than half of the LEP population in Massachusetts, are taught to read and write Spanish and also are instructed in Spanish in other academic subjects. Such examples have intensified the debate on bilingual education.

A recent study by the National Research Council, however, found that the arguments in favor of bilingual education were based on a number of myths. There was no evidence of long-term advantages in teaching LEP children in their native language. Further, teaching these children to read in English first, not in their native language, did them no harm. In contrast, emphasizing cultural and ethnic differences in the classroom caused stereotyping, did not improve the self-esteem of minority children, and reinforced the differences of those children from the others. Nor was there any research support for the idea that teachers who were themselves members of minority groups were more effective than others who worked with children from those same groups. The study concluded that the U.S. Department of Education's management of bilingual education research had been a total failure, wasting hundreds of millions of dollars, using the research agenda for political purposes to justify a program that had not proven its worth, and not making its research available to the educators who could use it to improve their school programs.

We would agree with Charles L. Glenn, a bilingual specialist, who insists that there is no reason to spend more years searching for a "model" teaching program, while another generation of language-minority students is damaged by inferior schooling. And there is certainly no reason to put any future research in the hands of the Office of Bilingual Education and Minority Languages Affairs (OBEMLA).[46]

We would leave considerable latitude to local authorities to deter-

---

46. Rosalie Pedalino Porter, Introduction to Charles L. Glenn, "Improving Schooling for Language Minority Children: A Research Agenda," a review of the National Research Council Study, *Read Abstracts Research and Policy Review*, May 1997, pp. 1–2.

mine their own needs in public education. But we reject "cultural maintenance" as a legitimate object of public education. U.S. citizens and residents alike have an indefeasible right to speak whatever language and practice whatever customs they please in their own homes. But the aim of public education should be to Americanize the immigrants — not to preserve their status as cultural aliens. Bilingualism serves to divide, not unite, Americans.

PART ONE

Benefits
and
Costs

*Kevin F. McCarthy and
Georges Vernez*

CHAPTER ONE

Benefits and Costs
of Immigration
The California Experience

Immigration, like any other complex socioeconomic phenomenon that affects a broad array of public and individual interests, involves both benefits and costs and thus confronts policymakers with making inevitable trade-offs between conflicting interests. We also would expect the size and nature of the trade-offs to vary over time depending on the volume of immigration; the education, skills, and other attributes of immigrants relative to native borns; the need for and public services available to immigrants; and a state's unique economic and social circumstances.

To learn more about the nature of the trade-offs involved with immigration, we have examined the demographic, economic, distributional, and institutional effects immigration has had in California over a thirty-year period from 1960 to 1990 (McCarthy and Vernez 1997). This chapter is based on this assessment and focuses primarily on economic and distributional effects. We begin with a brief review of the changes in immigration and the receiving environment that have taken place in California since 1960. We then examine the effects immigration has had over time on its labor market and economy, native-born workers, and the public sector.

Changing Immigration and Receiving Environment

Much has changed in California since the Immigration and Naturalization Act of 1965 abolished the national origin quotas that favored European immigration, opened the (previously closed) door to immigration from Asia and from Latin America, and established family reunification as the primary criterion for permanent legal immigration to the United States. The number of immigrants arriving in any given year has quadrupled; one out of ten immigrants is now from Europe down from nine out of ten; and increasingly more immigrants settle in California rather than in the rest of the nation. Finally, the economy has shifted from a manufacturing-based economy to an economy in which more than four out of every five newly created jobs require at least some college education.

NUMBER AND COMPOSITION OF IMMIGRANTS

From making a small contribution to the growth of California's population and labor force, immigrants have come to dominate it. In the 1960s, for instance, immigrants contributed only one out of every ten new workers to the labor force. By the late 1980s, immigrants were contributing the majority—more than one out of every two—of new workers to California's labor force. Over the past twenty years, we estimate that immigrants have contributed more than two-thirds to the growth of California's population including their children born in the United States, who now account for about 40 percent of the state's natural population growth. Today, more than one of every four California residents is foreign born compared to one in ten as recently as 1970.

In addition to volume, there have been three salient changes in the composition of immigrants. The first has been a steady decline in

the education of immigrants to California *relative* to native borns, from
an average gap of 1.8 years in 1970 to 2.6 years in 1990 (see table 1).
This growing relative shift in educational attainment between foreign
and native borns is most apparent at the lower levels of education,
where immigrants in the labor force are now *four* times more likely
than native borns to have less than twelve years of education compared
with two times twenty years earlier. This trend is also apparent at the
top of the educational distribution, where, in 1970, immigrants were
just as likely as native borns to have a college degree (13 vs. 15 percent)
but are now 30 percent less likely. The growth in the educational gap
between foreign and native borns has occurred despite an increase in
the educational attainment of foreign borns, from an average 10.4 years
in 1970 to 10.8 years in 1990. This is because the educational attainment of native borns has rapidly increased, from an average 12.2 years
in 1970 to 13.4 years in 1990. As we shall see in the next section, this
growing educational disparity between foreign and native borns has
shaped the various effects of immigration in significant ways, both
positive and negative.

A significant shift in countries of origin of immigrants has added a

Table 1   Educational Attainment of Labor Force by Immigration
           Status, California, 1970 and 1990 (in percent)

	1970		1990	
Years of Schooling	*Foreign Born*	*Native Born*	*Foreign Born*	*Native Born*
Less than twelve	46	28	37	9
Twelve	25	36	23	26
Thirteen to fifteen	16	21	21	38
More than sixteen	13	15	19	27
Total	100	100	100	100
Average Years of Schooling	*10.4*	*12.2*	*10.8*	*13.4*

SOURCE: 1970 and 1990 Public Use Sample of the U.S. Bureau of the Census.
NOTE: Includes all persons aged sixteen to sixty-four in the labor force.

new racial/ethnic diversity to immigration flows in the United States. In the 1950s, Europeans still dominated the immigration flows to California, with Mexicans (25 percent) and Asians (15 percent) forming distinct minorities. By the 1980s, Mexican and Asians were contributing about 40 percent of the flows each; Europeans were contributing only about 5 percent. These aggregate figures mask shifts in origin of immigrants within major regions of the world, most particularly Asians. Although Filipinos, Chinese, Japanese, and Koreans continue to come to California in large numbers, they have been joined by immigrants from Southeast Asia including Vietnam, Laos, and Cambodia. In addition, immigrants from Central America (now at 10 percent) and the Middle East make today's flow of immigrants to California the most diverse ever. Over time, and as a result of the higher fertility and younger age structure of immigrants, these flows are making California a state where no one racial/ethnic group will constitute a majority of the population. Today, non-Hispanic whites still constitute 55 percent of California's population, but in California's primary schools 40 percent of all students are of Hispanic origin, with Asians constituting 10 percent and non-Hispanic whites 47 percent.

This shift in the countries of origin of immigrants is also significant because it is the primary reason for the increasing gap in educational attainment between them and native borns. The dominance of immigrant flows from Central America and Mexico, where educational attainments of the overall population continue to be low (averaging seven to nine years in Mexico), is one reason for this trend. Indeed, nearly 60 percent of immigrants from Mexico reside in California.

A final salient change in the composition of immigration flows to California has been the increasing volume of illegal immigration. Although illegal immigration, most particularly but not exclusively from Mexico, has long been a feature of immigration flows to California, these flows have been estimated to have increased fivefold, from some 25,000 yearly in the late 1960s to some 100,000 to 135,000 in the first half of the 1980s to some 200,000 yearly in the second half of the 1980s

(Vernez 1991; Johnson 1996). The increase in the second half of the 1980s may be attributable to illegal immigrants seeking to take advantage of the ease with which legal permanent residence could be obtained under the 1996 Immigration Reform and Control Act's (IRCA's) Special Agricultural Workers (SAW) program. Some 700,000 previously illegal immigrants were amnestied under that program.[1] In the recessionary years of the early 1990s, flows of illegal immigrants were estimated at 100,000 annually (Johnson 1996).

UNIQUENESS OF CALIFORNIA IMMIGRATION

Several unique aspects of California's immigration likely make its effects on the state both greater than and different from the effects of immigration on the rest of the nation. One aspect is simply volume. Between 1960 and 1990, the share of foreign borns in the labor force grew sixteen times faster in California than in the rest of the country, going from 10 percent in 1960 to 26 percent in 1990 compared with an increase from 6 to 7 percent in the rest of the nation. Whereas immigration has played, at least until now, an insignificant role in most of the nation, it has been a major agent of change in places like California.

Another reason to expect the effects of immigration to be felt differently in California than in the rest of the nation is that immigrants to California are younger than in the rest of the nation: on average thirty-three years old compared with forty-two years old in the rest of the nation. They also have been in the United States for a shorter period of time. For instance, in 1990, the average length of stay of immigrants in California was eleven years, compared with fifteen years in the rest of the nation. Finally, and as noted above, whereas the educational gap between immigrants and native borns in California

---

1. An additional 800,000 illegal immigrants who had resided in the United States continuously since before January 1, 1982, were amnestied under IRCA.

has increased over time, in the rest of the nation it has remained constant, at 1.1 years from 1970 to 1990. In brief, there has been a negative educational selectivity of immigration to California relative to that of the rest of the nation. This pattern is mainly a result of the different pattern of immigration by country of origins: Whereas about 60 percent of California immigrants originate from low-education level countries—including Mexico, Southeast Asia, and Central America—this share is only 25 percent in the rest of the country.

CHANGES IN RECEIVING ENVIRONMENT

One important aspect of California's economy is that most of its newly generated jobs were filled by workers with at least some college education. More than eight out of every ten new jobs added to the economy between 1970 and 1990 were filled by a worker with at least some college. The balance was filled by high school graduates, and no new jobs were added to the economy that were filled by workers with less than twelve years of education (see table 2).

This pattern of job growth has had two notable consequences.

Table 2   New Jobs Filled by California Immigrants
               by Level of Education, 1970–1990

	NEW JOBS CREATED		JOBS FILLED BY IMMIGRANTS		*Share of Total New Jobs Filled by*
Years of Education	*In thousands*	*Percent*	*In thousands*	*Percent*	*Immigrants*
Less than twelve	16	.2	1,047	34.9	*
Twelve	1,034	15.0	658	21.9	63.6
Thirteen to fifteen	3,420	49.1	681	22.7	19.9
Sixteen plus	2,488	35.7	614	20.4	24.7
Total	6,960	100.0	3,001	100.0	*43.1*

SOURCE: 1970, 1980, 1990 Public Use Sample of the U.S. Census Bureau.
* Immigrants filled 52 percent of jobs previously filled by natives.

First, and more generally, it has contributed to the long-term increase in earnings disparities across workers with different levels of education. As the number of jobs available for low-educated workers has stagnated and the supply of low-educated workers has increased, their earnings have not only not grown but have decreased in real terms. The reverse has been the case for workers with some college or a college degree.

Second, and more specifically, as the education of native borns has increased, low-educated immigrants not only have filled most of the jobs requiring lower levels of education but have begun to replace native borns in those jobs. By 1990, 60 percent of those jobs filled by workers with less than twelve years of education were held by immigrants compared with 16 percent in 1970.[2] Immigrants also filled more than two-thirds of the new jobs given to workers with twelve years of education (see table 2). In contrast, immigrants filled less than 22 percent of jobs given to workers with some college or college graduates.

Economic Effects of Immigration

Keeping in mind the broad immigration trends outlined above, we now turn to the question of how those trends have affected a state that itself has been changing. In this section, we focus on three specific effects of immigration: its effects on (1) employers and indirectly the economy as a whole; (2) native-born workers who may be competing for jobs with immigrants; and (3) the demand for public services. We look at the extent to which these effects may have differed over time

---

2. Although immigrants now hold more than half the jobs previously held by native borns with less than twelve years of education, it does not necessarily mean that the first has displaced the second. As noted above, native-born new entrants in the labor force do so at increasingly higher levels of education and are filling the large number of new jobs requiring a postsecondary education.

during 1970–1990 as the number of immigrants increased and their educational levels decreased relative to those of native borns.

EFFECTS ON EMPLOYERS AND THE ECONOMY

As the number of immigrants has increased, their presence has increased in all occupations and all industries in the California economy, although unevenly. Immigrants' concentration in low-skilled occupations has increased relative to native borns, and their concentration in high-skilled occupations has decreased. This disparity in occupational distribution between immigrants and native borns is particularly sharp in low-skilled industries, including agriculture, nondurable goods manufacturing, construction, and personal services (see table 3). In these industries immigrants and native borns are separated by more than four years of schooling. Immigrants provide the majority of low-skilled labor, whereas native borns provide the supervisory and higher-skilled labor. This split is referred to in the literature as immigrants forming the bulk of the labor force in the "back room" while natives occupy the "front office." In contrast, immigrants working in high-skilled industries have similar educational characteristics, although they differ somewhat in their occupational distribution. Immigrants are less likely than native borns to work in occupations requiring knowledge of United States norms or certification or both, such as lawyers, teachers, and social and religious workers and are more likely to work in scientific and professional occupations including engineering, health, and computer-related occupations.

Regardless of where they work and what they do, *California employers have benefited from immigrants' lower costs and their relatively high productivity and entrepreneurial spirit.* The wages of California immigrants have been consistently and significantly lower than those of their native-born counterparts and lower than their immigrant counterparts in the rest of the country, even after controlling for years of education and occupation (see table 4). This comparative advantage

Table 3   Educational Distribution of the Labor Force by Type of Industry and Immigration Status, California, 1990

Industries	MEAN YEARS			LESS THAN TWELVE YEARS (PERCENT)			MORE THAN SIXTEEN YEARS (PERCENT)			Percent of Total Employment	Percent of Immigrants in Industries	Percent of All Immigrants
	I	N	All	I	N	All	I	N	All			
Low skilled [a]	8.6	12.7	11.0	57	15	33	7	17	13	19.2	40.2	28.0
Medium skilled [b]	11.2	13.2	12.7	33	10	15	18	21	20	47.9	23.4	49.7
High skilled [c]	13.5	14.1	14.0	11	4	5	39	38	38	32.9	15.5	22.3

SOURCE: 1990 Public Use Sample of the U.S. Bureau of the Census.

NOTES: I = immigrant; N = native.

[a] Includes agriculture, construction, nondurable manufacturing, personal services.

[b] Includes durable manufacturing, transportation, utilities, wholesale and retail trade, business/repair, and entertainment.

[c] Includes communications, finance, insurance, and real estate (FIRE), health education, other professional occupations, and government.

Table 4   Ratio of Mean Weekly Earnings of Immigrants
               to Native Borns in California and to Other Immigrants
               in the Rest of the Nation, 1960–1990

	RATIO TO CALIFORNIA NATIVE BORNS		RATIO TO IMMIGRANTS IN REST OF THE NATION	
Years of Schooling	1970	1990	1970	1990
Less than twelve	.92	.90	.98	.95
Twelve	.95	.84	.99	.96
Thirteen to fifteen	.95	.93	.96	1.09
Sixteen plus	.88	.87	.91	.99

SOURCE: 1970 and 1990 Public Use Sample of the U.S. Bureau of the Census.

with respect to cost of labor for California employers has increased over
time and has been holding across all levels of education from high
school dropouts to college graduates.

In addition, California employers have benefited from a further
labor cost advantage due to a relative lowering of educational levels of
its labor force relative to the rest of the nation. In 1960, California
enjoyed an overall comparative advantage in the average educational
attainment of its labor force of nearly a full year. By 1990, that comparative advantage had been reversed, with California average educational
attainment lagging that of the rest of the country by about two months.
This trend has affected both low- and high-tech industries (see table 5).
For instance, the average level of education in California's apparel and
textile industry has declined by more than two years relative to the rest
of the nation. A similar but smaller decline in relative education has
taken place between California and rest of the nation's respective labor
forces in the high-tech computer and accounting industries.

This relative deterioration of the educational attainment of California's labor force lowered the costs of labor to California employers
relative to their counterparts in the rest of the nation because the lower
a worker's level of education the lower his or her wages, even within
the same occupation. Thus, in 1990, for instance, a foreign-born

Table 5   Average Years of Schooling of Labor Force by Selected
               Industries in California versus the Rest of the Nation,
               1960–1990

Selected Industries	1960		1990	
	California	*Rest of Nation*	*California*	*Rest of Nation*
Apparel and textile	9.5	8.8	9.4	11.2
Computer and accounting	12.1	11.3	14.2	14.0
Electronic	11.9	10.9	13.0	12.8
Industries and related products	12.1	11.2	13.3	13.1
Construction	10.2	9.3	11.9	11.9
Overall	*11.2*	*10.4*	*12.7*	*12.8*

SOURCE: 1960 and 1990 Public Use Sample of the U.S. Bureau of the Census.

worker with less than twelve years of education was paid on average $7.80 an hour, a high school graduate, $8.90, and an immigrant with some college, $10.50. The wages of native-born workers of different levels of education follow a similar pattern, although their wages were consistently higher: $10.30 an hour for a native-born worker with less than twelve years of education and $11.90 for a native-born high school graduate. A similar relationship between hourly wages and educational attainment exists within most occupations including laborers, service-people, salespeople, clerical workers, and craftsmen/foremen.

Although cheaper, lesser-educated labor might not have provided a comparative advantage to California employers had it lowered productivity, there is no evidence that this occurred during most of the 1960 to 1990 time period. Table 6 compares the ratio of value added and capital investments per employee in California's manufacturing sector with that of the rest of the nation. The table also shows the California versus the rest of the nation ratio for the share of the labor force that is foreign born and for mean years of schooling and that California's value added has remained consistently higher than in the rest of the nation. This pattern has prevailed despite three other notable

Table 6   Indexes of California Productivity, Capital Investments,
              Dependency on Immigrant Labor, and Education Level of
              Labor Force in Manufacturing Relative to the Rest of the
              Nation, 1960–1992

Indexes	1960	1963	1967	1970	1972	1977	1980	1982	1987	1990	1992
Value added per employee		109	109		110	105		109	102		101
New capital investments per employee		105	87		84	80		108	98		88
Share of immigrant labor	140			227			371			456	
Mean years of education	109			107			102			99	

SOURCE: 1963 to 1992 U.S. Census of Manufacturing and 1960 to 1990 Public Use Samples of the U.S. Bureau of the Census.

trends: First, the share of immigrants in the manufacturing labor force has increased more than four times faster in California than in the rest of the nation; second, the mean years of schooling of the California labor force have declined relative to that of the nation; and, third, capital investments in manufacturing have been lower in California than in the rest of the nation.

This pattern for manufacturing as a whole holds across manufacturing industries making different products and requiring different mixes of low- and high-skilled labor such as the apparel and textile, computer and electronic equipment, and instruments industries. Productivity—value added per employee—in these as well as other industries has remained generally constant despite lower new capital investments and significant declines in average years of schooling in their labor force. Nowhere is this pattern more notable than in the apparel and textile industry, where the immigrant share has increased from 32 percent in 1960 to 75 percent in 1990 compared with an increase from

12 to 13 percent in the same industry in the rest of the nation. At the same time, mean years of education in California's apparel labor force have remained constant, at 9.4 years, while in the rest of the nation they have increased from 8.8 to 11.8 years. Despite this pattern and investments in new capital, which were similar in California to the rest of the nation, value added per employee in California's apparel industry remained consistently 10 percent higher than in the rest of the country to date.

The literature on immigration indicates that immigrants do not create major problems in the workplace (Vernez et al. 1996) and describes immigrants as being "hard working," "motivated," and possessing "a strong work ethic." Because of those traits, employers have reported preferring to hire immigrants over other workers (Ross and Tilly 1991).

The productivity of California manufacturing industries declined, however, in the mid-1980s and early 1990s, perhaps because of the combined effects of the long-term relative decline in the education of the California labor force and the lower investments in new capital made by California manufacturers during those years. In the early 1990s, California also experienced severe cutbacks in the defense sector and entered the deepest and longest recession the state has known in generations.

EFFECTS ON NATIVE-BORN WORKERS

Although large-scale immigration has benefited California employers and its economy more generally, it has done so at some cost to both natives and immigrants. As expected those costs—in the form of reduced job opportunities and earnings—have been primarily borne by native-born workers with less than twelve years of education or with a high school degree but without postsecondary training. Reduced job opportunities, in turn, have resulted in lower labor force participation, higher unemployment rates, and lower net in-migration of out-of-state workers into California.

Net annual immigration rates from other states in the United States into California were cut in half, from 4.6 in-migrants per thousand persons in the California labor force in the 1960s, when immigration was low, to 2.4 in-migrants in the 1970s, when the number of immigrants in California doubled. The in-migration rate during the 1980s climbed back somewhat, to 3.3 in-migrant workers per thousand as California's economy relative to that of the nation increased about twice as rapidly during that decade (32 vs. 17 percent) compared with 50 percent during the 1970s. A major shift in the educational distribution of in-migrants accompanied the decline in internal migration rates (see table 7). Net migration rates of native-born workers who were high school dropouts and high school graduates stopped or turned into net out-migration during the 1970s and 1980s. Net in-migrants to California are now exclusively college educated.

Apart from contributing to lowering net in-migration to California

Table 7   Net Migration Rates to California by Education and Immigration Status, 1965–1990

	NATIVE BORN			FOREIGN BORN		
Years of Education	1965– 1970	1975– 1980	1985– 1990	1965– 1970	1975– 1980	1985– 1990
Less than twelve	.3	−1.7	−2.4	4.3	1.2	−1.5
Twelve	3.6	−.5	0.0	7.5	5.8	1.1
Thirteen to fifteen	6.6	3.0	1.8	7.5	4.8	5.0
Sixteen plus	13.6	9.6	6.0	14.9	16.3	10.8
All	4.4	2.0	3.5	6.6	5.1	2.6

SOURCE: 1960, 1970, 1980, and 1990 Public Use Sample of the U.S. Bureau of the Census.

NOTE: Includes civilian persons aged sixteen to sixty-four in the labor force. The migration rate is the ratio of annual flow of people divided by the corresponding California population in the labor force at middecade (i.e., 1975 and 1985, respectively). Because the 1960 census did not ask about race and ethnicity, the migration rate for the 1965–1970 period were estimated using the 1970 population estimates by racial/ethnic groups. This bias introduced by this procedure is expected to be small because immigration was relatively small during the 1960–1970 time period.

from other states, immigrants have contributed to the long-term trends toward lower labor employment rates and earnings of high school dropouts and high school graduates. Overall the labor participation rates of native-born men decreased from 67 percent in 1970 to 47 percent in 1990 for high school dropouts and from 86 to 76 percent for high school graduates. We estimate that immigration contributed in the range of 10 to 30 percent to that decline. Employment rates of native borns with some college have remained constant.[3]

By contrast, the employment rates of native-born women have increased over this period of time but much less for low-educated than for college-educated women. The employment rates of women high school dropouts increased from 33 percent in 1970 to 35 percent in 1990, while the rates for high school graduates increased from 48 to 59 percent. We estimate that, without immigration, the growth in employment rates of these native-born women would have been 20 to 30 percent higher. The employment rates of women with some college were not affected by immigration; their rate of employment increased from 53 to 72 percent over the 1970 to 1990 period.

Overall, we estimate that by 1990 from 130,000 to 190,000 persons had dropped out of the labor force or were unemployed as a result of immigration. This represents from 1.0 to 1.5 percent of the adult population of working age.

There has also been a long-term downward trend in the growth of real earnings of all native-born men from 1970 to 1990. The percent decline in real earnings was higher for lower-educated men: a 24 percent drop for high school dropouts, 11 percent for high school graduates, and 3 percent for high school graduates with some college. College graduates are the only group that experienced an increase—5 percent—in their real earnings during this period of time. The size of the decline was more than twice as large during the 1980s as during

---

3. See McCarthy and Vernez (1997) for details on the analyses that led to this and other conclusions about the effects of immigration on native-born workers.

the 1970s for both high school dropouts and graduates. The reverse was true for native-born men with some college and college graduates.

Again we estimate that immigration contributed to the decline in real earnings of California's native-born male high school dropouts and graduates during the 1970s but did not contribute to further declines in their earnings during the 1980s. The estimated contribution of immigration varied between 15 to 75 percent of the total decline in real earnings during the 1970s depending on racial/ethnic groups, with Hispanics and African Americans having been most affected.

In contrast to native-born men, native-born women saw their real earnings increase during 1970 to 1990 at all levels of education with the exception of high school dropouts, who experienced a 10 percent decline in their real earnings. High school graduates experienced a 3 percent increase, and native-born women with some college or more experienced an increase in excess of 10 percent. We estimate that immigration had a downward effect on the earnings of native-born women high school dropouts and graduates during the 1970 time period only.

As noted above, the effects of immigration on the job opportunities and earnings of workers appear to have differed over time. During the 1970s, immigration affected primarily the earnings of less-educated workers—men and women—and net in-migration of workers from other states; effects on employment rates of California native borns were relatively small. During the 1980s, by contrast, immigration affected the employment rates of less-educated workers negatively and exclusively and net immigration from other states continued to be lower than in the past. Earnings were not affected during that decade. One explanation for this pattern is that job growth was much higher (30 percent) during the 1970s than during the 1980s, resulting in greater job opportunities that induced people to enter the labor market at higher rates than they would otherwise have done. In this relatively high-employment-growth context, immigration may have not so much increased competition for jobs as exercised a brake on the growth of wages.

EFFECTS ON DEMAND FOR PUBLIC SERVICES

Elsewhere (Vernez and McCarthy 1996) we have argued that the lack of comprehensive information on the use of public services by immigrants and the lack of a consensus on which services and which public revenues to include in estimates of the net public costs of immigration have made such estimates unreliable. Until appropriate data are collected and key accounting issues are resolved, new estimates will be just as unreliable and, generally, just as self-serving as previous ones have been.

Although a full accounting of the effect of immigration on California's public sector cannot currently be made, a few significant conclusions can be derived from what is known about immigrants' socioeconomic characteristics and their use of selected services by immigration status.

The first, and most significant, conclusion is that immigrants differ in the burden they place on public services in much the same way native borns do. What determines that burden for both native and foreign borns is not the immigration status of foreign-borns per se— whether legal or illegal—but those characteristics that determine eligibility for public programs, most frequently family income, family size and composition (particularly the presence of young children), and needs (DaVanzo et al. 1994). Hence, the lesser the human resources endowment—education and skills—of immigrants, the higher the demand they will impose on the federal, state, and local public sectors.

California immigrants with disproportionately lower levels of education than native borns command lower earnings. This, combined with the fact that they are more likely to be married and to have young children than native borns, means that they are more likely than native borns to need and use public services, most particularly services such as education and health care. This point is best illustrated with the case of education, the most expansive public service and one that is funded almost entirely with state and local revenues. The example of education will also illustrate how the effects of immigration on public services can cumulatively increase over time.

Steady increases in immigration flows since the 1960s have translated into increases in actual enrollments in California's primary and secondary schools only since the early 1980s (see figure 1). But they have been cumulatively building over time since the early 1970s owing to both the steady flow of immigrants of school age and the increasingly large number of children born to immigrant parents. This cumulative buildup of the demand on California's education system can readily be seen in table 8, which shows that the number of children from infancy to age eighteen declined by 90,000 during the 1970s. This decline would have been five times larger, however, without the entry of some 380,000 immigrant children. In the 1980s, these trends were reversed. The number of children from infancy to age eighteen

Figure 1   Enrollment in Kindergarten through Twelfth Grade,
                        California, 1970–1990

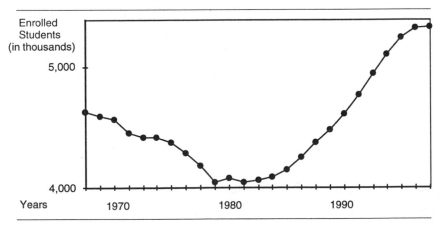

SOURCE: U.S. Department of Education (1994), table 43.

Table 8 Incremental Changes in Numbers of Immigrant and
Native School-Age Children in California, 1970–1990

Age Group	IMMIGRANTS		NATIVES		ALL	
	1970–1980	*1980–1990*	*1970–1980*	*1980–1990*	*1970–1980*	*1980–1990*
Infancy to eleven	184,630	110,214	−390,150	1,149,216	−205,220	1,259,430
Twelve to eighteen	190,720	229,275	−76,700	−265,398	114,020	−36,123
Total	*375,520*	*339,319*	*−466,850*	*883,818*	*−91,200*	*1,222,638*

SOURCE: 1970,1980, and 1990 Public Use Sample of the U.S. Bureau of the Census.

increased by 1.2 million, of which one-third were foreign born and two-thirds were native born. We estimated that about 40 percent of the native-born children were born to foreign-born parents. Hence, more than half (57 percent) of the enrollment growth during the 1980s was attributable to immigration.

The 1980–1990 increase in the size of the school-age population was concentrated in the 0 to 11 age cohort while the size of the 12 to 18 age cohort continued to decline slightly (see table 8). This means that the cumulative effects of past immigration had yet to be fully felt at the secondary school levels and certainly the state high schools as late as 1990. The effect of immigration on high schools began to be felt during the mid-1990s and will reach the postsecondary education system in the latter part of this decade.

A second conclusion, which has already been well documented in the service utilization literature, is that refugees are exceptionally high users of cash and other assistance programs in part because of their low participation in the labor force, their relatively low education (particularly refugees from Indochina), and hence their low wages and in part because, unlike other immigrants, they are eligible for all federal assistance programs upon arrival. For instance, refugees were estimated to be twice as likely to use public services of any kind — including welfare, medical assistance, and housing subsidies — than other immigrants

(Borjas and Hilton 1995; McCarthy and Vernez 1997)). In any given month, one in three refugees will use some form of medical assistance compared to one in ten for other immigrants and one in twelve for natives (McCarthy and Vernez 1997).

A third conclusion is that the full effects of the higher participation rates of elderly immigrants on supplemental security income (SSI) have yet to be fully felt. The dependency on SSI of elderly immigrants has increased significantly since 1970, when it was equal to that of native-born men and only slightly higher relative to native-born women (see table 9). By 1990, the dependency on SSI of immigrant men had increased by 50 percent, while that of native-born men had decreased by 50 percent. The differential pattern between foreign- and native-born women was similar, although somewhat less pronounced. Two factors have contributed to this differential pattern in dependency for elderly immigrants: The first is an increase in the reunification of elderly parents with their adult children that are already here. More than a third of recently arrived parents of present immigrants go on SSI within ten years of their arrival. This pattern is more pronounced among Asians than among Hispanics. The second reason is that the

Table 9   Adults Aged 65 or More Reporting Receiving Public
            Assistance Income by Gender and Immigration Status,
            California, 1970–1990 (in percent)

	MEN			WOMEN		
Age and Immigration Status	1970	1980	1990	1970	1980	1990
Adults aged sixty-five or more						
Recent immigrants	38.4	35.5	33.4	40.9	36.8	35.5
Earlier immigrants	11.4	13.1	15.0	'18.2	19.6	21.0
All immigrants	11.8	15.4	18.4	18.9	21.7	23.7
Natives	11.3	9.1	6.7	13.7	14.9	11.5

SOURCE: 1970, 1980, and 1990 Public Use Samples of the U.S. Bureau of the Census.

earlier cohorts of low-educated immigrants are beginning to reach retirement without sufficient Social Security and other savings to make them fully independent during their retirement years. This pattern is most pronounced among Hispanic immigrants, who typically have high labor force participation rates but command low wages during their entire working life in the United States (Schoeni et al. 1996).

These trends and the fact that California is the home of 33 percent of all immigrants in the nation, more than 40 percent of all immigrants with less than twelve years of education, and more than 40 percent of all refugees mean that increases in demand for public services have been primarily driven by immigration over the past ten to fifteen years. Because of these immigrants' relatively young ages and their higher fertility rates, this pattern will continue in the next ten to fifteen years regardless of the volume of future immigration flows.

Conclusions and Discussion

Immigration to California over the past thirty years has been larger, ethnically more diverse, relatively less educated, and younger than anywhere else in the nation. These factors go a long way toward explaining why immigration has come to be viewed differently in this state than in other parts of the country. These factors also underly the fallacy of attributing to California the benign, if not insignificant effects of immigration measured for the nation as a whole as has typically been the case. Surely, a 3-percentage point increase in the share of immigrants in a pool of more than 100 million workers over a thirty-year period might have a minimal effect. But a 16-percentage point increase in the share of immigrants in an economy that is six times smaller than the nation's is likely to generate effects that are both large and visible.

Indeed, immigration has resulted in significant economic benefits to the state of California and its people. California's economy has benefited from its immigrants' lower costs, relatively high productivity, and entrepreneurial spirit, which, in turn, have contributed to the more rapid growth of the state's economy relative to that of the rest of the nation throughout the 1970–1990 time period.

It has also resulted in some costs to low- and noncollege-educated native-born workers in the form of reduced earnings and reduced job opportunities. Reduced job opportunities have, in turn, resulted in lower labor force participation and higher unemployment rates for native-born workers with less than twelve years of education or with only a high school degree and lower net in-migration of out-of-state workers into California. We estimate that from 130,000 to 190,000 native-born workers, or 1.0 to 1.3 percent of the adult population aged sixteen to sixty-four, had dropped out of the labor force or were unemployed in 1990 in California because of immigration.

At the same time, immigrants in California have added to the demand for public services not because they are immigrants per se but because a significant share of them command low earnings and have larger families than native borns. California immigrants are also more likely to be refugees than are immigrants in other parts of the nation. In this sense, they contributed to, although were not the cause of, the state's fiscal deficit that developed when the economy entered a recession during the early 1990s.

Nowhere have the effects of immigration been greater than on the state's education system and on the supplemental security income for the aged program. The effect of past immigration on these services, as well as other public services such as health care, has yet to be fully felt and will steadily increase in the next decade or so regardless of the volume and composition of future immigration flows.[4]

---

4. Newly established restrictions on access to some federal assistance programs for new immigrants and noncitizens under the Personal Responsibility and Work Opportunity Reform Act of 1996 may temper growth on demand for welfare and Medicaid depending on whether or not the state decides to maintain access to these benefits for all or some noncitizen immigrants.

The multiplicity and complexity of the economic and distributional effects of immigration should make it clear that a simplistic account of benefits and costs is not feasible. For one thing, we can point to the direction of these effects but cannot measure their magnitude with any degree of certainty because we can only observe the net effects—at various points in time—of countervailing and constantly changing economic and labor force characteristics that interact with one another. A full account of costs and benefits of immigration also requires making value judgments about the relative importance of the various effects of immigration. To further complicate matters, immigration policy decisions made today may have little immediate effect, but significant long-term effects are difficult to predict since they are sensitive to the changes in economic conditions in the state, which themselves are difficult to anticipate. If any rules of thumb can be derived from our analysis of the long-term effects of immigration in California, they are that the volume of immigration matters but that educational and skill composition matters even more and that the balance of short-term benefits and costs of immigration does vary over time and may be reversed depending on changing economic conditions.

References

Borjas, George J., and Lynette Hilton. "Immigration and the Welfare State: Immigrant Participation in Means Tested Entitlement Programs." Working Paper 5372, National Bureau of Economic Research, 1995.

DaVanzo, Julie, Jennifer Hawes-Dawson, R. Burciaga Valdez, and Georges Vernez. "Surveying Immigrant Communities: Policy Imperatives and Technical Challenges." MR-247-FF, RAND Corporation, Santa Monica, Calif., 1996.

Johnson, Hans. "Undocumented Immigration to California, 1980–1993." Public Policy Institute of California, San Francisco, 1996.

Khoo, Sieu-Ean. "Correlates of Welfare Dependency among Immigrants in Australia." *International Migration Review* 28, no. 1 (spring 1994): 68–92.

McCarthy, Kevin F., and Georges Vernez. "Immigration in a Changing Economy." MR-858-OSD/CBR/FF/WFHF/IF/AMF, RAND Corporation, Santa Monica, Calif., 1997.

Moss, Philip, and Chris Tilly. "Raised Hurdles for Black Men: Evidence from Interviews with Employers." Paper presented at the annual conference of the Association for Public Policy Analysis and Management, Bethesda, Md., 1991.

Schoeni, Robert F., Kevin F. McCarthy, and Georges Vernez. "The Mixed Economic Progress of Immigrants." MR-763-IF/FF, RAND Corporation, Santa Monica, Calif., 1996.

Vernez, Georges. "The Current Situation in Mexican Immigration." *Science* 251 (March 1991): 1189–93.

Vernez, Georges, and Kevin F. McCarthy. "The Costs of Immigration to Taxpayers: Analytical and Policy Issues." MR-705-FF/IF, RAND Corporation, Santa Monica, Calif., 1996.

Vernez, Georges, Michael Dardia, Kevin F. McCarthy, Jesse Malkin, and Robert Nordyke. "California's Shrinking Defense Contractors: Effects on Small Suppliers." MR-687-OSD, RAND Corporation, Santa Monica, Calif., 1996.

Philip L. Martin

CHAPTER TWO

The Endless Debate

Immigration and
U.S. Agriculture

Labor is the problem of the twentieth century.
California fruit grower
H. P. Stabler in 1902,
quoted in Daniel 1981, 51

Introduction

California agriculture provides a case study of how an industry can remain dependent on an outside-the-community labor force for decades, usually by persuading the federal government to leave immigration doors ajar so that foreign workers willing to accommodate themselves to seasonal farmwork are available.

There are many reasons agriculture receives special treatment in immigration matters. Agriculture is considered a U.S. economic success story for its ability to provide U.S. residents with low-cost food and to generate a consistent trade surplus. Agriculture is one of the few U.S. industries in which the number of employers (about 750,000) is high relative to the number of employees (about 2.5 million), so that farm employers are far more important in employer organizations than farmworkers are in employee organizations. Third, agriculture is an old, widely dispersed industry familiar with obtaining government assistance.

Seasonal farm labor is almost always discussed in the United States as a problem. For farmers, the problem is cost and availability—how to get enough workers to fill seasonal jobs at "reasonable" wages. Farmers argue that the biological production process, the competitive nature of the markets in which their commodities are sold, and the nature of farmwork make it impossible for farmers to compete with nonfarm employers for workers.

Worker advocates, in contrast, define the farm labor problem as too little work at too low wages, meaning that most farmworkers wind up with below-poverty-level incomes. Not surprisingly, both farmers and worker advocates look to government to resolve the farm labor problem as each side has defined it. Farmers, especially those in California, long ago learned that the cost and availability problem could be dealt with most easily through immigration; if there were enough immigrants without other U.S. available job options, then there would be a sufficient seasonal labor force for each farm. Just as farmers cooperated to get government to develop water facilities so that all had access to cheap water, so farmers learned to cooperate to persuade government to keep border gates open so that all had access to immigrant labor.

Farmers traditionally won the immigration-for-agriculture argument for political and economic reasons. Farmworker advocates were divided on a strategy: For most of the twentieth century, more worker advocates wanted to break up large farms that depended on armies of seasonal workers than wanted to treat large farms the same as nonfarm employers for immigration and labor law purposes.

Two economic factors worked against worker advocates. First, in a booming nonfarm economy, farmworkers found it easier to achieve upward mobility by shifting to the nonfarm economy than by fighting for change within the farm labor market, which helps explain why, even today, the average seasonal farmwork career is less than ten years. Second, farm wages—lowered by the availability of immigrant workers—raised land prices, giving farm employers an incentive to make investments that protected their asset values (i.e., making political contributions to maintain access to immigrant workers).

Immigrant farmworkers provide a classic example of the trade-offs inherent in immigration policy making. Permitting Mexican farmworkers to enter the United States helps hold down farm wages and thus food prices. The immigrants are eager to come, the farmers are eager to employ them, and, because of their presence, Americans have more money to spend on nonfood items.

What is the trade-off? Some of the Mexican workers settle in the United States, and they and their children are encouraged by low farm wages to move to urban areas to improve their lot. If they and their children succeed in urban labor markets, then the U.S. immigration miracle of giving opportunity to the poor of other countries is repeated. If they do not, then rural poverty in Mexico becomes rural and eventually urban poverty in the United States.

U.S. Agriculture

Agriculture is a frequently misunderstood industry. Farming is often considered a crown jewel of the economy, a testament to the fact that only about 9 percent of the average "consumer unit's" annual expenditures ($30,700 in 1993) were for food eaten at home.[1] The United

---

1. The approximately 100 million "consumer units" in the United States in 1993 spent an average of $30,700. The U.S. population in 1993 was 258 million, so the average consumer unit contained about 2.6 persons. The five largest expenditure items in 1993 were housing, $9,600; transportation, $5,500; food, $4,400; personal taxes, $3,000; and personal insurance and pensions, $2,900. Food expenditures included $2,700 for food eaten at home, 9 percent of total expenditures, or about $52 a week. The major items were meat and poultry, on which spending averaged $735; fruits and

States also runs a $20 to $30 billion annual surplus in agricultural trade.

This picture of efficiency, however, is clouded by the fact that most U.S. farms lose money farming and that government payments typically account for one-fourth of net farm income. A handful of large farms produce most of the nation's food and fiber. The largest 5 percent of all farms, each a significant business, account for over half of the nation's farm output, while the smallest two-thirds of all farms account for only 5 percent of all farm output. These small farms, on average, lose money farming.[2]

Most American farms are family farms—defined by the U.S. Department of Agriculture (USDA) as those that can operate with less than the equivalent of one and a half year-round hired hands. Most of these farms are operated by non-Hispanic whites; in 1992 the Census of Agriculture reported that there were 1.9 million U.S. farms and that more than 80 percent were operated by non-Hispanic whites. Many of

---

vegetables, $445; cereals and bread, $435; and dairy products, $295. In addition, consumer units spent an average of $225 on nonalcoholic beverages and $270 on alcoholic beverages. About 60 percent, or $270, of the fruit and vegetable expenditures were for *fresh* fruits and vegetables—about $135 for fresh fruits and $135 for fresh vegetables, the commodities most likely to use immigrant farm labor. Over fifty-two weeks, this means that the average consumer unit spent $5.20 a week on fresh produce.

Farmers received about 19 percent of the average retail price for fresh fruits in 1993 ($26 of $135) and 23 percent of the retail price of fresh vegetables ($31 of $135), so that farmers get $57, or 21 percent, of the $270 average retail expenditures on fresh fruits and vegetables. Farm labor, including supervisory labor, typically represents about one-third of farmers' costs of production for fresh fruits and vegetables, or farm labor represents about $8.60 of the $26 that the average U.S. consumer unit spends on fresh fruit and $10.20 of spending on fresh vegetables. This means that the average conumer unit of 2.6 persons in 1993 spent $19 on farm wages and benefits for fresh fruits and vegetables.

2. *Statistical Abstract of the United States*, 1992, p. 649. There were 2.1 million farms with a gross cash income of $186 billion in 1990. The largest 107,000 farms each sold farm products worth $250,000 or more and accounted for 56 percent of gross cash income. The smallest 1.3 million farms each sold farm products worth $20,000 or less and accounted for 5 percent of gross cash income. These small farms lost $500 million farming.

these farmers are sideline farmers, but others report long hours of work; thus about two-thirds of U.S. farmwork is done by farmers and their unpaid family members.

The subsector of U.S. agriculture that is most closely associated with Mexican migrants are the seventy-five thousand U.S. farms that hire workers to produce Fruits and nuts, Vegetables and melons, and Horticultural specialties (FVH) such as flowers and nursery products. Even the seventy-five thousand number exaggerates; the largest 10 percent of these FVH farms account for 80 percent of U.S. fruit and vegetable production and employment. Most U.S. farms, then, as well as most fruit and vegetable operations, are small, family-run operations, but seasonal factories in the fields account for most U.S. farmworker employment; it is their efforts that have led to immigration exceptions for agriculture.

Immigration policy and immigrants are linked to fruit and vegetable agriculture because immigrants constitute almost two-thirds of the industry's current workforce and nearly all the entrants to the seasonal fruit and vegetable workforce. The USDA's National Agricultural Worker Survey (NAWS), for example, reported in 1990 that most hired workers on crop farms were recent immigrants from Mexico and that 75 percent of them worked in fruit and vegetable agriculture (see box 1).

California farmworkers are more likely to be Mexican born, to be employed by farm labor contractors rather than directly by growers, and to live in nonemployer-provided housing than farmworkers in other parts of the United States. The percentage of male and unauthorized farmworkers is about the same in California as in the rest of the United States (see figure 1). As with most hired farmworkers interviewed in the NAWS, few California farmworkers speak English (11 percent in 1990–91) and few finished high school (13 percent).

Few young Americans dream of growing up to be farmworkers. In the past, it was feared that farmworker children would be trapped in the migrant stream by their inadequate education. Most of the

Box 1   National Agricultural Worker Survey Profile of Some 2 Million
         Seasonal Agricultural Services (SAS) Farmworkers, 1989–1991

1. *Demographic Characteristics*: Most farmworkers are male, young, married immigrants with special agricultural worker (SAW) status
   - 73 percent are male; 67 percent are thirty-five or younger (median age, thirty-one), 17 percent are twenty or younger
   - 58 percent are married; 52 percent have children; 40 percent do farmwork unaccompanied by their families
   - 60 percent are foreign born, including 55 percent who were born in Mexico
   - 70 percent are Hispanic
   - 29 percent are SAWs (580,000 of an estimated two million) and have a median seven years of U.S. farmwork experience
   - 10 percent are unauthorized (200,000 of two million); these young workers (median age, twenty-three) have only two years of U.S. farmwork experience
   - 53 percent of all SAS workers have eight or fewer years of education (median, 8 years); 65 percent speak primarily Spanish
   - 57 percent of the workers live with their families at the work site; 85 percent of the persons fifteen and older in households work
2. *Farmwork and Earnings*: Most workers experience extensive seasonal unemployment and have low annual earnings
   - workers have a median eight years experience doing SAS farmwork; U.S. citizens and green card immigrants average eleven to twelve years, while unauthorized workers average just two years experience
   - workers on average spend 50 percent of the year, or twenty-six weeks, doing SAS work for 1.7 farm employers, 20 percent, or ten weeks, unemployed, 15 percent, or eight weeks, doing non-SAS work, and 15 percent, or eight weeks, traveling abroad
   - 75 percent of all crop workers are employed in fruits or vegetables
   - 77 percent are hired directly by growers, usually to harvest crops
   - median earnings were $4.85; workweeks averaged thirty-seven hours for SAS earnings of $180, and, for twenty-six weeks, $4,665
   - less than half of the workers have unemployment insurance or workers' compensation coverage; 21 percent have off-the-job health insurance
   - 28 percent live in employer-provided housing
3. *Other Work and Income*: Farmworkers are poor but not dependent on welfare
   - 46 percent of all SAS workers have below-poverty-level incomes; the poverty rate is highest for unauthorized workers (77 percent)
   - 36 percent also do non-SAS farmwork; such work paid a median $4.50 an hour and is preferred to farmwork (i.e., layoffs push these workers into farmwork)
   - 58 percent are unemployed sometime during the year; 50 percent of these unemployed are jobless less than two months; only 28 percent of jobless farmworkers apply for unemployment insurance
   - 40 percent of the workers spend an average of nineteen weeks abroad each year
   - median individual incomes are $5,000 to $7,500; median family incomes are $7,500 to $10,000; 50 percent of the families are below the 1989 poverty line of $12,675 for a family of four
   - 55 percent of the workers own assets, usually a vehicle
   - 16 percent get food stamps; 3 percent, Aid to Families with Dependent Children

SOURCE: U.S. Department of Labor 1991a and 1991b

NOTES: Based on quarterly interviews with 7,242 farmworkers (for some questions) employed in SAS between the fall of 1989 and 1991. SAS is most of crop agriculture; it probably includes 80 percent of all farmworkers, 70 percent of all farm jobs, and 60 percent of farm wages paid.

Figure 1   Characteristics of U.S. and California Farmworkers, Mid-1990s (by percentage)

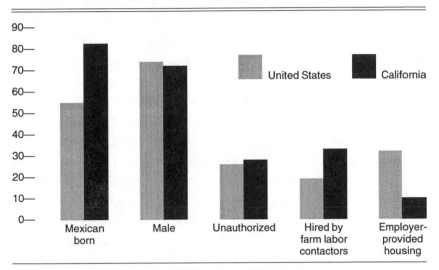

SOURCE: U.S. Department of Labor (1993b) and unpublished data.

evidence today indicates that many farmworker children do farmwork alongside their parents as teens, but, if they attend U.S. schools, they tend to take nonfarm jobs by age eighteen or twenty. The high turnover farm workforce is reproduced abroad; most new entrants to the farm workforce were born in rural Mexico. Increasingly, new farmworkers, so-called new-new migrants—indigenous peoples from southern Mexico and Central America, such as non-Spanish-speaking Mixtec Indians—have begun to enter the U.S. farm workforce in significant numbers

Farmers and Immigration Reform in the Mid-1980s

When the congressional hearings on illegal immigration that eventually culminated in the Immigration Reform and Control Act of 1986 began in 1981, the positions of farmworker and farmer advocates were not well developed. United Farm Workers (UFW) representative Stephanie Bower, for example, testified on September 30, 1981, that the UFW supported "imposing sanctions on employers who hire illegal aliens . . . [but since] laws covering farm workers have been rarely enforced . . . we strongly urge that a large budget for staff and operations be allocated to enforce sanctions."[3] The UFW also supported issuing counterfeit-proof Social Security cards to all workers, including farmworkers, to verify their legal right to work in the United States.

The National Council of Agricultural Employers (NCAE) testified that it had not yet developed a position on employer sanctions but that, if there were to be a sanctions law, "we [agriculture] must have some means to offset a worker shortfall if there are not enough U.S. workers to fill the needs of agricultural employers."[4] The NCAE offered two reasons sanctions might lead to farm labor shortages: "they [illegal alien farmworkers] will move to other jobs where they may get 12 months out of the year employment," . . . and many of "those people" (illegal aliens) "do not want amnesty," so if they must "choose amnesty" in order to work in the United States, "they may just opt [to go] back to Mexico."[5]

When the immigration reform bill was introduced by Senator Alan Simpson (R-Wy.) and Representative Romano Mazzoli (D-Ky.) in 1982, it included sanctions on U.S. employers who knowingly hired illegal aliens, amnesty for some illegal aliens in the United States, and a streamlined H-2 nonimmigrant worker program that allowed temporary farmworkers to fill temporary U.S. jobs if American workers were unavailable at government-set wage and working conditions. Western farm employers were not satisfied with the prospect of a government certification process standing between them and the Mexican workers

---

3. Senate Serial J-97-61, 1981, p. 78.
4. Ibid., p. 125.
5. Senate Serial J-97-61, 1981, p. 125.

to whom they had become accustomed. They argued that they could not plan their need for seasonal labor because they produced perishable commodities, that they lacked the free housing required to obtain H-2 workers, and that farmworker unions might urge the government not to approve their requests for alien workers on the grounds that U.S. workers were available.

In January 1983, representatives of most U.S. farm employers met in Dallas, Texas, to decide whether to press for further changes in the H-2 program to accommodate Western growers or to seek a new foreign worker program. The decision was made to seek a new foreign worker program. The Farm Labor Alliance (FLA), a coalition of twenty-two farm organizations, was created to press for such a program in Congress.

The FLA wanted a flexible guest-worker program under which legal nonimmigrant workers would be confined to farm jobs while in the United States and U.S. farmers would not be required to go through a certification process to employ them. Both Senator Simpson and Representative Mazzoli opposed such a free agent guest-worker program, arguing that it was hard to justify a guest-worker program in legislation designed to reassert control over immigration. Free agent guest workers, they argued, would be difficult to regulate in a manner that would not undermine the wages and working conditions of U.S. farmworkers.

Representatives Leon Panetta (D-Calif.) and Sid Morrison (R-Wash.) introduced the FLA's guest-worker program as an amendment to the Simpson-Mazzoli bill in the House in 1984. To the surprise of many observers, the House approved the Panetta-Morrison guest-worker program in June 1984 in what the *New York Times* described as one of the year's top ten political stories.[6] In 1985, the FLA got then

6. John Norton, undersecretary of agriculture in the mid-1980s and a major lettuce grower, said that "Leon Panetta carried the ball for California on the Panetta-Morrison

Senator Pete Wilson (R-Calif.) to offer another version of the Panetta-Morrison program; after Wilson agreed to cap the number of guest-workers at 350,000, Wilson's guest-worker program was approved by the Senate.

When the House considered immigration reform in 1986, Representative Peter Rodino (D-N.J.) asserted that he would try to block legislation that included a Panetta-Morrison or Wilson-type guest-worker program, for agriculture. During the summer of 1986, Representative Charles Schumer (D-N.Y.) negotiated a compromise legalization program, with Representative Panetta representing employer interests and Representative Howard Berman (D-Calif.) representing worker interests; this "Schumer compromise" was a key element in permitting the Immigration Reform and Control Act (IRCA) of 1986 to be enacted.

IRCA's Agricultural Provisions

IRCA included three major agricultural provisions: deferred sanctions enforcement and search warrants, the special agricultural worker (SAW) legalization program, and the (revised) H-2A plus the new replenishment agricultural worker program. Each provision had anticipated and unanticipated consequences.

DEFERRED SANCTIONS

Before IRCA, the Immigration and Naturalization Service (INS) enforced immigration laws in agriculture by having the border patrol drive into fields and apprehend aliens who tried to run away. Farmers pointed out that the INS was required to obtain search warrants before

---

amendment. . . . He did a superb job of trying to represent California's labor needs . . . he's been a real champion of the industry." *California Farmer*, June 21, 1986, p. 7.

inspecting factories for illegal aliens and argued that the INS should similarly be obliged to show evidence that illegal aliens were employed on a farm before raiding it. IRCA extended the requirement—that the INS have a search warrant before raiding a workplace for illegal aliens—from nonfarm to agricultural workplaces.

The search warrant provision was gained by the farmers' argument that farms should be treated like factories. Farmers simultaneously argued, however, that farms, unlike factories, were extraordinarily dependent on unauthorized aliens and that sanctions should not be enforced while the legalization program for farmworkers was under way. Sanctions enforcement was thus deferred in most crop agriculture until December 1, 1988.

LEGALIZATION

IRCA created two legalization programs: a general (I-687) program, which granted legal status to illegal aliens if they had continuously resided in the United States since January 1, 1982, and the SAW (I-700) program, which granted legal status to illegal aliens who had done at least ninety days of farmwork in 1985–1986. Because farmers and farmworker advocates testified that many illegal workers were paid in cash, it was easier for illegal farmworkers to become legal immigrants than it was for nonfarm aliens.[7]

No one knows how many illegal aliens were employed in U.S. agriculture in the mid-1980s. Most farmers and farmworker advocates accepted a USDA estimate that there were 350,000 illegal aliens employed in agriculture, and this number became the maximum number

---

7. A SAW applicant, for example, could have entered the United States illegally in early 1986, left after doing ninety days of farmwork, and then applied for SAW status from abroad. An applicant was permitted to apply for the SAW program with only an affidavit from an employer asserting, for example, that the worker named in the letter had done ninety days of work in virtually any crop. The burden of proof then shifted to the INS to disprove the alien's claimed employment.

Table 1   Legalization Applicants

Characteristic	LAW [a] (in percent)	SAW [b] (in percent)
Age fifteen to forty-four	80	93
Male	57	82
Married	41	42
From Mexico	70	82
Applied in California	54	52
Total Number of Applicants	1,759,705	1,272,143

SOURCE: *INS Statistical Yearbook*, 1991, pp. 70–74

[a] Persons filing I-687 legalization applications

[b] Persons filing I-700 legalization applications. About eighty thousand farmworkers received legal immigrant status under the pre-1982 legalization program.

of Group-1 SAWs.[8] However, in a major surprise, *1.3 million aliens* applied for SAW status, or almost three-fourths as many as applied for the general legalization program, even though it was widely asserted that only 15 to 20 percent of the undocumented workers in the United States in the mid-1980s were employed in agriculture.

SAW applicants turned out to be mostly young Mexican men (see table 1). Their median age was twenty-four, and half were between twenty and twenty-nine. Since SAWs had to be employed in 1985–1986 to qualify, there were few SAWs under fifteen, compared with 7 percent of the general legalization applicants. More than 80 percent of all SAW applicants were male, and 42 percent were married. In a few limited surveys, it appeared that SAWs who had an average of five years of education earned between $30 and $35 daily for 100 days of farm-work in 1985–1986.

The SAW program was rife with fraud. Farmworker advocates testified that many unauthorized workers were paid in cash, meaning that

---

8. Group-1 SAWs did at least ninety days of SAS work in each of the years ending in May 1, 1984, 1985, and 1986. Group-2 SAWs, by contrast, did ninety days of SAS work only in the year ending May 1, 1986. Over 90 percent of all SAW applicants were in the Group-2 category.

unauthorized aliens were permitted to apply for legalization with only a letter from a U.S. farm employer asserting that the named person had done at least ninety days of farmwork. Most SAW applicants, in fact, submitted a letter, often signed by a farm labor contractor rather than a farmer, that asserted "Juan Gonzalez picked tomatoes for 92 days in Salinas for me in 1986."

A careful analysis of several hundred applications suggested that most could not be correct (Martin, Luce, and Newsom 1988). The ninety-day requirement is relatively stiff; in most surveys, less than half of all hired farmworkers find ninety days of farmwork in a typical year. But, in an unusual twist in U.S. immigration law, after the SAW application was filed, the burden of proof then shifted to the INS to "disprove" the alien's claim, something the INS rarely did. For example, few farmworkers outside the coastal valleys of California do ninety days of farmwork in one location; thus the assertion of thousands of persons that they picked raisins for ninety days around Fresno must be false since the raisin harvest season is, at most, eight weeks, or fifty-six days, long.

In the spring of 1987, an early Oregon strawberry crop, as well as fears of IRCA in Mexico, led to cries of a farm labor shortage, and Representative Vic Fazio (D-Calif.) succeeded in requiring the INS to establish a border entry program for illegal farmworkers. Under this program, a foreigner could arrive at a U.S. port of entry on the U.S.-Mexican border, assert that she did farmwork as an illegal alien in the United States for ninety days in 1985–1986 but had no records of such employment, and could enter the United States with a ninety-day work permit to contact the old employer, obtain the letter certifying employment, and apply for SAW status.

Workers lined up at the ports of entry, and entrepreneurs offered to rent them work clothes, provide instruction in farming practices, and give geography lessons to the thousands of Mexicans seeking to enter the United States. Almost 100,000 Mexicans entered the United States in 1987–1988 under this border entry program, even though, near the end of the program, more than 95 percent of those who applied were rejected. Many made ludicrous assertions. When asked how they picked strawberries, for example, several applicants asserted that "we got out our ladders and climbed the strawberry tree."

ADDITIONAL FARMWORKERS

Many unauthorized aliens were believed to be "trapped" in farmwork by lack of English, skills, and documents. By granting farmworkers legal status, the expectation was that nonfarm employers of unskilled workers, such as hotels and factories, would recruit SAWs, so that farm employers would have to gradually improve wages and working conditions to retain them. With sanctions and stepped-up border enforcement preventing additional illegal aliens from entering the United States, the expectation was that the low-wage labor market would gradually tighten.

Farmers, however, won another special exception that discouraged adjustments in crop choices and labor strategies. IRCA included *two* programs through which U.S. farmers could obtain foreign workers if they faced labor shortages: the revised H-2A nonimmigrant worker program and the replenishment agricultural worker (RAW) program.

Two major ways to import foreign workers are to tie them to a particular employer with a contract or to permit the foreigners to be free agents in the labor market. Schemes to reduce macrolabor shortages usually involve immigrants who are free agents in the labor market, whereas programs that aim to curb microlabor shortages usually require the government to certify each employer's request for foreign workers and then tie the nonimmigrant worker to a particular vacant job with a contract.

The H-2A program is a contractual program. In exchange for having the government certify that the farmer faces a genuine labor shortage, the farmer is free to recruit workers wherever and however he pleases, and the foreign workers are required to remain with the employer who brought them into the United States or face deportation.

Farmworker advocates dislike the H-2A program, arguing that H-2A nonimmigrants are "captives" of their U.S. farm employers. In a strange bedfellows alliance, California farmers, who feared that the United Farm Workers union might send them workers whenever they did the required advertising for U.S. workers, and legal services attorneys, who found it difficult to persuade H-2A workers to make complaints and enforce their contracts, established the RAW program.

The RAW program would have been a first in U.S. immigration history. If the U.S. government projected a farm labor shortage, then RAWs could be "admitted" to fill U.S. vacant farm jobs.[9] To protect farmers from government interference, however, there would be no certification that U.S. workers were not available. To protect the RAWs, they would be free agents in the United States, able to move from farm to farm. The immigration anomaly was that, after doing at least ninety days of farmwork for three years, the RAW could become a legal immigrant; five years of U.S. farmwork would enable a RAW to become a naturalized U.S. citizen.

Neither the RAW nor the H-2A program has admitted any additional legal foreign workers since the mid-1980s, largely because illegal immigration continued and document fraud enabled farm employers and unauthorized workers to satisfy IRCA. RAW admissions depended on national calculations of farm labor "need" and supply, and these calculations did not produce the necessary prediction of a labor shortage to justify the issuance of RAW visas; thus the RAW program expired on September 30, 1993.

H-2A admissions require employers to request alien workers. The U.S. Department of Labor added staff to handle the expected 200,000

---

9. Farmers and the INS were chagrined to learn that more than 90 percent of the 700,000 persons who registerd for the RAW program provided U.S. addresses; farmers complained that simply legalizing illegal aliens would not add to the farm labor supply.

H-2A applications a year, but instead admissions shrank, from about 30,000 in 1989 to 15,000 in 1995. The shrinkage of the H-2A program was due in large measure to the mechanization of the Florida sugarcane harvest, which in the mid-1980s employed nine thousand H-2A, mostly Jamaican, cane cutters. US Sugar, the nation's largest employer of H-2A temporary foreign workers for over more than fifty years, announced in June 1995 that it would harvest all its sugarcane by machine in 1996.

IRCA's Agricultural Effects

Immigration reforms should have had at least two effects in agriculture: farmworkers should have become legal U.S. workers, and farmers should have adjusted to fewer newly arrived unauthorized workers from Mexico.

IRCA has not had these effects in agriculture. There are several reasons, including a continued influx of unauthorized workers and less rather than more effective enforcement of immigration and labor laws in agriculture. The demand for labor-intensive fruit and vegetable commodities, both in the United States and abroad, has increased, encouraging increased plantings of the crops that tend to rely on foreign workers.

One of the most dramatic changes in the farm labor market as a result of IRCA is the switch from "undocumented" workers to "falsely documented" workers. Illegal immigrants who do farmwork are usually among the poorest and least sophisticated workers in the United States. IRCA may well be remembered as a stimulus to illegal immigration for spreading work authorization documents and knowledge about them to very poor and unsophisticated rural Mexicans and Central Americans, encouraging many first-time entrants from these areas.

In the mid-1990s, pre-IRCA legal farmworkers, newly legalized SAWs, and a continued influx of illegal aliens have produced an ample

Figure 2   Harvesting Fresno Raisins: Wages and Seasonal Relocations,
                1987–1994

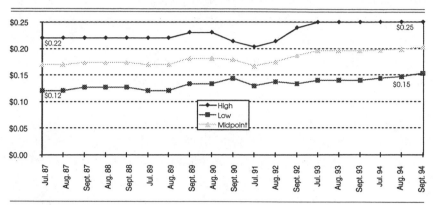

SOURCE: California Employment Development Department, Report 881A.

supply of seasonal workers, giving farmers little incentive to improve wages and working conditions. Study after study confirms the fact that most farmers have not raised wages, improved working conditions or housing, or otherwise made adjustments to recruit and retain legal workers.[10]

The singlemost labor-intensive activity in U.S. agriculture is the harvest of raisin grapes around Fresno, California. Some fifty thousand workers are involved in a six-week effort to cut bunches of grapes from 200,000 acres of vines and lay them on paper trays to dry in the sun. The piece-rate wages paid to workers rose less than 25 percent between 1987 and 1994, even though the minimum wage rose 27 percent in 1988 (see figure 2).

Most farmworkers have been paid the same per hour worked or unit of work done since the late 1980s; farmworker earnings have nonetheless declined in many instances because, with more workers, each does fewer hours of work. Farmworker profiles indicate that a typical

10. These studies are summarized in the *Final Report of the Commission on Agricultural Workers* (Washington, D.C.: Government Printing Office, 1992).

seasonal worker is available for farmwork about forty weeks a year, finds
work for twenty to twenty-five weeks, or seven hundred to one thousand
hours; at $5 an hour, then, farmwork generates $3,500 to $5,000 an-
nually.[11]

Seasonal farmworkers have also been affected by the post-IRCA
tendency of farm operators to hire more seasonal workers through in-
termediary farm labor contractors (FLCs). In California, the "market
share" of FLCs appears to have risen from about one-third of all job
matches in the early 1980s to more than half in the early 1990s. Employees of FLCs are worse off in several ways, including the tendency
of FLCs to pay lower wages to recently arrived immigrants.

Many FLCs condition employment on worker acceptance of housing away from the work site and then charge workers for both housing
and rides to work. Housing away from the farm, usually in barracks-
style accommodations, costs each worker $25 to $35 weekly; the private
rural taxis (*raiteros*), which provide rides to work sites, typically charge
each worker $3 to $5 daily. A worker getting $200 weekly (forty hours
at $5 an hour) often has $50, or 25 percent, less take-home pay if he or
she is employed by an FLC because of these housing and taxi charges.

The ability to hire "documented illegal" workers through FLCs
has meant that most farmers plan on a future of continued immigration. In state after state, labor-intensive agriculture has expanded:
Washington apple acreage has risen by about 35 percent since 1986,
strawberry and broccoli acreage has increased in California, and thou-
sand-acre blocks of oranges have been planted in southern Florida.

---

11. The Department of Labor National Agricultural Worker Survey (NAWS),
which probably includes a disproportionate share of the long-season and year-round
workers who do most of the days of farmwork done by hired workers, reports that median
earnings in 1989 were $7,500 for thirty-seven weeks of work. These SAS workers were
young (median age, thirty), male (75%) foreign born (75%), and poorly educated
(median, six years of education; 75 percent cannot read English well. SAWs are about
40 percent of the NAWS sample, and post-IRCA "documented illegals" are about 10
percent. *Findings from the NAWS: A Demographic and Employment Profile of Perishable
Crop Farm Workers* (Washington, D.C.: U.S. Department of Labor, July 1991).

When asked about the labor assumptions that went into these plant-ings, many of which will not need harvest workers until the mid-1990s, the answers are a sheepish we didn't think about labor or we assumed seasonal labor would be available at the minimum wage, "as it always has been."

IRCA created the Commission on Agricultural Workers (CAW) to review the effects of IRCA and especially its SAW provisions on the farm labor market. On the basis of case study research and hearings, the commission made three major findings. First, the commission con-cluded that the majority of SAW-eligible undocumented workers gained legal status but did so through a flawed worker- and industry-specific legalization program that was "one of the most extensive im-migration frauds ever perpetrated against the U.S. government."[12]

Second, the commission found that, although the SAW program legalized many undocumented farmworkers, the continued influx of illegal workers prevented newly legalized SAWs from obtaining im-provements in wages and benefits. Third, the commission reported that the farm labor market continues to leave the average farmworker with below-poverty-level earnings.

The commission recommended that federal and state governments take steps to develop a legal farm workforce, to improve social services for farmworkers and their families, and to improve the enforcement of labor laws. In response to IRCA's failure to reduce illegal immigration, the commission recommended more enforcement and a fraud-proof work authorization card. To combat declining real farm wages, the absence of benefits such as health insurance, and the exclusion of some farmworkers from federal and state programs that would make them eligible for unemployment insurance benefits and workers' compen-sation, the commission recommended that the federal government provide more services to farmworkers and their children and that farm-workers be covered under protective labor laws. Finally, the commis-

---

12. Reprinted in the *Sacramento Bee*, November 12, 1989, p. Al.

sion recognized that federal and state agencies today have a limited ability to enforce farm labor laws and recommended that enforcement efforts should be better coordinated and targeted.

What Next?

The federal government has permitted immigration to be a subsidy for the labor-intensive fruit and vegetable subsector of U.S. agriculture. This immigrant labor subsidy encourages the expansion of an industry in which the majority of workers earn below-poverty-level incomes. Farmworker poverty is widely recognized, but there is unlikely to be an effective solution to reduce it until the question of who is responsible for the farmworker's plight is confronted.

It is often argued that poor farmworkers are the price that must be paid for cheap food. There is a trade-off between farm wages and food prices, but the savings to the average consumer are small. In the case of the fresh fruits and vegetables that immigrant workers harvest, farm wages typically account for less than 10 percent of the retail price of a head of lettuce or a pound of apples. Doubling farm wages, and thus practically eliminating farmworker poverty, would raise retail food prices by less than 10 percent.

Retail food prices may not even increase if the U.S. government reversed its historical policy and aimed to increase rather than depress farm wages because the demand for farm labor is typically more elastic than the supply. When wages rise, farmers usually find ways to get farmwork done with less labor; the resulting technological changes sometimes wind up reducing consumer prices.

This is what happened when the U.S. government eliminated the supply of Mexican farmworkers to the U.S. tomato processing industry.[13] In 1960, a peak forty-five thousand workers (80 percent braceros)

---

13. Tomatoes are native to South America. Commercial U.S. production began in

were employed to handpick 2.2 million tons of the processing tomatoes used to make ketchup from 130,000 acres. In 1996, about fifty-five hundred workers were employed to ride on machines and sort almost twelve million tons of tomatoes harvested from 360,000 acres, a record crop.

Most of the early 1960s predictions about what would happen without braceros turned out to be wrong. In the early 1960s, headlines in farm magazines read "Without Braceros, Tomato Growers Will Slash Acreage" (*California Farmer*, July 6, 1963, p. 5). Tomato industry leaders were unanimous that California would "never again reach the 100,000 to 175,000 acres planted [as] when there was a guaranteed supplemental labor force in the form of the Bracero" (ibid.). The director of the California Department of Agriculture testified that, without braceros, "we could expect a 50 percent decrease in the production of tomatoes" (U.S. House of Representatives 1963, 61).

The bracero program ended, and those predictions turned out to be wrong. In 1960, the average American consumed forty-four pounds of processed tomato products. In 1994, per capita consumption of processed tomato products was about seventy-five pounds. The real price of processed tomatoes in California fell, from $30 a ton in 1960–1961 to $22 a ton in 1970–1971 (Brandt and French 1981, 92). Cheaper tomatoes permitted the price of ketchup and similar products to drop, helping fuel the expansion of the fast food industry.

The tomato case provides one example of what happens when wages rise. Farm wages in relation to farm machinery prices remained low throughout the bracero era, rose sharply in the 1960s and 1970s, and then began to fall as illegal immigration increased.

---

the 1880s. The United States produces about 20 percent of the world's tomatoes. Cannery or processing tomatoes are harvested by cutting the plant and shaking off the tomatoes. The tomatoes are then sorted by color as they move past an electronic eye and loaded onto twenty-five-ton trucks for delivery to processing plants. The tomatoes are washed, screened to remove debris, and then either sliced or processed into tomato paste.

Bibliography

Bean, Frank, Barry Edmonston, and Jeffrey Passel, eds. 1990. *Undocumented Migration to the United States: IRCA and the Experience of the 1980s.* Washington, D.C.: Urban Institute Press

Brandt, Jon, and Ben French. 1981. *An Analysis of Economic Relationships and Projected Adjustments in the U.S. Processing Tomato Industry.* Research Report 331. Berkeley, Calif.: Giannini Foundation.

Brown, G. K. 1984. "Fruit and Vegetable Mechanization." In P. Martin, ed., *Migrant Labor in Agriculture: An International Comparison.* Berkeley, Calif.: Giannini Foundation.

California Assembly Committee on Agriculture. 1965. "The Bracero Program and Its Aftermath: An Historical Summary." Sacramento, April 1.

Congressional Research Service. 1980. "Temporary Worker Programs: Background and Issues." Prepared for the Senate Committee on the Judiciary, February.

Cook, Roberta, et al. 1991. *NAFTA: Effects on Agriculture.* Vol. 4, *Fruit and Vegetable Issues.* Park Ridge, Ill.: American Farm Bureau Foundation.

Cornelius, Wayne, Philip Martin, and James Hollifield, eds. 1994. *Controlling Immigration: A Global Perspective.* Stanford, Calif.: Stanford University Press.

Elac, John. 1961. "The Employment of Mexican Workers in US Agriculture, 1900–1960." University of California at Los Angeles, May.

Fuller, Varden. 1942. "The Supply of Agricultural Labor as a Factor in the Evolution of Farm Organization in California?" Ph.D. dissertation, University of California at Berkeley, 1939. Reprinted in *Violations of Free Speech and the Rights of Labor Education and Labor Committee* [The LaFollette Committee]. Washington, D.C.: Senate Education and Labor Committee.

Garcia y Griego, Manuel. 1981. "The Importation of Mexican Contract Laborers to the United States, 1942–1964: Antecedents, Operation, and Legacy." Working Paper 11. Program in U.S.-Mexican Studies, University of California at San Diego.

Martin, Philip, Stephanie Luce, and Nancy Newsom. 1988. "Researchers Present Mid-Term Review of SAW Program." *Ag Alert.* April 20, pp. 8–9.

Martin, Philip, and Edward Taylor. 1990. "Immigration Reform and California Agriculture a Year Later." *California Agriculture* 44, no. 1 (January–February): 24–27

Martin, Philip, Edward Taylor, and Philip Hardiman. 1988. "California Farm Workers and the SAW Legalization Program." *California Agriculture* 42, no. 6 (November–December): 4–6

Martin, Philip, Wallace Huffman, Robert Emerson, Edward Taylor, and Refugio Rochin, eds. 1995. "Immigration Reform and US Agriculture." Publication 3358. Berkeley, University of California, Division of Agriculture and Natural Resources.

Martin, William. 1966. "Alien Workers in US Agriculture: Impacts on Production." *Journal of Farm Economics* 48 (December): 1137–45.

U.S. Commission on Agricultural Workers. 1993. "Commission on Agricultural Workers Report," Appendix II.

Peter Brimelow

CHAPTER THREE

The Case for Limiting Immigration

> *I didn't read his book, but I do know this: We are a society committed to equal opportunity, and in 1965 we rejected national origins as a basis of immigration.*
> —Immigration and Naturalization Commissioner Doris Meissner, *New York Times Magazine*, October 27 1996.

I was somehow unsurprised to read Doris Meissner's claim, made in a fawning *New York Times Magazine* profile, that she had not read my book *Alien Nation*. It had stirred up a certain amount of fuss the previous year by demonstrating that the 1965 Immigration Act had accidentally triggered an influx vastly larger, more exclusively nonwhite and (importantly) relatively less skilled that anything promised at the time. This is the indisputable reality. But many people absolutely do not want to see it discussed. I'm just an immigrant (from Britain, via Canada) doing a dirty job.

I was, however, fascinated to see Meissner justify the disastrous

1965 Act in the name of "equal opportunity." Of course, this is absurd on its face. America's current immigration system is highly discriminatory. It has choked off immigration from Europe, the traditional homeland of Americans. It has allowed about a dozen mostly Third World countries to shoulder aside all others and monopolize legal immigration.

What Meissner apparently means by "equal opportunity" is "wilful blindness to racial and ethnic reality." This pathological antiracism on the part of the American elite proves my thesis in *Alien Nation*: current immigration policy can best be viewed as Hitler's posthumous revenge upon the country that defeated him.

□ □ □

The case against America's current immigration policy develops inexorably from three fundamental points.

Point #1 in the case against immigration:
Immigration today is a big deal.

It is a characteristic of the American immigration debate that even the simplest statement of fact meets with deep and persistent denial from immigration enthusiasts. Thus Professor Julian L. Simon of the University of Maryland, in his famous 1990 proimmigration polemic *The Economic Consequences of Immigration*, states flatly: "*Contemporary immigration is not high by U.S. historical standards.*" I saw this claim repeated uncritically by Simon disciples and others in reviews of *Alien Nation* in 1995, although I explicitly addressed and refuted it there. Quite obviously, a lot of people are deeply and emotionally attached to the comforting thought that this has all (yawn) happened before (ho hum . . .)

Of course, this is not strictly logical. How today's immigration compares with U.S. historical standards is ultimately irrelevant. The real question is: can today's immigration be absorbed? It hardly matters whether the floodwaters have reached the record level set in 1900—if, in the interim, a city has been built on the flood plain.

But the fact is that the recent immigration peak of 1990–1991 towers far above the previous record set in 1907, during the First Great Wave at the turn of the century. During the whole Great Wave decade, from 1901 to 1910, about 8.7 million immigrants arrived in the United States. In the decade just passed, 1981–1990, legal immigration into the United States amounted to some 7.3 million. Which means that, counting illegal immigrants—who were not a factor in the earlier period, when the borders were more or less open—1981–90 probably matched and may well have exceeded the earlier record.

Moreover, for most of American history, immigration has risen and fallen very sharply. On a chart, it looks like a sawtooth mountain range. *These pauses are the hidden dimension of immigration history—critical to the process of assimilation.* But after 1965, immigration has been building in a strikingly consistent way. It looks like a ramp . . . or a spring-board.

Unlike previous waves, the post-1965 immigration does not seem to be affected very much by economic conditions in the United States—such as the 1990–1991 recession that helped to turn President George Bush out of his job.In fact, the rising trend line over the entire period since the 1965 act came into effect has been generally smooth—suspiciously smooth.

Why? There are two obvious reasons. Firstly, the emphasis placed by the 1965 act on "family reunification" rather than the importation of workers to fill specific labor needs. Secondly, the modern American welfare state. There is new and disturbing evidence that the post-1965 Great Wave immigrants are going on welfare in sharply higher proportions than in the past. (See chapters 1 and 4, this volume.)

Both of these factors have served to uncouple immigration from American economic conditions . . . And, not coincidentally, from American economic needs.

Immigration enthusiasts, of course, protest that you can't just look at absolute numbers of immigrants. You have to look at immigration relative to the American population.

For example, during the previous Great Wave in the first years of the twentieth century, the total U.S. population was rising through the level of only a third of what it is today. The census recorded just over ninety million Americans in 1910, when just over one million immigrants arrived. But there were just over 250 million Americans in 1993, when about one million legal immigrants were reported. So in 1910, immigration amounted to just over ten per thousand of the American population. But in 1990, immigration amounted only to four per thousand.

But the fact is that, even when you look at current immigration relative to U.S. population, it is still significant. Expected immigration levels above a million a year through the 1990s will work out at above five per thousand, well above lows in the 1845–1920 "Immigration Era," itself an aberration in American history. Adding three million annual gross illegal immigrants—almost twelve per thousand—would take the total to Immigration Era peaks.

Furthermore, absolute numbers matter—absolutely. They matter in at least two ways.

Firstly, comparisons can be deceptive. Expressing immigration relative to host population size causes something of a statistical mirage. A moment's simple arithmetic shows you why: it is mathematically impossible to maintain any very high proportion of immigrants, relative to a country's host population, as the host population grows. After all, immigration has never been *relatively* higher than when the second Pilgrim Father came down the gangplank. That increased the Plymouth Colony's population by 100 percent in just a few seconds.

Secondly, concentrations can cause trouble. Immigrants do not spread all across the United States in a thin, tactful layer just four one-hundredths of a native-born American thick. They invariably accumulate in specific localities. When the immigrants' absolute numbers in these localities pass a certain point, their communities achieve a critical mass. Their alien languages and cultures become, at least for a while, self-sustaining. And the natives start asking themselves, "Are we still living in America?"

For example, the Cubanization of the Miami area has become legendary. But Cuban immigration since 1960 has only been about 650,000—a fraction of the nineteen million immigrants who have come to the United States since 1960. The Cuban community in Florida, with its American-born offspring, is probably about 500,000. It has been, however, enough to transform the area.

Moreover, there is the issue of *net immigration*—another hidden dimension of American immigration history. Although you don't hear as much about it, as many as a third of the 1880–1925 Great Wave seem eventually to have gone back home. Significantly more of the post-1965 Great Wave immigrants seem to be staying in the United States. One estimate of current net immigration, both legal and illegal, has been made by Jeffrey S. Passell and Barry Edmonston of the Urban Institute of Washington, D.C.

> Net immigration in the 1900–1910 decade was 4.9 million—well below the 8.2 million *net* figure we estimate for the 1980s. In fact, our estimates suggest that the 1970s (not the 1980s) were most comparable in terms of net immigration to the 1900–1910 decade, with the 1980s *clearly* exceeding all other decades.

Why? Passel and Edmonston don't say. But there is one obvious difference between early-twentieth-century and late-twentieth-century America: the welfare state. To put it brutally: the failures are no longer winnowed out. Instead, they are encouraged to stay—at the expense of the American taxpayer.

(In my opinion, focusing on net immigration is a way to conclude the curious theological dispute among economists about whether welfare is a "magnet," itself evidence of the moralism paralyzing the immigration debate. Whether or not immigrants come for welfare, they clearly stay for it.)

The decisive element in the historical argument, however, is this: at the beginning of this century, the U.S. birthrate was much higher than it is now. Now American Anglos are below replacement levels. So post-1965 Great Wave immigrants are having a proportionately much higher demographic impact on America than the pre-1925 Great Wave.

Immigration in the 1980s contributed a significantly higher proportion of population growth (37.1 percent) than it did in the legendary 1900–1910 decade (27.8 percent). In fact, immigration also contributed a high share of population growth in the 1970s (32.6 percent).

And after immigrants arrive in the United States, they have children. So the true impact of immigration is the proportion of immigrants *and their descendants* in the American population. The demographer Leon Bouvier projects that immigrants and their descendants will make up about two-thirds U.S. population growth during the 1990s. Thereafter, they will supply *virtually all* population growth.

By 2050, the Census Bureau estimates that the U.S. population will have reached 391 million. By Bouvier's count, at that point more than a third (36 percent) of the U.S. population will be post-1970 immigrants and their descendants—a staggering 139 million people.

"Oh, but they'll assimilate," insist the immigration enthusiasts. "They always have."

To which the only possible answer is: *they'd better.*

This question of assimilation greatly concerned Americans during the 1890–1920 Great Wave. They instituted a systematic campaign of "Americanization." And, in the end, they shut immigration off almost completely.

But the question is much more acute today. For the first time, virtually all immigrants are racially distinct "visible minorities." They come not from Europe, previously the common homeland even for the 1890–1925 Great Wave about which Americans were so nervous.

Instead, these new immigrants are from completely different, and arguably incompatible, cultural traditions. And they are coming in such numbers that their impact on America is enormous—inevitably, within the foreseeable future, they will transform it.

By 2050, the Census Bureau projects, whites will constitute only 52.7 percent of the U.S. population. Hispanics will constitute 21.1 percent, blacks, 15.0 percent, Asians, 10.1 percent, and "other" 1.1 percent. But in 1960, whites were nearly 90 percent of the population. Blacks made up virtually all the balance—Asians and Hispanics were mere trace elements.

There is no precedent for a sovereign country undergoing such a rapid and radical transformation of its ethnic character in the entire history of the world.

Point #2 in the case against immigration:
there is no economic rationale for immigration on this scale.

The American immigration debate has been focusing, albeit rather ineffectually, on the issue of government book-keeping—what is the fiscal burden of immigration? Yet this issue is not only disgustingly technical: it's really fairly trivial. Even Professor Donald Huddle's much-cited $40 billion loss estimate is small compared to the $5 trillion U.S. economy. (Although, we should remember, it's certainly substantial when a few states and cities have to pay it all).

The immigration debate should be refocused. The question—the economic question—should be: is immigration actually necessary for economic growth?

The answer, perhaps surprisingly, is: *certainly not.* Immigration does very little that the host country cannot achieve, possibly better, by other policies.

Immigration does generate instant population growth. The host country can't achieve instant population growth by other policies. And an instantly larger population can be very useful if you are seizing a continent or fighting a war (at least before high-tech weapons).

But, from an economic standpoint, instantly acquiring more people is not so obviously useful. A country's living standard is expressed by its output per capita, not just its sheer output. The economies of Britain and China had about the same output in the early nineteenth century. But Britannia could afford to rule the waves while China was starving because British output was fifteen times higher *per capita* than the Chinese.

Just acquiring more people is not enough. In an increasingly technical age, what will count is not the quantity of people but their quality—and the quality of their ideas.

This insight casts a stark new light on much American immigration history. For example, Professor Richard A. Easterlin, writing in the *Harvard Encyclopedia of Ethnic Groups*, has argued that the vast immigration into the United States in the nineteenth century "probably did not alter substantially the growth of output per capita."

The innovations that drove American economic growth such as mass production in manufacturing, Easterlin points out, were already celebrated worldwide by 1850 when mass immigration was only just getting under way. In the next hundred years, both France and Germany outstripped the United States in per capita output growth.

"Immigrants built America," immigration enthusiasts always claim. Well, not quite, as it turns out. The colonial stock Americans had things rolling along pretty well before mass immigration began. The immigrants just climbed on the bandwagon.

And what about the present situation—with large numbers of immigrants arriving who are far more unskilled relative to the host population? Even if they enter the workforce smoothly and cause total output to grow, their greater numbers must cause output *per head* to fall. And if their marketable skills are minimal, and their entry is not smooth but causes social stress, it's possible that even total output may not grow much more than it would have done anyway. Even, perhaps, less.

This is the specter haunting the United States in 2050—that the American population may be 30 percent larger than it would have been without immigration; but its native stock no richer and its overall national income little greater than would have been achieved anyway.

Oddly, American economists have made very little effort to measure the overall economic benefits of immigration. But the answer seems to be clear: immigration doesn't contribute that much to economic growth. Professor George Borjas's estimate, using a Harberger Triangle application, suggests native-born Americans have recently received a net benefit of about $6 billion annually, or one-tenth of 1 percent of gross domestic product (GDP) (*Journal of Economic Perspectives*, spring 1995). This is less than his estimate of the fiscal burden of immigration, which means immigration is a net economic loss. And even if this "immigration surplus" exists, other policy measures could potentially generate far more—deregulation, lower taxes.

America is being transformed for—nothing.

(Note that Borjas's calculation suggests that the immigration surplus could be higher if the immigrants were skilled. But even if all the immigrants currently in the United States—about ten percent of the total workforce—were skilled, the resulting surplus would still be only $54 billion. That's less than 1 percent of GDP, hardly worth the massive changes immigration involves. And it would require admitting that the current system is broke and needs fixing, which its advocates adamantly refuse to do.)

Naturally, immigration enthusiasts have trouble accepting this. They are shocked to hear that the gains from immigration are so trivial. Particularly if they live New York or California, where its effects are very visible. How can it be? they ask. And they start telling stories about immigrant entrepreneurs.

Well, you can fit a lot of Korean convenience stores, and even Silicon Valley electronics start-ups, into $6 billion. (Indeed, even if immigrants ran the entire computer industry, software and hardware, that would only account for just over 2 percent of gross national product—some \$120 billion annually.)

Moreover, the gross flows in each direction—immigrants earning more, natives earnings less—are much larger. Remember that because of Political Correctness in the immigration debate, anecdotes about displaced natives or immigrants on welfare don't get equal time.

Further evidence in support of Borjas's back-of-the-envelope calculation comes from other immigrant countries. A 1991 study by the Economic Council of Canada and a 1985 study by the Committee for Economic Development of Australia both found that the beneficial effects of mass immigration were nugatory.

The underlying point here: labor is only a small element in economic growth. "However surprising it may seem to laymen, capital and labor are relatively minor as factors of production," Professor Peter Bauer [Lord Bauer of Market Ward] the famous British development economist, told me when I was writing *Alien Nation*. "For example, the work of Simon Kuznets [such as his *Modern Economic Growth: Rate, Structure and Spread*] showed that increases in capital and labor together accounted for no more than 10 percent of the West's increase in output over the last two hundred years and possibly less. The balance was caused by technical innovation—new ideas."

This is the explanation for the great counter-example hanging like the sword of Damocles over the immigration enthusiasts' polemics: the extraordinary economic success of Japan since World War II. Despite its population of only 125 million and virtually no immigration at all, Japan has grown into the second-largest economy on earth. Its GDP has gone up nearly ten times since 1955 and is now about perhaps half that of the United States', which has barely tripled in the same period.

Incredibly, although his book is called *The Economic Consequences of Immigration*, Professor Simon does not mention the Japanese experience at all. Directly asked about it in 1990 by *Forbes Magazine*'s Jim Cook, he in effect struck out. "How Japan gets along I don't know," he said. "But we may have to recognize that some countries are *sui generis*."

In 1993, I followed up in another *Forbes* article by asking Julian Simon directly: given Japan's apparent demonstration that growth through innovation is a viable alternative, is immigration actually necessary for the U.S. economy?

"I've never said it's *necessary*," he replied.

QED!

Point #3 in the case against immigration: what is at issue is not
immigration in principle but immigration in practice—a public
policy: the fatally flawed 1965 act and the system based on it.

Even now, many Americans still simply do not realize what is causing this ethnic revolution that is transforming their country. They tend to assume that some kind of natural phenomenon is at work— that Hispanics, for example, went from an estimated 2.6 percent of the U.S. population in 1950 to 9 percent in 1990 because they somehow started sprouting out of the earth like spring corn.

Americans tend to assume this partly because they are, in fact, regularly told that a natural phenomenon is at work. The standard American media treatment of demographic and multicultural issues simply slides right over the role of immigration.

Thus *Time* magazine proclaimed happily in its April 9 1990 cover story ("What Will the U.S. Be Like When Whites Are No Longer the Majority?") that

> the "browning of America" will alter everything in society, from politics and education to industry, values and culture

and that, of course, "it is *irreversibly* the America to come." [my emphasis].

Buried in eight pages of text was this one weasel phrase: "If current trends in immigration and birthrates persist." Even here, the reference to birthrates is misleading, because it includes births to immigrants. Six-sevenths of the Hispanic population, and five-sixths of the Asian population, are due to immigration since 1900, most of it since 1970.

The point cannot be emphasized too strongly: The current wave of immigration is wholly and entirely the result of government policy. Specifically, it is the result the Immigration Act of 1965, and the further legislation of 1986 and 1990.

The three classic questions of immigration policy are how many get admitted? who? and how is this enforced? All are uniquely within the power of American government officials. Even if they prefer to let these questions be decided, as often at present, by default.

U.S. immigration policy was not transformed in 1965 without debate. There was a debate. It just bore no relationship to what subsequently happened.

Today, it is astonishing to read the categorical assurances given by the 1965 Immigration Act's supporters. "What the bill will not do:" summarized its floor manager, Immigration Subcommittee chairman Senator Edward Kennedy (D.-Mass.):

> First, our cities will not be flooded with a million immigrants annually. Under the proposed bill, the present level of immigration remains substantially the same. . . . Secondly, the ethnic mix of this country will not be upset. . . . Contrary to the charges in some quarters, [the bill] will not inundate America with immigrants from any one country or area, or the most populated and deprived nations of Africa and Asia. . . . In the final analysis, the ethnic pattern of immigration under the proposed measure is not expected to change as sharply as the critics seem to think.

Every one of Senator Kennedy's assurances has proven false. Immigration levels *did* surge upward. They *are* now running at around a million a year, not counting illegals. Immigrants *do* come predominantly from one area—some 85 percent of the 16.7 million legal immigrants arriving in the United States between 1968 and 1993 came from the Third World: 47 percent from Latin America and the Caribbean, 34 percent from Asia. (What's more, nearly half of all the 1968–1993 immigration came from Spanish-speaking countries, dramatically contrasting with the First, polyglot Great Wave and enough to establish for the first time the possibility of permanent "bilingual"— more accurately, Spanish-language— enclaves in the United States) Also, immigrants *did* come disproportionately from one country: 20 percent from Mexico. Indeed, 85 percent of legal immigration came from just 10 of the 191 sovereign countries in the world and not even the largest.

Finally, and above all, the ethnic pattern of immigration into the United States *did* change sharply. In fact, it could hardly have changed more sharply. And the ethnic mix of the country *has*, of course, been upset.

Why were the 1965 Act's supporters all so wrong? The kindest answer must be staggering technical incompetence. They simply did not think through just how the immigration system that they had put together would really work.

Properly speaking, the United States does not have an immigration system. It has an immigration shambles. The basic elements of the system remain those of the 1965 Act.

- *An overall ceiling or worldwide quota for immigration to the United States.* Since the 1990 Act, it has been set at 700,000.

- *Every country treated equally.* All are entitled to contribute a maximum number of immigrants (recently 25,620) to the United States.

But remember that there are 191 independent countries in the world. And 191 into 700,000 goes 3,644.9 times—far less than the 25,620 to which each country is supposedly entitled. If one country fills its quota, others can't.

- *Within each country quota, the highest priority given to "family reunification."* The details get complicated, but U.S. citizens and resident aliens are variously allowed to import spouses, adult children with spouses and children, brothers and sisters with spouses and children. All get preference over immigrants with skills but no relatives.

So there's a tendency over time for "family reunification" to crowd out skilled would-be immigrants from the same country, with the result that skill levels in each country's immigrant flow starts to decline. And skilled workers from other countries, which might be already getting crowded out from the worldwide quota, competing indirectly have even more difficulty getting in to start their own "family reunification" chain.

(I put "family reunification" in inverted commas because, after all, the immigrant would achieve the truest reunification with all of his family if he returned home. Indeed, "family reunification" permits immigrants, after their arrival, to acquire and import foreign spouses, forming new families that never existed to be "disunited" in the first place.)

This is what has happened to European immigration. At first sight, the 1965 Act treated all countries equally. But its workings, as they developed, choked off, as a practical matter, immigration from the historic homeland of America. De jure discrimination *in favor of* Europe (some Southern and Eastern Europeans were always able to come here, unlike Asians) was replaced by de facto *discrimination against* Europe.

It's a common allegation that Europeans no longer wanted to emigrate. But in fact the 1965 Act cut back a continuing flow from Europe.

The number of British immigrants, for example, had been running at 20,000 to 30,000 a year. It was immediately reduced by more than half and has never recovered. In 1991, it was about 13,000. (The damage done to the number of Canadian immigrants was even more dramatic. It had been running close to 40,000 a year; it fell to below a quarter. In 1991, it was just over 10,000.)

The British reaction is instructive. Always inclined to emigrate, they did not stop when their access to the United States was curtailed. They continued to leave Britain at a rate of 100,000 to 200,000 a year. What seems to have happened is that they, along with other Europeans, were simply diverted elsewhere—for example, between 1965 and 1991, some 540,000 British emigrated to Canada; a substantially larger number emigrated to Australia. All told, there are now estimated to be some three million British citizens living overseas.

This illustrates an observation by Professor Borjas, in his seminal *Friends or Strangers: The Impact of Immigrants on the U.S. Economy* (1990): U.S. immigration policy does not exist in a vacuum. There is a worldwide market for immigrants—especially skilled immigrants. With its 1965 reform, the United States in effect reduced its competitive "offer" to European emigrants. Indeed, in many cases it ceased to make an offer at all. So they went elsewhere. And they took their skills—which tend to be higher than those of Third World immigrants—with them.

- *No limits on "refugees" and "asylees."* Outside any country quotas, refugees and asylum seekers have been admitted in numbers determined each year in consultation between the president and Congress. Recently these numbers have been rising under various political pressures. In 1993, 127,000 refugees were approved for admission into the United States, and there were 110,000 applications for asylum from people already in the United States. The backlog of asylum applications is mounting quickly: by 1993, some 333,000 were pending.

The truth is that "refugees" and "asylees" have become just a special sort of expedited (and subsidized, because eligible for welfare) immigration.

Virtually all pretence that refugees are fleeing war or persecution was abandoned in 1989, when Senator Frank Lautenberg (D.-N.J.) succeeded in passing legislation requiring that all Jews from the territory of the former Soviet Union (plus members of two small Christian minorities) Ukrainian Catholics and Evangelical Protestants, should be presumed to be "refugees" for the purpose of admittance to the United States.

Remember, this was *after* the collapse of communism. And the Jews at least, whether persecuted or not, certainly had a place to go: Israel. Still, nearly fifty thousand ex-Soviet "refugees" arrived in the United States in 1993, of whom 80 percent are thought to be Jewish. In 1994, when the Lautenberg Amendment was quietly extended for the third time, for another two years, some fifty-five thousand ex-Soviet "refugees" were expected.

No reform of this extraordinary special interest privilege was even suggested in the failed 1996 immigration reform.

A final immigration end-run, opened in the 1990 Act, illustrates how corrupt the debate has become:

- *The "diversity lottery."* An additional forty to fifty thousand visas were set aside for a group of countries deemed to have been underrepresented—squeezed out—of the 1965–1990 stampede. They were to be allocated by lottery (thus totally passing up any chance to ensure that those immigrants met American needs).

By "diversity," of course, the politicians meant the exact opposite. In fact, they were trying to restore some European immigration, above all for relatives of Senator Kennedy's Massachusetts constituents. But, of course, this could not be admitted. However, several African countries are among those eligible for the lottery. Which has enabled the late Jerry Tinker, Senator Kennedy's veteran immigration aide, to justify the provision as follows: "Now an unemployed Nigerian can immigrate to the U.S. for work."

Sure. But it does help if the unemployed Nigerian is an Irish citizen. Some 40 percent of the lottery slots were reserved exclusively for them.

Besides reducing America's "offer" to skilled immigrants, the inflexible, statute-bound 1965 system has other grave weaknesses.

For example, there is no more important foreign policy problem facing the United States than the stabilization of the lands comprising former Soviet bloc. And there could be no surer way of binding that region into the civilized world than allowing, for a period at least, the immigration to the United States of hundreds of thousands of its tormented (although, incidentally, highly skilled) populace.

They would be rescued from Eastern Europe's economic collapse. They would remit monies to their families back home, a form of foreign aid far more efficiently targeted than any government-to-government grant. They would provide some personal inoculation against the anti-American demagoguery into which the politics of these newly liberated societies might easily degenerate. And many of them would eventually return home—as large proportions of immigrant waves always do—with capital, skills, and the vital experience of functioning in a free, capitalist society.

But today the United States simply does not have the flexibility to accept large numbers of Eastern Europeans. Such a change in policy would require legislation, which would never pass a Congress where immigration is entirely held hostage by ethnic lobbies. And anyway, the result of the post-1965 immigration binge is that ordinary Americans are heartily sick of immigration and want no more. One of the great strengths of the United States has been carelessly, culpably, dissipated.

□   □   □

So America is being transformed by accident, in a way that is unprecedented in the history of the world, to no particular economic benefit, entirely through public policy. Those of us who point this out are under no obligation to explain our motives. It is incumbent upon those who support this extraordinary situation to explain theirs. Neuroses about Nazis don't count.

I suggest Americans think about immigration this way: In the Presidential debate of 1980, Ronald Reagan flourished this pre-cut cardboard cutlass at the audience to remind them of the foreign and domestic record of Jimmy Carter:

> Are you better off than you were four years ago? Is it easier for you to go and buy things in the stores than it was four years ago? Is there more or less unemployment in the country than there was four years ago? Is America as respected throughout the world as it was? Do you think that our security is as safe, that we're as strong as we were four years ago? . . . If you don't think that this course that we've been on for the last four years is what you would like to see us follow for the next four, then I could suggest another choice that you have.

If the 1965 Act had done what its supporters said it would do, immigration would have been held to (say) 350,000 a year. The U.S. population in 1990 would have been 239 million instead of 250 million. According to the 1965 bill's advocates, the U.S. ethnic balance would not have been altered at all. That means that the American population would still be what it was in 1960: almost 89 percent white (including maybe 1 percent or so Hispanic white, which the 1960 Census did not break out).

If there had been no immigration at all after 1970, according to the Urban Institute's Jeffrey Passel and Barry Edmonston, the American population in 1990 would have been an estimated 230 million — about 20 million lower than it is today. Blacks would have been 12 percent, Asians 1 percent, Hispanics 5 percent. And non-Hispanic whites would have been about 82 percent. (The Urban Institute's estimate of non-Hispanic whites tends to be lower than the U.S. Census figures.)

In the end, Americans have to ask themselves very specific questions about the immigration flood unleashed upon their country by the politicians in 1965:

> Has the mass immigration triggered by the 1965 reform made me and my family better off? Has it made it easier or harder for us to work, to educate our children, to live our lives? Has it resulted in more or less congestion? pollution? racial tension? crime? Do I feel it has made America respected for its generosity—or despised for its gullibility? Are we stronger because immigration brought diversity? Or weaker because it brought divisiveness? Has the post-1965 immigration enabled us to achieve anything that we could not have managed on our own?
>
> What if the 1965 act had worked as promised and there were fewer immigrants? Or if immigration had been stopped completely in 1965?
>
> Would America be a happier or unhappier place than it is today?

Well? *Well?* —30—

George J. Borjas

CHAPTER FOUR

Immigration and Welfare

A Review of the Evidence

Introduction

The historical debate over immigration policy in the United States has traditionally focused on two questions: do immigrants take jobs away from native workers? and can immigrants assimilate easily into the United States? The explosive growth of entitlement programs in the past few decades introduces an additional question into the policy arena: do immigrants pay their way in the welfare state?

The conventional wisdom regarding immigrant participation in welfare programs has changed drastically in recent years. Blau's (1984) study, which analyzed data drawn from the 1976 Survey of Income and Education, concluded that immigrant households had a lower probability of receiving public assistance than U.S.-born (or "native") households.[1] A number of recent studies, beginning with Borjas and Trejo (1991), have shown that this conclusion is no longer true—immigrant households are now more likely to receive social assistance than native households.

---

1. See also Simon (1984), Tienda and Jensen (1986), and Jensen (1988).

This chapter uses data drawn from the decennial censuses, as well as from the Survey of Income and Program Participation, to trace the evolution of immigrant participation in welfare programs during the past two decades. The key implication of the data is striking and can be easily summarized: immigrant participation in welfare programs is on the rise. As a result, immigrants now receive a disproportionately high share of the public assistance benefits distributed in the United States.

Results from Census Data

To summarize the main trends in immigrant welfare participation over the past two decades, we can use data from the 1970, 1980, and 1990 Public Use Samples of the decennial censuses.[2] The household is the unit of observation. A household is classified as an immigrant household if the household head was born outside the United States and is either an alien or a naturalized citizen. All other households are classified as native households. The year of immigration of the household is determined by the household head's year of arrival in the United States. The empirical analysis is restricted to households not residing in group quarters and headed by persons who are at least eighteen years of age.

I classify a household as receiving public assistance if any member of the household received public assistance income in the calendar year before the census. The *cash benefit* programs for which the census reports public assistance income include Aid to Families with Dependent Children (AFDC), supplemental security income (SSI), and general assistance. The censuses do not contain any information on the

---

2. Borjas (1995) presents a more detailed discussion of the evidence obtained from decennial census data.

household's participation in noncash assistance programs, such as food stamps and Medicaid.

Table 1 reports the welfare participation rates (i.e., the percent of households receiving public assistance) calculated in the various censuses. The source of the concern over immigrant participation in welfare programs is clear: in 1970, immigrants were slightly less likely, on average, to receive cash benefits than natives. By 1980, the direction of the differential had reversed and immigrants were about 1 percentage point more likely to receive public assistance. During the 1980s, the "welfare gap" widened between immigrant and native households. Whereas native households experienced a decline in the welfare participation rate, immigrant households experienced an increase. By 1990, the welfare participation rate of immigrant households was 9.1 percent, or about 1.7 percentage points higher than the participation rate of native households.

Two distinct factors explain the disproportionate increase in welfare participation among immigrant households. More-recent immigrant waves have relatively higher welfare participation rates than earlier waves (see table 1). For example, in 1970 only 5.5 percent of the most recently arrived immigrant households (i.e., households that have been in the United States fewer than five years) received public assistance; by 1990, 8.3 percent of the newly arrived immigrant households were receiving cash benefits. This rate of increase exceeds the respective rate in the native population from 6.0 to 7.4 percent. The fact that more-recent immigrant waves are more likely to receive cash benefits mirrors the well-known fact that more-recent immigrant waves are relatively less skilled than earlier waves.[3]

Table 1 also indicates not only that recent waves are more "welfare-prone" but that the welfare participation rate for a specific wave of immigrant households increases over time. Even though only 5.5

---

3. Borjas (1985) was the first study to document the fact that skills were declining across successive immigrant waves.

Table 1   Welfare Participation Rates of Native and Immigrant Households, 1970–1990
(percent of households receiving public assistance)

Group	ALL HOUSEHOLDS			MALE–HEADED HOUSEHOLDS			FEMALE–HEADED HOUSEHOLDS		
	1970	1980	1990	1970	1980	1990	1970	1980	1990
Natives	6.0	7.9	7.4	3.7	4.7	4.4	14.8	16.1	13.5
All immigrants	5.9	8.7	9.1	4.5	6.4	6.9	10.4	14.7	14.4
Noncitizens	7.4	9.9	10.5	5.7	7.2	7.7	13.9	19.1	18.7
Citizens	5.4	8.0	7.6	4.0	5.9	6.1	9.4	12.5	11.0
Cohort									
1985–1989 arrivals	—	—	8.3	—	—	7.0	—	—	13.2
1980–1984 arrivals	—	—	10.7	—	—	8.3	—	—	19.1
1975–1979 arrivals	—	8.3	10.0	—	6.9	7.3	—	14.6	19.1
1970–1974 arrivals	—	8.4	9.7	—	5.8	6.7	—	19.1	18.7
1965–1969 arrivals	5.5	10.1	9.8	4.4	7.0	6.7	11.7	20.5	17.8
1960–1964 arrivals	6.5	9.2	8.4	4.9	6.3	6.2	14.5	18.3	13.6
1950–1959 arrivals	4.9	7.1	6.7	3.5	4.8	5.1	12.1	14.1	10.3
Pre–1950 arrivals	6.2	9.3	8.1	4.7	7.3	7.0	9.8	12.3	9.4
Sample Size									
Immigrants	86,201	298,045	357,294	64,980	214,502	256,999	21,221	83,543	100,295
Natives	58,958	72,733	423,468	46,653	52,635	290,228	12,305	20,098	133,240

SOURCE: Public Use Samples of the U.S. Census.

percent of the households that migrated between 1965 and 1969 received public assistance in 1970, the welfare participation rate of this group increased to about 10 percent in both 1980 and 1990. Similarly, households who arrived between 1975 and 1979 had a welfare participation rate of 8.3 percent in 1980 and 10.0 percent in 1990.

The census data reveal that these trends occur among both male-headed and female-headed households. Among male-headed households, for example, the participation rate of the most recent wave increased by 2.6 percentage points between 1970 and 1990, as opposed to the 0.7 percentage point rise experienced by male-headed native households over the same period. Similarly, among female-headed households, the welfare participation rate of the most recent wave increased by 1.5 percentage points, in contrast to the 1.3 percentage point decline experienced by female-headed native households.

The recent resolution of the debate over welfare reform addressed much of the concern raised by these statistics by making noncitizens ineligible for most types of public assistance. It is of interest, therefore, to discover whether the welfare participation rates differed between the naturalized and noncitizen populations before this legislation. Table 1 also reports the trends for these two immigrant groups. Noncitizens typically have much higher welfare participation rates than citizens. It is worth noting, however, that the "welfare gap" between the naturalized and native households grew in the 1970–1990 period. In 1970, naturalized citizens had lower welfare participation rates than natives: 5.4 percent versus 6.0 percent. By 1990, naturalized citizens had slightly higher welfare participation rates: 7.6 percent versus 7.4 percent for natives. The fact that the trends in the naturalized citizen population resemble those found among noncitizens, as well as the fact that noncitizen households can easily choose to change their status, suggests that the recent "solution" may not be that effective in the long run.

The census data also reveal substantial differences in welfare propensities among national origin groups. Table 2 reports the welfare

Table 2   Welfare Participation Rates in 1990,
by National Origin Group

	ALL IMMIGRANTS		PRE–1980 ARRIVALS	
Country of Birth	Percent on welfare	Sample size	Percent on welfare	Sample size
Europe				
Austria	4.3	2,407	4.5	2,299
Czechoslovakia	4.9	2,320	4.9	2,111
France	4.8	2,613	5.9	2,054
Germany	4.1	17,198	4.2	16,143
Greece	5.5	4,196	5.6	3,851
Hungary	5.1	3,142	5.1	2,943
Italy	5.4	15,220	5.6	14,626
Poland	5.7	9,437	5.9	7,645
Portugal	7.1	3,903	7.6	3,293
USSR	16.3	7,133	10.1	5,387
United Kingdom	3.7	14,928	4.1	12,279
Yugoslavia	5.3	3,339	5.7	3,000
Asia				
Cambodia	48.8	1,560	24.4	317
China	10.4	9,804	11.1	6,034
India	3.4	8,092	4.2	4,572
Iran	7.5	4,317	4.1	2,747
Japan	2.3	4,860	3.7	2,551
Korea	8.1	8,286	8.6	4,163
Laos	46.3	2,197	34.1	595
Lebanon	7.3	1,722	8.8	1,039
Philippines	9.8	13,839	10.5	9,312
Taiwan	3.3	4,005	4.2	1,660
Vietnam	25.8	7,170	15.9	3,288
North and South America				
Argentina	4.8	1,972	5.7	1,445
Canada	4.8	18,398	5.1	16,401
Colombia	7.5	4,713	8.9	2,972
Cuba	16.0	16,472	15.3	13,197
Dominican Republic	27.9	5,124	29.9	3,280
Ecuador	11.9	2,279	13.8	1,631
El Salvador	7.3	6,047	10.2	2,409
Guatemala	8.7	2,982	11.4	1,426
Haiti	9.1	3,359	9.7	1,781
Jamaica	7.5	5,512	8.7	3,793

Table 2   (*continued*)

Country of Birth	ALL IMMIGRANTS		PRE–1980 ARRIVALS	
	Percent on welfare	*Sample size*	*Percent on welfare*	*Sample size*
North and South America (*continued*)				
Mexico	11.3	68,076	12.8	47,630
Nicaragua	7.8	2,144	11.8	825
Panama	9.0	1,488	8.7	1,131
Peru	5.9	2,304	7.8	1,268
Africa				
Egypt	5.5	1,578	6.7	1,039
Ethiopia	5.9	601	3.0	181
Nigeria	3.2	1,164	3.3	449
South Africa	1.6	680	1.6	361
Australia	3.7	834	3.8	569

SOURCE: 1990 Public Use Sample of the U.S. Census.

participation rates for selected groups in 1990. Only about 2 to 4 percent of the households originating in South Africa, Taiwan, or the United Kingdom receive public assistance, as opposed to 11 to 12 percent of the households originating in Ecuador or Mexico and nearly 50 percent for households originating in Laos or Cambodia. These statistics suggest a major "structural shift" between two types of immigrant households. In particular, refugee households tend to exhibit much higher rates of welfare participation than nonrefugee households. Households originating in Cambodia or Laos had a welfare participation rate of near 50 percent; those originating in Vietnam had a welfare participation rate of 25.8 percent; and those originating in Cuba or the Soviet Union had a participation rate of 16 percent. Moreover, the participation rate of refugee households remains high even after a decade in the United States. Refugee groups that are thought of as being economically successful, such as the pre-1980 Cubans (i.e., Cubans who migrated before the Mariel flow), had a welfare participation rate of more than 15 percent in 1990.

The high propensity of refugee households to enter (and stay in) the welfare system may be the result of government policies designed to ease the transition of refugees into the United States. Persons who enter the country as refugees or political asylees have immediate access to a wide array of social services and programs that neither other legal immigrants nor natives qualify for. The impact of this introduction to the welfare state seems to be both profound and long lasting.

Because refugees accounted for 12 percent of the immigration flow in the 1970s and 17 percent of the immigrant flow during the 1980s, it is possible that some of the trends observed across cohorts in the past twenty years can be directly attributable to the relative growth in the number of refugee households.[4] It is important, therefore, to determine if the same trends are observed among nonrefugee immigrant households.

The U.S. Census, however, does not contain any information on the type of visa used by a particular household to enter the United States. To approximate the refugee population, therefore, we can classify *all* households who originate in the main refugee-sending countries as refugees (all other households are classified as nonrefugees). The thirteen refugee-sending countries—Afghanistan, Bulgaria, Cambodia, Cuba, Czechoslovakia, Ethiopia, Hungary, Laos, Poland, Romania, Thailand, the former USSR, and Vietnam—accounted for 90.4 percent of the refugees awarded permanent residence status during the 1970s and for 90.5 percent in the 1980s.

Table 3, which illustrates the trends in immigrant participation rates for nonrefugee and refugee households, shows that both types of immigrants are now more likely to be enrolled in welfare programs. In 1970, 5.6 percent of nonrefugee households received public assistance,

---

4. These percentages are obtained by dividing the number of refugees granted permanent residence by the total size of the immigrant flow: the denominator excludes the population of illegal aliens who received amnesty (and who were granted permanent residence status) in 1989 and 1990.

Table 3   Welfare Participation Rates of Immigrant Households,
1970–1990, by Refugee Status

Group	NONREFUGEE HOUSEHOLDS			REFUGEE HOUSEHOLDS		
	1970	1980	1990	1970	1980	1990
All immigrants	5.6	8.2	7.8	7.1	11.6	16.1
Cohort						
1985–1989 arrivals	—	—	5.3	—	—	30.5
1980–1984 arrivals	—	—	7.4	—	—	25.9
1975–1979 arrivals	—	5.6	8.6	—	23.6	18.5
1970–1974 arrivals	—	7.5	9.2	—	15.9	14.9
1965–1969 arrivals	3.3	8.8	9.1	16.7	16.9	13.9
1960–1964 arrivals	4.7	8.4	8.2	13.1	12.1	9.6
1950–1959 arrivals	4.7	7.1	6.8	5.5	7.2	8.2
Pre–1950 arrivals	6.4	9.7	8.4	5.5	7.4	6.6
Sample size						
Immigrants	67,767	248,515	303,489	18,434	49,530	53,805

SOURCE: Public Use Samples of the U.S. Census. Refugee households are households originating in Afghanistan, Bulgaria, Cambodia, Cuba, Czechoslovakia, Ethiopia, Hungary, Laos, Poland, Romania, Thailand, the USSR, and Vietnam.

as opposed to 7.1 percent of refugee households. By 1990, nonrefugee households had a welfare participation rate of 7.8 percent, as opposed to 16.1 percent for refugee households.

Perhaps the most surprising finding revealed by the census statistics is that immigrants' participation in welfare programs tends to increase the longer they reside in the United States. To investigate the importance of this assimilation effect in more detail, it is of interest to track a specific immigrant cohort, defined in terms of both year of migration *and* age at arrival, across the various censuses. Table 4 summarizes the empirical evidence. It is evident that tracking specific age groups across censuses reveals the existence of sizable assimilation effects into welfare both in the entire immigrant population and among nonrefugees. Consider, for example, the sample of nonrefugee households who arrived between 1965 and 1969 and who were between eighteen and thirty-four years old in 1970 (meaning that most persons in the sample

Table 4   The Impact of Assimilation on Welfare Participation Rates
             (in percent)

Cohort	Age Group	1970	1980	1990
Natives	18–34 in 1970	5.1	6.4	5.6
	35–49 in 1970	4.5	7.2	8.1
	18–34 in 1980	—	6.7	6.2
	35–49 in 1980	—	6.7	6.2
Immigrants 1965–69 arrivals	18–34 in 1970	3.2	7.4	8.2
	35–49 in 1970	5.7	10.1	11.7
	18–34 in 1980	—	7.6	8.0
	35–49 in 1980	—	8.0	8.1
Immigrants 1975–79 arrivals	18–34 in 1980	—	5.8	7.8
	35–49 in 1980	—	8.8	9.8
Nonrefugees 1965–69 arrivals	18–34 in 1970	2.6	7.2	8.0
	35–49 in 1970	3.1	8.7	10.9
	18–34 in 1980	—	7.7	8.2
	35–49 in 1980	—	7.5	7.6
Nonrefugees 1975–79 arrivals	18–34 in 1980	—	4.2	7.0
	35–49 in 1980	—	5.5	8.4
Refugees 1965–69 arrivals	18–34 in 1970	9.3	9.4	10.0
	35–49 in 1970	15.2	15.1	14.4
	18–34 in 1980	—	6.2	5.9
	35–49 in 1980	—	11.9	11.6
Refugees 1975–79 arrivals	18–34 in 1980	—	18.1	14.0
	35–49 in 1980	—	23.6	16.1

SOURCE: Public Use Samples of the U.S. Census.

migrated as young adults). This group of immigrant households had
an initial welfare participation rate of 2.6 percent (much less than that
of similarly aged natives). By 1980, however, the participation rate had
risen to 7.4 percent, and by 1990, to 8.0 percent (or about 2.4 percentage points above that of comparable natives). Similarly, nonrefugee
households who arrived between 1965 and 1969 and were between
thirty-five and forty-nine in 1970 (meaning that they migrated as prime-
age adults) had an initial welfare participation rate of 3.1 percent,

which increased to 10.9 percent by 1990. During a twenty-year period, therefore, the participation rate of nonrefugees increases by about 5 percentage points relative to that of native households.

The table also indicates that, if we track specific cohorts of immigrants, refugee households do *not* move out of the welfare system. For example, among refugee households who arrived in the United States between 1965 and 1969 and who were aged thirty-five to forty-nine in 1970, the participation probability fell from 15.2 to only 14.4 percent between 1970 and 1990. Similarly, the refugees who entered the United States between 1960 and 1964 and who were aged thirty-five to forty-nine in 1970 experienced a decline in participation probability from 11.6 percent to 11.3 percent during the twenty-year period.

The descriptive data reported in table 4, therefore, clearly indicate that the typical nonrefugee immigrant assimilates *into* welfare, whereas the typical refugee has a high welfare participation probability throughout the life cycle.

Results from the Survey of Income and Program Participation

Although the trends uncovered by census data have raised serious concerns over the impact of current immigration policy on welfare expenditures, the immigrant-native participation rate gap *in cash benefit programs* is not numerically large. As we saw, in 1990 immigrants had a 9.1 percent probability of receiving cash benefits as compared with 7.4 percent for natives. The census, however, does not provide any information on noncash transfers, such as food stamps, Medicaid, and housing subsidies, so we do not know the extent to which immigrants participate in these other (and more expensive) components of the welfare state.

We can fill in this information by using data drawn from the 1990 and 1991 panels of the Survey of Income and Program Participation (SIPP).[5] The SIPP is a panel survey that collects monthly data by interviewing the same individuals every four months. During the interview, each respondent is asked about his or her economic experiences during the previous four-month period, including benefits received from a large number of means-tested entitlement programs. In the SIPP panels used in this study, the households were reinterviewed at four-month intervals for eight waves, providing us with thirty-two monthly observations for each household.

The SIPP collects information on all persons in the household, one of whom is called the "reference person," or "householder," the person who either owns the house or whose name it is rented under. If the house is owned jointly by a married couple, either the husband or the wife may be listed as the reference person. We restricted our analysis to the sample of persons who were householders in the first month of the panel (effectively making the household the unit of analysis), and we then followed the household's welfare participation history over the course of the thirty-two-month sample period.[6] The SIPP files contain information on whether any person in the household participated in a number of public assistance programs. To increase sample size (and improve statistical reliability), we pooled the data in the 1990 and 1991 panels and calculated the probability that a household participated in the various programs during a typical month in the early 1990s.

Table 5 shows that immigrant households (i.e., households where the householder is foreign born) are more likely to participate in practically every one of the major means-tested programs. The typical immigrant household had a 4.4 percent probability of receiving benefits from the AFDC program, as compared with only 2.9 percent for native

---

5. Borjas and Hilton (1996) provide a more detailed discussion of the empirical evidence revealed by the Survey of Income and Program Participation.

6. The analysis is restricted to households that were interviewed throughout the entire thirty-two-month sample period. Borjas and Hilton (1996) show that this sample restriction does not lead to a substantial bias in the estimates.

Table 5   Average Monthly Probability of Receiving Various Types
of Means-Tested Benefits in 1990/1991 (in percent)

Type of Benefit	Native Households	Immigrant Households
Cash programs		
Aid to Families with Dependent Children (AFDC)	2.9	4.4
Supplemental security income (SSI)	3.7	6.5
General assistance	0.6	0.8
Noncash programs		
Medicaid	9.4	15.4
Food stamps	6.5	9.2
Supplemental food program for women, infant and child (WIC)	2.0	3.0
Energy assistance	2.3	2.1
Housing assistance (public housing or low-rent subsidies)	4.4	5.6
School breakfasts and lunches (free or reduced price)	6.2	12.5
Summary statistics		
Receive any cash benefits	7.3	10.8
Receive cash benefits or Medicaid	10.0	15.7
Receive cash benefits, Medicaid, or vouchers (which include food stamps, WIC, and energy assistance)	12.3	18.2
Receive cash benefits, Medicaid, vouchers, or housing assistance	14.1	20.7
Receive any type of assistance (cash benefits, Medicaid, vouchers, housing assistance, or school breakfasts and lunches)	16.3	26.1
Number of households	25,340	2,449
Number of observations	810,880	78,368

SOURCE: 1990/1991 Survey of Income and Program Participation.

households. Similarly, over 9 percent of immigrant households received food stamps, as opposed to only 6.5 percent of native households. Finally, 15.4 percent of immigrant households were covered by Medicaid, as compared with only 9.4 percent of native households.

The data suggest that census-based studies (which focus on cash benefits) understate the extent to which immigrant households benefit from welfare programs. To measure the "true" incidence, we can define five increasingly broader measures of welfare benefits: (1) participation in *any* cash benefit program; (2) participation in cash benefit programs or Medicaid; (3) participation in cash benefit programs, Medicaid, or voucher programs (voucher programs include food stamps, WIC, and energy subsidies); (4) participation in cash benefit programs, Medicaid, voucher programs, or housing subsidies; and (5) participation in cash benefit programs, Medicaid, voucher programs, housing subsidies, or the National Breakfast and Lunch School Program. The bottom panel of table 5 reports the participation rates in these measures of public assistance.

If we restrict our attention to cash benefits, immigrants are more likely to receive welfare but not by much. The immigrant-native difference in participation rates is 3.5 percentage points. When we expand our definition of welfare to include Medicaid, voucher programs, and housing assistance, the immigrant-native gap widens to 6.6 percentage points. In fact, nearly 21 percent of immigrant households received at least one of these benefits during the typical month.[7]

As with the census data, the SIPP reveals a lot of dispersion in welfare participation among national origin groups in the immigrant population. Table 6 shows that *some* groups have high participation rates. About 36 percent of the households originating in Mexico, 42 percent of those from the former Soviet Union, and over 50 percent of those originating in the Dominican Republic received some type of benefit (defined as cash benefits, Medicaid, vouchers, or housing subsidies). Moreover, the welfare participation rates experienced by some immigrant groups exceeds that of native groups with high participation rates. For example, 33 percent of Hispanic natives and 39 percent of black natives participated in some welfare program.

We can also use the SIPP to investigate the distinction between refugees and nonrefugees to explain the high usage rates among im-

---

7. The inclusion of school lunches and breakfasts increases the gap even further, to nearly 10 percentage points. These school-related benefits, however, have different take-up decisions and do not have the same types of negative connotations as other welfare programs.

migrants. Even though the SIPP files do not report whether a particular household entered the United States with a refugee visa, we assume that immigrants originating from the main refugee-sending countries are refugees.[8] The data reported in Table 6 suggest a large difference in the extent to which refugees and nonrefugees receive both cash benefits and other programs: 20 percent of nonrefugee and 28 percent of refugee households participate in some welfare program. Nonrefugee households, however, have substantially larger welfare participation rates than native households (where the participation rate is 14.1 percent). In other words, the welfare gap between immigrants and natives cannot be explained away by the presence of a large number of refugee households.

Do Immigrants Pay Their Way?

The question of whether immigrants pay their way in the welfare state looms large over the current policy debate. As with all accounting exercises, this one is fraught with questionable assumptions. Passel and Clark (1994), for example, find that immigrants pay over $27 billion more in taxes than they took out of the welfare and schooling systems; Huddle (1993) concludes that the net costs of immigration exceeded $40 billion in 1992.[9]

Regardless of which calculation one wishes to believe, there are some facts about the costs of immigrant participation in welfare programs that are indisputable and do not depend on accounting assumptions. The SIPP reports the dollar value of the benefits received in many of the programs, with each household reporting the value of cash benefits and vouchers received. There is no information, however, on

---

8. The refugee-sending countries identified in the SIPP are Cuba, Czechoslovakia, Hungary, Poland, the former USSR, and Vietnam.

9. Other accounting exercises include North (1983) and Parker and Rea (1993). A critical survey of the literature is given by Rothman and Espenshade (1993).

Table 6   Average Monthly Probability of Receiving Benefits in 1990/1991, Selected National Origin Groups (in percent)

Country of Birth	AFDC	SSI	Food Stamps	Medicaid	Housing Subsidies	School Lunches	Cash, Medicaid, Vouchers, Housing	Number of Households
Europe								
Germany	0.8	1.6	4.1	4.3	1.5	2.1	7.3	113
Greece	0.0	2.9	1.4	4.6	2.6	2.6	7.7	33
Italy	1.7	6.0	2.4	8.7	6.4	1.6	17.2	90
Poland	2.1	3.3	4.9	7.7	3.7	2.3	10.7	61
Portugal	0.3	3.9	0.3	5.5	2.7	6.3	10.5	31
United Kingdom	0.2	2.4	2.5	5.2	2.9	2.4	9.6	95
USSR	7.5	17.8	30.9	40.6	11.0	7.3	41.8	38
Asia								
China	0.3	8.0	1.3	11.8	6.3	6.3	14.3	114
India	1.5	1.3	1.9	7.2	4.5	3.2	11.7	55
Japan	0.0	7.8	1.0	7.8	0.0	3.1	9.3	33
Korea	0.1	2.7	0.2	4.2	2.4	6.7	7.3	62
Middle East	5.1	12.8	12.4	22.8	1.2	9.4	23.5	66
Philippines	1.1	7.3	3.1	10.8	3.6	2.5	15.2	96
Vietnam	30.3	24.1	29.7	44.9	18.6	28.6	48.6	48

North and South America								
Canada	1.6	1.7	0.7	4.4	4.4	1.2	9.6	108
Central America	4.3	5.8	11.3	22.8	7.4	25.7	31.5	99
Cuba	0.6	17.5	15.6	22.7	8.9	5.6	27.5	126
Dominican Republic	23.9	19.8	38.3	47.1	15.3	29.7	50.9	56
Jamaica	1.3	6.8	3.3	11.0	2.5	9.3	12.8	45
Mexico	6.9	6.2	17.0	26.8	7.9	35.6	36.0	505
Refugees	7.4	13.6	16.9	24.1	9.5	8.8	27.9	312
Nonrefugees	3.8	5.5	8.0	14.1	4.9	12.6	19.7	2,137
All natives	2.9	3.7	6.5	9.4	4.4	6.2	14.1	25,340
White natives	1.5	2.5	4.0	6.5	3.1	3.9	10.5	21,170
Black natives	12.1	12.2	23.3	28.8	14.6	22.0	38.8	2,600
Hispanic natives	10.0	9.9	19.4	26.0	10.3	18.5	33.4	1,247

SOURCE: 1990/1991 Survey of Income and Program Participation.

Table 7   Percentage of Dollar Benefits Distributed to
                 Immigrant Households

Type of Benefit	1990/1991
Cash programs	16.0
Aid to Families with Dependent Children (AFDC)	16.6
Supplemental security income (SSI)	18.4
Voucher programs (food stamps, WIC, and energy assistance)	11.2
Food stamps	11.5
Cash programs and voucher programs	14.5
Other programs	
Medicaid	14.1
Housing assistance (public housing or low–rent subsidies)	9.9
School breakfasts and lunches	19.0
All programs	13.8
Percent of households that are foreign born	8.0
Percent of persons living in foreign-born households	8.8

SOURCE: 1990/1991 Survey of Income and Program Participation (SIPP). The SIPP provides information on the dollar value of the benefits received by the household in cash and voucher programs. The dollar value of the benefits received by "other programs" is imputed using state–specific administrative data; see text for details.

the value of the benefits received from Medicaid, housing subsidies, or school breakfasts and lunches. We used administrative data specific to the household's state of residence to impute a dollar amount for benefits received by a household under each of these programs. For example, to calculate the value of the benefits received from Medicaid, we multiplied the number of persons in the household covered by Medicaid times the per-recipient cost in the state.[10]

We used those benefit amounts to calculate the fraction of benefits that are received by immigrant households. Table 7 shows that

---

10. The state-specific per-recipient cost for Medicaid was obtained from U.S. House of Representatives (1986, 1992). The state-specific per-recipient cost for school lunches was obtained from U.S. Bureau of the Census (1986, 1992). We could not find state-specific costs for housing subsidies and for the school breakfast program, so we used the national per-recipient cost. These data are reported in U.S. House of Representatives (1986, 1992).

Table 8   Accounting of Welfare Expenditures and Taxes Paid by
            Immigrant Households in 1990 (in billions of dollars)

	TAX RATE		
	20%	30%	40%
Dollar value of benefits from means-tested programs received by immigrant households (13.8% of $181.3 billion)	$25.0	$25.0	$25.0
Nonwelfare income received by immigrant households	$284.7	$284.7	$284.7
Taxes paid by immigrant households	$56.9	$85.4	$113.9
Taxes allocated to means-tested entitlement programs (8.9% of taxes paid)	$5.1	$7.6	$10.1
Fiscal burden on native taxpayers imposed by immigrant households (if marginal cost equals average cost)	$19.9	$17.4	$14.9

immigrant households account for a disproportionately large fraction of the costs of these programs. In the early 1990s, 8.0 percent of households were foreign born and contained 8.8 percent of all persons in the country. These immigrant households accounted for 16.6 percent of the costs of the AFDC program, 18.4 percent of the costs of SSI, 11.5 percent of the costs of food stamps, 14.1 percent of the costs of Medicaid, and 19.0 percent of the costs of subsidized school breakfasts and lunches. In sum, the 8.8 percent of persons residing in immigrant households accounted for 13.8 percent of the costs of the programs, almost 60 percent more than their representation in the population.

As noted earlier, accounting exercises that assign a dollar figure to the tax burden imposed by immigration inevitably incorporate a number of hidden and questionable assumptions. Table 8 illustrates the problem by reporting a back-of-the-envelope calculation of the costs and benefits of immigration. As we have seen, the SIPP data imply that immigrant households receive about 13.8 percent of the benefits distributed. In 1990, the total expenditures on means-tested entitlement programs was $181.3 billion (U.S. Bureau of the Census 1992, 357).[11]

---

11. Actually, expenditures on means-tested entitlement programs totaled $186.4

If we assume that immigrants received a 13.8 percent share of these expenditures, immigrants then accounted for $25.0 billion of expenditures in all means-tested entitlement programs.

The next step in the calculation is to compute the taxes that immigrants pay. According to the 1990 census data, immigrant households earned a total income (net of welfare payments) of $284.7 billion. There are no nationwide estimates of the total tax burden (i.e., one that includes federal, state, and local taxes) faced by the immigrant population. Table 8 provides estimates of total taxes using three alternative tax rates: 20, 30, and 40 percent.

If the tax rate were 30 percent, for example, immigrant households would pay about $85.4 billion in taxes. The calculations thus indicate that immigrants pay more in taxes ($85.4 billion) than they take out of the welfare system ($25.0 billion). But this comparison is misleading. It is, in effect, saying that immigrant taxes are only used to fund their use of entitlement programs. One can justify this assumption by arguing that all other government programs provide pure public goods and that expenditures in these programs would be the same whether or not we had immigration. It is likely, however, that immigrants increase the congestion associated with the provision of many of these public goods (e.g., more-crowded schools, parks, jails, and roads). Therefore, the marginal cost of providing these services to the immigrant population is not zero.

Obviously, different assumptions about the marginal cost of providing services will lead to different conclusions about whether immigrants pay their way in the welfare state. If the marginal cost is zero, immigrants make a substantial contribution to the U.S. Treasury. If the marginal cost equals the average cost, however, then immigrants should be charged for the costs of the various government programs *as*

---

billion. The figure reported in the text nets out expenditures on Indian Health Services and on pensions for needy veterans from the total because few immigrants are likely to qualify for these programs.

if they were natives. In 1990, 91.1 percent of taxes were used to pay for programs other than means-tested entitlement programs.[12] If we charge immigrants 91.1 percent of their tax payments for using these other programs, then only 8.9 percent of immigrants' taxes are left to fund their use of means-tested entitlement programs. As reported in table 8, immigrants would then contribute only $7.6 billion to the funding of the entitlement programs. The tax burden resulting from immigration would then be on the order of $17 billion.

As this back-of-the-envelope calculation suggests, accounting exercises can lead to radically different conclusions about whether immigrants pay their way. Because we do not have any estimates of the impact that immigrants have on expenditures in a vast array of nonwelfare programs, accounting exercises that claim that immigration has a huge fiscal impact (either positive or negative) should be interpreted with a great deal of caution. The data, however, *do* unambiguously indicate that immigrants receive a disproportionately high share of welfare benefits.

Summary

This chapter uses data drawn from the decennial censuses and from the Survey of Income and Program Participation to review the trends in immigrant welfare participation during the past two decades. The empirical evidence convincingly shows that immigrant participation in welfare programs has risen rapidly for two distinct reasons. First, more-recent immigrant waves are more likely to receive public assistance. Second, immigrants "assimilate" into welfare, so that the probability that immigrants participate in welfare programs actually in-

---

12. In 1989, total government expenditures totaled $2,031 billion, of which $181.3 billion (or 8.9 percent) was allocated to means-tested entitlement programs; see U.S. Bureau of the Census (1992, 357).

creases (relative to that of natives) as they age. By the early 1990s, about 21 percent of immigrant households received some type of public assistance, as compared with 14 percent of native households.

As a result of these trends, the costs associated with immigrant participation in public assistance programs may be substantial. By the early 1990s, immigrants made up about 8 percent of the households, but these immigrant households accounted for 13.8 percent of the public assistance dollars disbursed in the United States.

The adverse impact of immigration on welfare expenditures has already had an important influence in the policy debate over welfare reform. The resolution of this debate, as exemplified by the legislation enacted in 1996, is to essentially prohibit most noncitizens from receiving many types of public assistance. There are good reasons to suspect that this resolution to the problem will not be effective in the long run. By restricting public assistance to noncitizens, the reform creates an important economic incentive for less-skilled immigrants to apply for naturalization. Indeed, the number of naturalization applications has risen rapidly since the enactment of California's Proposition 187 in 1994. If many noncitizens choose to become naturalized as a result of the legislation, it is doubtful that restricting aid to noncitizens will have a major impact on welfare expenditures in the long run. As a result, the debate over whether immigrants pay their way in the welfare state may have to be revisited in the near future.

References

Blau, Francine D. "The Use of Transfer Payments by Immigrants." *Industrial and Labor Relations Review* 37 (January 1984): 222–39.

Borjas, George J. "Assimilation, Changes in Cohort Quality, and the Earnings of Immigrants." *Journal of Labor Economics* 3 (October 1985): 463–89.

———. "Immigration and Welfare, 1970–1990." *Research in Labor Economics* 14 (1995): 251–80.

Borjas, George J., and Lynette S. Hilton. "Immigration and the Welfare State: Immigrant Participation in Means-Tested Entitlement Programs." *Quarterly Journal of Economics* 111 (May 1996): 575–604.

Borjas, George J., and Stephen J. Trejo. "Immigrant Participation in the Welfare System." *Industrial and Labor Relations Review* 44 (January 1991): 195–211.

Clark, Rebecca L., and Jeffrey S. Passel. "How Much Do Immigrants Pay in Taxes? Evidence from Los Angeles County." Working Paper PRIP-UI-26, Urban Institute, Washington, D.C., Program for Research on Immigration Policy, August 1993.

Fix, Michael, and Jeffrey S. Passel. *Immigration and Immigrants: Setting the Record Straight.* Washington, D.C.: Urban Institute, 1994.

Huddle, Donald. "The Costs of Immigration." Manuscript, Rice University, July 1993.

Jensen, Leif. "Patterns of Immigration and Public Assistance Utilization, 1970–1980." *International Migration Review* 22 (spring 1988): 51–83.

North, David. "Impact of Legal, Illegal, and Refugee Migration on U.S. Social Service Programs." In Mary Kritz, ed., *U.S. Immigration and Refugee Policy.* Lexington, Mass.: D.C. Heath, 1983.

Parker, Richard A., and Louis M. Rea. "Illegal Immigration in San Diego County: An Analysis of Costs and Revenues." Report to the California State Senate Special Committee on Border Issues, Sacramento, Calif., September 1993.

Passel, Jeffrey S., and Rebecca L. Clark. "How Much Do Immigrants Really Cost? A Reappraisal of Huddle's 'The Cost of Immigration.'" Working Paper, Urban Institute, Washington, D.C., February 1994.

Rothman, Eric S., and Thomas J. Espenshade. "Fiscal Impacts of Immigration to the United States." *Population Index* 58 (fall 1992): 381–415.

Simon, Julian L. "Immigration, Taxes, and Welfare in the United States." *Population and Development Review* 10 (March 1984): 55–69.

Tienda, Marta, and Leif Jensen. "Immigration and Public Assistance Participation: Dispelling the Myth of Dependency." *Social Science Research* 15 (December 1986): 372–400.

U.S. Bureau of the Census. *Statistical Abstract of the United States, 1992.* Washington, D.C.: U.S. Government Printing Office, 1992.

U.S. House of Representatives. *Background Material and Data on Programs within the Jurisdiction of the Committee on Ways and Means (Green Book).* Washington, D.C.: U.S. Government Printing Office, various issues.

U.S. Immigration and Naturalization Service. *Statistical Yearbook of the Immigration and Naturalization Service, 1991.* Washington, D.C.: U.S. Government Printing Office, 1992.

Roy Beck

CHAPTER FIVE

The High Cost
of Cheap
Foreign Labor

The costs of immigration do not fall primarily on the nation but on the local communities and the individuals in the occupations where foreign workers and their families concentrate. Although many owners of business and capital may view immigrants—whether low skilled or high skilled—primarily as a source of cheap labor, those workers can be quite expensive to the rest of the members of a community. And although some private organizations may promote immigration as a way for them to express charitable feelings, the other members of a community may end up paying most of the costs.

In myriad ways, a community subsidizes those who benefit from high immigration. Some of the subsidy is monetary: social services to foreign workers who do not earn enough money to rise above poverty; issuance of new school bonds to educate the foreign workers' children; additional infrastructure to handle an expanding population that cannot pay enough taxes to cover the costs; social services to American workers who lose jobs or drop into poverty wages because of the foreign job competition.

Other costs to a community are less tangible but probably more disconcerting to the American people. They involve changes—many of which are considered *losses* by natives—in the quality of life in a community. My journalistic research in local communities—and of scholarly studies doing the same—finds that high immigration tends to lengthen the time it takes people to travel to work; it tends to increase air pollution, to add pressures on already vulnerable environmental resources, to deteriorate the quality of the schools primarily through overcrowding, to add transience to a community while diminishing social cohesiveness, to decrease public safety, and to change the ambiance and lifestyle of a community.

Economic Dynamism and Social Disintegration on the Prairie

Two prairie towns featured in a 1972 *Fortune* magazine vividly illustrate some of the high costs of cheap foreign labor. A picture of the citizens of Spencer, Iowa, filled the magazine cover. Inside, the article on small cities also saluted Garden City, Kansas. Both cities were said to be prospering economically while continuing to offer their residents the "uniquely American lifestyle" of a small town. The article extolled the small towns' low crime and taxes, an idyllic environment for children, friendliness, an absence of an underclass, and a strong sense of community unity (Loving 1975).

Much has changed since then. Garden City has become home to thousands of immigrants; Spencer has not. Spencer has retained most of the attributes that so impressed the *Fortune* writer; Garden City has not.

Congress has made the decision that the nation should move in a Garden City–like direction. And it is Garden City that provides a glimpse of the future for all American communities and the price they may be forced to pay for Washington's immigration policies—if they aren't paying them already.

In some ways, immigrant-enlarged Garden City looks to be the more successful of the prairie towns. The two were about the same size in 1972. Since then, Spencer has barely grown to eleven thousand, but Garden City now is more than twice that size. Spencer quickly faded from national attention; Garden City received continuing national recognition through the 1980s and 1990s as a meat-processing boomtown and a home of increasing cultural diversity.

Garden City measures up well under a "bigger is better" standard. Not only has its population surged, but it has many more jobs—a 55 percent increase between 1980 and 1988 alone. By 1991, *Kansas Business Review* could boast that the town had added seventeen eating and drinking establishments and thirty-nine new retail stores, including a new shopping center anchored by J. C. Penney and Wal-Mart (Broadway and Stull 1991).

But below those obvious signs of growth lies a much grimmer picture of the costs to Garden City natives of having industries that rely heavily on immigrants. Garden City's conditions moved toward Third World standards as Third World immigrants arrived. By 1987, for example, the county had the second-highest birthrate in Kansas and was the only county in which less than 50 percent of the mothers received adequate prenatal care. In the first five years of recruiting immigrant workers into Garden City, confirmed cases of child abuse and neglect tripled. Garden City taxpayers now have a much heavier load of impoverished residents to support. Even as the number of jobs expanded, the unemployment rate rose 50 percent between 1979 and 1986, partly because of the number of immigrants who were injured on the job or who found they weren't willing to put up with the conditions at the meatpacking plants.

Economic growth based on low-wage immigrant labor "had the effect of reducing relative income levels," said the *Kansas Business Review*. Per capita income for the county, in comparison to the rest of Kansas, dropped throughout Garden City's "booming" 1980s.

Because of the low wages and the high number of children of the foreign workers, many of the immigrant families couldn't make ends meet on their incomes. The taxpayers had to supplement the workers' food, medical care, and other basic needs. The taxpayer-supported psychiatric hospital experienced sustained admissions, as did treatment centers for alcoholism. Health care availability in the county deteriorated as the doctor-resident ratio grew worse by about a third.

According to a team of scholars writing in the *Aspen Institute Quarterly*, Garden City has been typical of the way taxpayers subsidize most industries that expand in Midwestern cities using immigrant labor. The Mid-Nebraska Community Services, for example, experienced a huge increase in the demand for social services after the introduction of immigrant labor into its region. Use of the food pantry rose 405 percent, and programs for the homeless experienced a 1,000 percent jump in activity after the first year. Lexington, Nebraska, the site of a major immigrant worker center, saw its crime rate rise to the highest in the state, twice the state average (Hackenburg 1993).

The Aspen Institute scholars noted that a "local community assumes it will benefit from a growing payroll and improved purchasing power. However, the case of Lexington demonstrates that the economic expansion may not be sufficient to support new-worker households at the living standards of older residents. The unexpected result is a net gain in poverty and expanded demands for understaffed and underfinanced health and social services. Less visible costs are reflected in the need for new education programs and expanded police protection." In part because governments give industries tax incentives to expand their immigrant-reliant operations, the tax receipts do not expand sufficiently to meet the additional needs of the immigrant workers. The native taxpayers have to pay a subsidy to the industries in the form of higher taxes and deteriorated services. In Garden City— which once typified the very term *heartland*—residents watched as their crime rate rose steadily and violent crimes nearly doubled in the county, while crime in the rest of Kansas was dropping.

The superintendent of Garden City schools in 1990 had to acknowledge the highest dropout rate in Kansas. Trying to provide a good climate for education was increasingly difficult with a growing student body—a 37 percent increase over one six-year period—and immigrant students who often seemed just to be passing through, thanks to chronic absenteeism and a turnover of almost one-third of the student body each year. Minority enrollment—mostly Southeast Asian, Mexican, and Central American—had hit 36 percent by 1989. While the school system struggled to find teachers who could speak Vietnamese and Spanish, the racial imbalance among the elementary schools grew so stark that the school board proposed busing, only to cancel it after vigorous protest from the natives. Taxpayers consented three times to major bond issues to build new schools for the immigrant children. But according to Professors Michael Broadway and Donald D. Stull, who did in-depth studies of the town, "the struggle to provide a sufficient education for all of Garden City's children is being lost."

A sense of unity and egalitarianism has been lost amid all the transience. A longitudinal analysis of families enrolling their children in the Garden City school district for the first time found that 40 percent of them had left within a year. Another 20 percent were gone at the end of the second year.

Some Garden City people approve of the immigrant influx. They occupy the same professional sector as those who seem to speak favorably about immigration in most local communities: educators, clergy, and other people who provide government or private relief services to the immigrants. Those residents are proud that Garden City is now more "cosmopolitan," with bilingual education, ethnic festivals, and social service challenges like the big cities. They like the national attention they have received about their cultural diversity. For the overwhelming majority of residents, however, high immigration has brought few benefits and many costs, not the least of which is an irreparably changed style of community living—a change the residents never asked Congress to make.

Complexity in Comparisons between Immigrant Towns and Nonimmigrant Towns

In visiting and studying numerous other cities and towns across the country that have experienced new streams of immigrants in the last two decades, I found that most followed similar patterns of change to those found in Garden City. The changes there do not seem to just be part of an overall national trend that is independent of immigration, for such changes have missed Spencer, Iowa, which has thus far avoided being caught in the new immigration tidal wave. Unlike most immigration cities, Spencer has retained its more egalitarian qualities; it is a community without stark contrasts between haves and have-nots, without escalating social tensions, and without a sense that its best days of community are in the past.

Spencer has had to fight harder than Garden City to keep its over-all economy strong. In essence that is because Garden City "stole" a lot of Spencer's jobs. Federal immigration policies played a key role in that "theft." Meatpacking had been the chief industry of Spencer through the 1970s. But after years of Congress creating a surplus labor market through the mass importation of lower-skilled foreign workers, some meatpacking industries devised a strategy to open up new plants in places like Garden City and to staff them with lower-paid immigrants. As a result, tens of thousands of American workers earning unionized wages lost their jobs in plants such as the one in Spencer so that foreign workers could have lower-paying jobs (some in the same plants but most in new plants such as the ones in Garden City).

That is an important image to retain when looking at economic comparisons between immigration and nonimmigration cities. To do direct year-by-year economic comparison between Spencer and Garden City entails complex challenges. During the early 1980s, for example, "nonimmigrant" Spencer definitely would look weaker in several economic indexes than "immigrant" Garden City. Those results might cause somebody to conclude that immigration is good for economic growth. Anybody knowing the meatpacking history, however, would see through those kinds of results. Immigrants not only bring harm (as well as benefits) to the cities where they settle, but they bring harm to the cities where they don't settle. Had Congress not provided the immigrant labor pool used by the industries of Garden City (and other such places), Spencer's economy likely would have been stronger during the 1980s.

That factor often is lost when comparing fast-growing coastal immigration cities with nonimmigration cities like Memphis and Detroit, which can look economically pale in comparison. The rapid inflow of foreign laborers into the coastal cities attracts industry to take advantage of the cheap labor. Without the immigrant-bloated labor markets on the coasts, however, the interior cities, with their labor markets of underemployed native workers, would have looked more attractive for industrial expansion.

Yet another factor that is commonly missed in comparing cities is that many of the American workers in immigration cities who are hurt by foreign workers don't get measured as a cost for those cities because they move to nonimmigration cities. To the extent that those mobile workers do poorly, their cost gets counted not against the immigration city but against the nonimmigration city.

A Theoretic Basis for the Wisdom of the People

Numerous comparative statistical surveys of cities as well as econometrics modeling have fed us varying and seemingly contradictory conclusions about the costs of immigration to communities. Some economists find striking costs; others do not. Yet most Americans who actually live in the communities and work in the occupations where significant immigration occurs overwhelmingly feel that the costs of immigration in their communities and in their occupations have far outweighed the benefits.

These Americans are not just imagining that something has gone wrong in those immigration-impacted communities and occupations. Median wages and working-class incomes have been stagnant or declining during the last two decades of immigration. That immigration is numerically more than quadruple the traditional U.S. average, or the level, during the previous forty years.

A recent study by the *Washington Post*, Harvard University, and the Henry J. Kaiser Family Foundation examined the perception gap between the way economists and other Americans view the economy. Most economists—who also happened to report that their own personal circumstances have improved considerably—look at the overall American economy and declare it healthy and promising. But most Americans are pessimistic; they believe that the economy only helps some people and that they are most likely to come out on the short end. In reality, the study found that the Americans with the on-the-ground view of the economy probably have the more accurate view. The study concluded that a growing disparity in this nation is dividing the country into a small group of "prosperous, optimistic winners" and a much larger group of "struggling and increasingly embittered losers." It wasn't that economists were providing faulty data but that they were not focusing on the economic facts that were the most important to the people (Chandler and Morin 1996).

But has Washington's reinstituting mass immigration been a cause or just a coincidental factor in the growing disparities? There have been massive restructurings of the economy and domestic social mores, as well as changes in trade laws and global competition. In that complicated mix, it is not easy to determine how much of the depression of U.S. wages and increase in economic disparity is the result of increased immigration.

A number of prominent economists, however, note that immigration would theoretically cause both wage depression and economic disparity. The *Post* series noted that we have not seen economic disparity like this since the turn of the last century. Interestingly, that is the last time we had a major surge in immigration.

That is no coincidence, according to economist Jeffrey Williamson. Economic inequality in America was greatest from 1820 to 1860 and from the 1890s until World War I. Those periods coincided with the two previous major waves of immigration. According to Williamson, increased fertility and immigration foster income inequality. Despite having democratic institutions, abundant resources, and a reputation as a workingman's country, America during those periods of nineteenth-century immigration surges was a land of jarring inequality.

Economist Peter H. Lindert (1977) has noted that American inequality lessened when immigration was curtailed. When World War I abruptly cut off most immigration to the United States, the huge gap between rich and poor closed incredibly fast: "Within three years' time, pay gaps dropped from historic heights to their lowest level since before the Civil War." But just as quickly, inequality grew as soon as mass immigration resumed after World War I, so that later in the 1920s, "income looked as unequal as ever."

It should not be surprising that the law of supply and demand has not been repealed. Increasing the supply of labor tends to decrease its value and vice versa. The economist Harry T. Oshima has explained how tight labor markets not only make employers pay more for scarce labor but greatly stimulate a country's creativity. When immigration was restricted around 1915 and again in the mid-1920s, employers were forced to raise wages. That induced the employers to press for major advances in mechanization. The resulting new technological applications of gasoline and electric machines made it possible to mechanize enough unskilled operations and handwork to release many workers into more skilled jobs. Growth in output per worker hour was phenomenal, making it possible to raise wages still further. Because of the increasing demand for skilled workers, American parents realized that they would need to spend more money to help their children gain a better education. This contributed to lower birthrates and thus to slower labor force growth and thus to tighter labor markets and thus to higher wages, which pushed manufacturers to push the skill levels of their workers up even further. In this cycle of productivity and wage gains—each feeding on the other—the United States became a middle-class nation.

But since 1965, Congress has denied the country the opportunity for this "virtuous circle" by flooding the labor markets with foreign workers.

Williamson and economist Timothy J. Hatton (1994) have written that all standard mainstream economic models predict that migration will tend to lower wages where immigrants settle. But many economists have had difficulty designing measuring models that actually prove that this is happening. In the meantime, common sense and daily experience allow most Americans to feel that they have all the proof they need.

Stagnant wages and growing economic inequality are the chief causes of the following five major costs that communities must bear as the result of high immigration:

INFRASTRUCTURE

Immigrants—through their arrival from other countries and through their fertility rates being much higher than the natives'—are the chief cause of U.S. population growth today. Since 1970 immigrants and their descendants have caused the majority of U.S. population growth and are projected to cause some 90 percent of it between now and 2050. The majority of population growth in most cities is due either directly to immigration or to the arrival of native-born Americans fleeing high-immigration centers. In many cities, immigrants account for all the population growth.

The United States is not even close to meeting the infrastructure maintenance needs for its own population of 265 million. Yet it runs a massive immigration program that is projected to add another 110 million people to the country over the next five decades (in addition to some 20 million people among Americans whose families were here before 1970).

Those 110 million additional immigrants and their descendants are not likely to create or gain the kinds of jobs that will provide sufficient taxes in the future to cover the price of the infrastructure they will need. A 1996 study of California immigrants, for example, found that their earned incomes were 62 percent lower than those of natives. A body of literature suggests that even when natives are added to most communities they are unable to pay for the extra infrastructure they require. It appears highly unrealistic to think that the current flow of immigrants could do so.

Until we get our infrastructure house in order, can there be any rationality in Congress forcing the population upward? It is relatively simple to gauge when our infrastructure is ready for more immigrants—when a significant portion (say 50–70 percent) of our backlogged infrastructure needs are met.

EDUCATION

The U.S. Census Bureau projects that between 1992 and 2003, school enrollment nationwide will increase by nearly nine million students. The vast majority of them will be immigrants or the children of immigrants (*Statistical Abstract* 1994).

America is faced with a daunting challenge of building enough classrooms to accommodate all the children immigration policies have added and are on course to add in the future. Texas needs to complete two schools every *week*—indefinitely—to keep up. The pace is even tougher in California, which needs to build an entire school every *day*, seven days a week, fifty-two weeks a year (California Department of Education 1991).

Who is going to pay for all the classrooms for the nine million additional students? Probably not the immigrants, according to a major study by the Rand Corporation of the school districts where most immigrants settle: "The one common characteristic of most immigrant children is poverty" (McDonnell and Hill 1993).

It is highly unlikely that immigrants will pay the approximately $15,000 per child it costs to build new schools, says physics professor Albert Bartlett of the University of Colorado. And that doesn't count the actual annual cost of more than $5,000 to educate the child. Taxpayers are not keeping up; education is suffering.

When looking at the crumbling big-city school systems of the country, it is not nearly as important that Congress ask what caused the problems as to ask what would make it easier to improve the educational quality of big cities? (1) add tens of thousands of additional foreign students to the overstressed school systems each year? (2) or allow the local school districts to try to catch up to the current overdemand on the system without Congress increasing the demand? When urban school districts stop asking for more money and report that success is the norm rather than failure, then Congress could consider importing more foreign students.

WELFARE

For years, public officials have talked about, debated, legislated, and administered plans for moving Americans out of welfare and into full-time jobs. In 1996, Congress and President Clinton enacted a tough plan aimed at pushing 2.5 million adults from welfare to jobs.

The problem as always is the jobs. The government can train, motivate, cajole, and coerce people on welfare, but it can't succeed unless there are jobs for the welfare recipients to take. More than twenty years of wage depression, due in part to high immigration, is making welfare reform difficult. The evidence is widespread.

In 1990 the Center on Budget and Policy Priorities, looking back over studies of welfare work programs, reported that only a tiny percent of welfare recipients secured "a stable source of employment that provides enough income for a decent standard of living (at least above the poverty line) and job-related benefits that adequately cover medical needs" (Porter 1990). That same year, the Brookings Institution could not find any welfare work program that raised the income of welfare recipients more than $2,000 above public assistance levels (Burtless 1990).

In *Forgotten Americans* (1992), John E. Schwartz and Thomas J. Volgy wrote: "No matter how much we may wish it otherwise, workfare cannot be an effective solution. Among the most important reasons for this is the absence of enough steady, decent-paying, full-time jobs to go around" because "low-wage employment riddles the economy." Sociologists Frances Fox Piven and Richard A. Cloward—in the 1993 revision of their classic *Regulating the Poor: The Functions of Public Welfare*—pointed out that with the labor market "flooded with immigrants from Asia, from Mexico and other Central and South American countries . . . there was no evidence, in short, that business required the labor of AFDC mothers."

Chalk up at least a portion of the Americans trapped in welfare dependency as part of the human cost of Washington's decision to add a million or more foreign workers to the economy each year. And include the monetary cost of taxpayers' having to continue to support those people on welfare. "Welfare reform presents new challenges as thousands of Americans now receiving public assistance will be required to enter the labor market," Susan Martin, executive director of the bipartisan U.S. Commission on Immigration Reform, said in 1995. "The commission believes that it is not in the national interest that they should face additional competition from unskilled foreign workers" (Martin 1995).

Unfortunately, the same Congress that passed welfare reform in 1996 voted down legislation that would have begun to cut off one of the largest flows of lower-skilled foreign workers: adult relatives of recent immigrants. By allowing the continuation of that adult relative stream, Congress gave its approval to an endless chain of lower-skilled foreign workers migrating to compete with lower-skilled Americans who cannot find jobs. Congress should not consider allowing further unskilled immigrants into the country until virtually all former welfare recipients who want a job find one.

DOMESTIC TRANQUILITY

Americans are substantially agreed that immigration has not made their communities calmer, more peaceful places to live. In 1992, a *BusinessWeek* poll found that 59 percent of Americans said that immigration had worsened race relations in the cities. And 55 percent of respondents told Gallup pollsters in 1993 that the diversity of cultures brought in by immigrants "mostly threatens" American culture.

To say that the imposition of a foreign culture into an American community is disruptive is not necessarily to say there is anything negative about that foreign culture itself. The point is that differing cultures often tend to clash. And no matter how admirable the traits of a foreign culture, it can produce less than admirable results when introduced too rapidly and in too large of a dose into the middle of a community. Most people anywhere in the world feel a strong right to surround themselves with whatever local culture they prefer. Americans have not been happy when the influx of immigrants has seemed to threaten their local way of life. The higher the volume of immigration, the higher has been the sense of threat and resulting tensions.

The problems that U.S. communities encounter when large numbers of immigrants enter from other countries is not unique to Americans, according to a 1995 study by the National Center for Policy Analysis. Immigration can create a type of cultural diversity, which anthropologists identify as a universal source of social conflict and often a barrier to personal freedom and economic progress, the author stated. The role of culture in a society is to standardize human contact so that people can make reasonably confident assumptions about the reactions of other people. "Multiculturalism sounds fine in theory," said Gerald R. Scully, the author, "but we find that where there are multiple cultures there's almost always conflict. Most homogeneous cultures have more civil and political freedom, while culturally heterogeneous ones have less." The study (Scully 1995) by the free market–oriented think tank found that increasing the number of languages and cultures in a country harmed economic progress: "Even if different groups live together peacefully, the lack of a common language and common norms reduces cooperation and increases the cost of transacting."

The criticism of cultural diversity tends to grate on the ears of Americans who think of their country as a great respecter and appreciator of diversity. That sense of national identity is so ingrained in many altruistic Americans that immigration trumps all other issues; the belief is that the more diversity the better, no matter the cost. Much of the confusion may come from the fact that few people alive have experienced American diversity—until recent years—under conditions other than the low immigration flows following 1924. Many have falsely assumed that because the diversity of the 1950s and 1960s was good for society, more diversity would be even better. But the diversity of national origins was a delightful spice during that period because it was in small enough proportions that the minority cultures could achieve common bonds with the majority culture.

The truism that too much immigration will kill healthy multiculturalism seems to apply everywhere, despite claims in a number of national newsmagazines and newspapers that New York City is an exception. "Civil War in Los Angeles, but Civil in New York," read a headline over an article in *USA Today* saying that "in New York City, people and politicians are not upset about immigration" (Puente 1995). The statement was half-right: A group of politicians *has* made aggressive proimmigration statements.

In fact, though, New York residents disagree with their local officials about immigration and are not at all happy that some 30 percent of the population is foreign born. An Empire State Survey in 1993, for example, found that New York City residents by a two to one margin said that immigration was making the city a worse place to live. Even the majority of the immigrants there said immigration was deteriorating the city (McFadden 1993).

New York City was not always this way. During the decades of low immigration in this century, it was "a city that enjoyed tranquility and civility to an extent quite unimaginable today," in the words of essayist Jonathan Yardley (1995). New York City during that time was "a model and an ideal" for the rest of the nation, says author David Gelernter. U.S. senator Daniel Patrick Moynihan (1994) points out that New York City today "is immeasurably worse in nearly every aspect of urban life: violent streets, disintegrating families and crumbling infrastructure." The city once had "the most admired urban school system in the world, the finest housing, the best subways and in many ways the best-behaved citizens." New York City always has been an immigration center, but during its golden years the flow was modest and nourishing instead of torrential and eroding.

The proliferation of so-called gated communities may be the clearest and most disturbing sign that "the problems of the city will continue to get worse, and someday there may be no 'city' left," says Roger K. Lewis (1995), professor of architecture at the University of Maryland. Americans buying walled-off homes in both the city and the suburb are not just seeking to escape the problems of the city, he says, "They are abandoning the whole *idea* of city—its culture, its physical form, its intellectual and commercial vitality, its complexity and unique capacity for accommodating disparate individuals within a shared environment."

The drive of so many Americans for protection, exclusion, and separation in gated communities is fueled by immigration, a growing underclass, and a restructured economy, according to Edward J. Blakely, professor of planning and development at the University of

Southern California. He and Mary Gail Snyder of the University of California at Berkeley studied the gated communities and found them to be popular throughout California, Texas, Florida, and in the cities of New York, Chicago, and Phoenix. All but Phoenix have high concentrations of immigrants—and Phoenix is filling up with native-born urban refugees who have been traumatized by the social breakdown in California. Would it not make sense for Congress to wait until there are sustained signs that most American communities have figured out how to live peacefully and comfortably with the current levels of ethnic, racial, and cultural diversity before forcing more on them?

LIFESTYLE

At present immigration levels, America's population (excluding Alaska) in just a few decades will be as dense as that of the Europeans. Because Europe's population has already stabilized, it won't be long until Americans will be even more crowded than the Europeans. Will Americans adjust well and readily, considering the history of so many Americans insisting on a high degree of personal freedom, personal space, and proximity to natural areas?

Those are not frivolous wants on the part of Americans and likely are deep psychological needs, says Debbie Biniores-Egger, an analytic psychologist. A native of Arkansas who now is a Swiss citizen, she believes most Americans might find it psychologically difficult to adjust to a European-type congestion: "I'm committed to the premise that what we create on the outside in our society has a relationship to the inner psyche of a population. Americans have a total sense of open boundaries. This is in essence the American culture" (interview with author, August 10, 1994). The Swiss, like other Europeans, have evolved a very different culture within their dense population to preserve their privacy and to limit opportunities for personal conflict, she says. Thus they consent to and encourage their government to force the protection of personal boundaries.

Managers of U.S. parks and wilderness areas can attest to Americans' deep need for solitude and nonurban experiences. The problem is that, with 265 million Americans, the open spaces no longer are sufficient; Americans are loving nature to death. There isn't much more wilderness left to set aside and open up to the public. In 1993, Congress opened up 353 square miles at South Colony Lakes in Colorado's Sangre de Cristo mountains. Within two years, it was so crowded that rangers were contemplating limiting the number who could visit. In state and national parks near population centers, reservations and daily visitor limits are becoming more common as the national population grows by nearly three million a year (Finley 1995).

One would hope that federal officials would carefully study the desire of Americans to live in European-style density—as well as European-style regimentation and regulation—before their immigration policies leave Americans only a choice between that lifestyle and eradicating much of the nation's natural heritage.

Meanwhile, Congress runs its relentless population growth program, and native-born Americans are fleeing the immigration centers by the tens of thousands, according to demographer William H. Frey of the University of Michigan. It is not just the core cities that Americans are deserting but the suburbs, which have been surrounded by layer upon layer of new suburbs. "Phoenix sprawls into the desert at the rate of an acre an hour; greater New York City stretches clear into Pennsylvania; strip malls, traffic, fear of crime have wrecked the tranquil 'burbs of Ozzie and Harriet's time," trumpeted the opening lines of a special *Newsweek* report. The endless urban sprawl is a fairly clear signal that millions of Americans are unhappy with the never-ending growth in population centers and that they continue to try to establish themselves on or beyond the urban edges (Adler 1995).

Like latter-day Daniel Boones, the urban refugees want more elbow room. They seek to get away from the things of the city and move far enough out so they can see nature or get to it quickly. But as long as the United States continues to grow by some three million a year, there always are more people moving in next door. As Frances Emma Barwood told *Newsweek* about a popular development on the edge of Phoenix: "The people who bought houses in Phase One were told they'd be surrounded by beautiful lush deserts, but instead they're surrounded by Phases Two and Three."

A small percentage of the urban refugees are giving up on seeking the "edge" around the immigration centers of the coasts and are moving to the interior. Their presence, plus the smaller movements of foreign migrants into the interior, is creating minisprawls and changing cultures in a way not at all appreciated by the interior's residents. In Phoenix, native-born Americans fleeing immigration-weary California are fueling a rampaging sprawl. According to the *Arizona Republic*, on the lips of seemingly every resident is the great fearful declaration "We don't want to become another Los Angeles." The newcomers immediately sing the same refrain, hoping that they will be the last to arrive. But Congress continues to pour hundreds of thousands of foreign citizens into California, and the natives there continue to flee (Nilsson 1995).

Hundreds of thousands of Americans have been moving out of California. Almost a quarter of departing Californians move to the South. About half of them move to other western states. The flight is rapidly changing the ambiance of the mountain states.

Most of the residents of the previously sparsely populated mountain states are unhappy with the influx from both the West and the East Coasts. Housing prices are driven up, pollution increases, schools get crowded, the old views of beautiful mountains are filled with condos and tract homes. Many communities and Americans remain whose lives are not yet forcibly transformed by the new immigration wave, but as long as Congress allows immigration above historically beneficial levels, no American in any community—no matter how remote—can feel beyond the reach.

Federally Coerced Community Upheaval Not Economically Necessary

It is important to note the obvious: None of that immigration-caused upheaval would have occurred without the federal government's actively running such a large immigration program. The common justification for the federal government causing such unrequested changes to communities is that foreign workers are necessary because they are filling jobs that Americans won't do. Such a claim is nearly always false.

For example, consider meat-cutting jobs, which today pay relatively low wages for work that is the most dangerous in America. Just fifteen years ago, before industry began fully taking advantage of the surplus labor pool provided by federal immigration programs, nearly all those jobs were filled by Americans making high wages and working under safe conditions. Although there have been major structural and technological changes in the industry, there is no doubt that the meat packers would still be hiring all the meat cutters they needed from among American workers had Washington not given them a foreign alternative. In my book *The Case against Immigration* (W.W. Norton, 1996), I detailed the sad history of how Congress colluded—wittingly or unwittingly—with maverick, union-busting meatpacking companies to destroy one of the best middle-class blue-collar occupations of America. Likewise, President Grover Cleveland had allowed the meatpacking companies to use foreign labor to battle the unions and maintain inhumane working conditions at the turn of the century (Beck 1996). It was only during the period of low immigration, from 1925 to 1965, that pay and working conditions improved to middle-class standards. Thanks to Washington's renewal of mass immigration since 1965, the working conditions of Upton Sinclair's *The Jungle* have returned (Stull and Broadway 1990).

One occupation after another has become an "immigrant job" in the high-immigration cities. But when I travel almost anywhere in the United States that is at least a hundred miles from a coast, I find native-born Americans making the beds, washing the dishes, running the cash registers, driving the cabs, and doing the construction. Obviously, Americans will do those jobs if the employer is forced to offer the pay and working conditions acceptable to American workers. In the case of Garden City, the local workforce was not large enough meet the big meat packers' needs when they first built there. But those same companies had eliminated an even larger number of jobs in places like Kansas City and Spencer. If Congress had not provided the companies with foreign workers, they would have had to entice their fired workers or other underemployed and unemployed Americans to move to Garden City. If we do not need foreign workers, one has to wonder why the federal government insists on continuing to import hundreds of thousands of them each year at such a high cost to local communities and to wage-earning Americans, both native and foreign born.

Bibliography

Adler, Jerry. "Bye, Bye Suburban Dream." *Newsweek*, 15 May 1995.

Beck, Roy. *The Case against Immigration: The Moral, Economic, Social and Environmental Reasons for Reducing Immigration Back to Traditional Levels*. New York: W. W. Norton, 1996. See chapter 2 for immigration history and chapter 6 for case study of meatpacking industry.

Blakely, Edward J, and Mary Gail Snyder. "Fortress Communities: The Walling and Gating of American Suburbs." *Landlines* (newsletter of the Lincoln Institute of Land Policy).

Broadway, Michael. "Beef Stew: Cattle, Immigrants and Established Residents in a Kansas Beefpacking Town." In Louie Lamphere, Alex Stepick, and Guillermo Grenier, eds., *Newcomers in the Workplace: Immigrants and the Restructuring of the U.S. Economy*. Philadelphia: Temple University Press, 1994.

Broadway, Michael, and Donald D. Stull. "Rural Industrialization: The Example of Garden City, Kansas." *Kansas Business Review* 14 (summer 1991).

Burtless, Gary, ed. *A Future of Lousy Jobs: The Changing Structure of U.S. Wages.* Washington, D.C.: Brookings Institution, 1990.

Businessweek/Harris Poll, June 1992.

California Department of Education. "California Schools Bursting at the Seams," 3 September 1991.

Chandler, Clay, and Richard Morin. "Reality Check: The Economic Perception Gap." *Washington Post*, 13–15 October 1996.

Fehr, Stephen C. "Traffic Taking Toll on Wilson Bridge." *Washington Post*, 2 September 1994.

Finley, Bruce. "Vanishing Wilderness: Recreation Surge Scars Landscapes." *Denver Post*, 3 September 1995.

Hackenberg, Robert A., et al. "Meat Processing and the Transformation of Rural America: The Emergence of a New Underclass?" *Aspen Institute Quarterly* 5 (spring 1993).

Hatton, Timothy, and Jeffrey G. Williamson. "International Migration 1850–1939: An Economic Survey." In Hatton and Williamson, eds., *Migration and the International Labor Market 1850–1939.* New York: Routledge, 1994.

Lewis, Roger K. "Gated Areas: Start of New Middle Ages." *Washington Post*, 9 September 1995.

Lindert, Peter H. *Fertility and Scarcity in America.* Princeton, N.J.: Princeton University Press, 1977.

Loving, Rush, Jr. "Small Town That Has Kept Its Vigor." *Fortune*, April 1972.

Martin, Susan. "How Much Immigration We Need—and the Rules for Who Can Stay." *Washington Times*, 27 June 1995.

McDonnell, Lorraine M., and Paul T. Hill. *Newcomers in American Schools: Meeting the Educational Needs of Immigrant Youth.* Santa Monica, Calif.: RAND Corporation, 1993.

McFadden, Robert D. "Immigration Hurting City, New Yorkers Say in Survey." *New York Times*, 18 October 1993.

Moynihan, Daniel Patrick. "A Cry for My City." *Reader's Digest*, January 1994.

Nilsson, Joel. "State Trust Lands Hold Key to Desert Preservation." *Arizona Republic*, 7 May 1995.

Oshima, Harry T. "The Growth of U.S. Factor Productivity: The Significance of New Technologies in the Early Decades of the Twentieth Century." *Journal of Economic History* 44 (March 1984).

Piven, Frances Fox, and Richard A. Cloward. *Regulating the Poor: The Functions of Public Welfare*. New York: Vintage Books, 1993.

Porter, Kathryn H. *Making Jobs Work: What Research Says about Effective Employment Programs for AFDC Recipients*. Washington, D.C.: Center on Budget and Policy Priorities, March 1990.

Puente, Maria. "Civil War in Los Angeles, but Civil in New York," *USA Today*, 3 July 1995.

Schwartz, John E., and Thomas J. Volgy. *Forgotten Americans*. New York: W. W. Norton, 1992.

Scully, Gerald R. *Multiculturalism and Economic Growth*. Washington, D.C.: National Center for Policy Analysis, 1995.

Shultz, Richard H., and William J. Olson. *Ethnic and Religious Conflict: Emerging Threat to U.S. Security*. Washington, D.C.: National Strategy Information Center, 1994.

Statistical Abstract of the United States. Washington, D.C.: U.S. Department of Commerce, 1994.

Stull, Donald D., and Michael J. Broadway. "The Effects of Restructuring on Beefpacking in Kansas." *Kansas Business Review* 14 (fall 1990).

Williamson, Jeffrey. *Inequality, Poverty and History: The Kuznets Memorial Lectures*. Cambridge, Mass.: Blackwell, 1991.

Yardley, Jonathan. "We Have Met the Future and It Is Us." *Washington Post Book World*, 11 June 1995.

PART TWO

Rules
and
Regulations

Stephen H. Legomsky

CHAPTER SIX

Employer Sanctions
Past and Future

Illegal immigration has been a front-page issue for several decades. Today, however, the subject is practically leaping off the page. Whether the subject is California Proposition 187, asylum reform, birthright citizenship for children of undocumented aliens, law enforcement funding levels, welfare eligibility rules, incarceration of undocumented alien criminal offenders, or federal reimbursement for state expenditures, illegal immigration has become a core element of American political discourse.

The Illegal Immigration Reform and Immigrant Responsibility Act of 1996 (IIRIRA)[1] is merely the most recent congressional foray into the area (among many others) of illegal immigration. Until 1986, efforts to reduce illegal immigration generally emphasized the detection and apprehension of undocumented aliens at the border and in the interior. The Immigration Reform and Control Act of 1986 (IRCA)[2] fundamentally altered that strategy. With IRCA, Congress attempted

---

1. Public Law 104-208, 110 Stat. 3009, Div. C, 104th Cong., 2d sess., September 30, 1996.
2. Public Law 99-603, 100 Stat. 3359, 99th Cong., 2d sess., November 5, 1986.

to reduce the undocumented alien population in two ways: through legalization, which would make most of the undocumented population "documented," and through sanctions on employers of aliens not authorized to work.

Employer sanctions became permanently etched in the American consciousness in 1993, when it became known that Zoe Baird, President Bill Clinton's choice for attorney general, had been employing an undocumented couple as domestic workers. The resulting uproar eventually doomed her nomination.[3] Somewhat similar problems plagued the president's second choice, Judge Kimba Wood.[4]

For a variety of reasons considered below, employer sanctions remain controversial. Would the country be better off with them or without them? What are the still unsettled empirical questions on which the magnitudes of the competing benefits and costs depend? And how might the employer sanctions program be modified to enhance the benefits and reduce the costs? Those are the questions this chapter will address. First, though, it is necessary to provide some basic background information on undocumented aliens generally and on employer sanctions in particular.

Background

UNDOCUMENTED ALIENS AS A PROBLEM

The central mission of employer sanctions is to remove the incentive for undocumented aliens to enter, and to remain in, the United States. I use the phrase *undocumented aliens* to cover all aliens who are not in possession of valid immigration documents. For present purposes, they can be thought of as consisting almost entirely of two large

---

3. *New York Times*, January 22, 1993, p. A-1.
4. Ibid., February 6, 1993, p. A-2.

groups: those who entered the United States by evading inspection and those who entered on lawful temporary visas but then overstayed.

By their nature, undocumented aliens are hard to count. The commissioner of the Immigration and Naturalization Service recently estimated the total undocumented alien population at 3.8 million, divided roughly evenly between those who entered without inspection and those who overstayed.[5]

Why is undocumented immigration such a concern? Some of the reasons are intangible. If the rule of law is the thread that preserves the social fabric, then mass violations of federal law weaken the public order. If democracy is what legitimates government power, then violations of valid laws thwart democratic rule. And if sovereignty means anything at all, surely it means that a nation may decide whom to admit into its territory.

Other social costs are more tangible, though their magnitudes are often unknown. These include public benefits, incarceration of those undocumented aliens who commit crimes, increased competition for jobs, the costs associated with law enforcement, the exacerbation of overpopulation and the attendant environmental impact, a public backlash toward legal immigrants, the exploitation of undocumented aliens by employers, and physical dangers to the aliens at the border, including drownings and abuse.[6]

---

5. Testimony of the Honorable Doris Meissner before the Judiciary Committee of the U.S. Senate, June 15, 1994; see also 71 Interpreter Releases 827 (Federal Publications Inc., June 27, 1994). For a detailed study of the methods and problems in estimating this population, see U.S. General Accounting Office, "Illegal Aliens — Despite Data Limitations, Current Methods Provide Better Population Estimates," GAO/PEMD-93-25, August 1993.

6. See generally Robert L. Bach and Doris Meissner, "Employment and Immigration Reform: Employer Sanctions Four Years Later," Carnegie Endowment for International Peace, 1990, pp. 4–5; Michael Fix and Paul T. Hill, "Enforcing Employer Sanctions: Challenges and Strategies," Rand Corporation and Urban Institute, 1990, pp. 11–15. As for the drownings, see *Migration World Magazine* 24, no. 3 (1996): 10. On the subject of abuse of aliens by border patrol officials, see Bill Ong Hing, "Border Patrol Abuse: Evaluating Complaint Procedures Available to Victims," *Georgetown*

EMPLOYER SANCTIONS AS A SOLUTION

Proposals to bar the employment[7] of undocumented aliens began to surface in the early 1950s,[8] but not until the mid-1970s did those proposals begin to attract serious attention.[9] By 1986, public concern about unauthorized immigration had reached politically significant levels. At the same time, long-standing concerns that sanctions legislation would provide new impetus for job discrimination persisted.

In the end, it took a coalition of disparate groups to break the impasse. Sanctions proponents accepted provisions that would bar both national origin and citizenship status discrimination under certain limited circumstances.[10] In addition, the final package included ambitious programs to legalize the immigration status of certain of those aliens who had already been living in the United States for prescribed numbers of years.[11] The combination was able to command majorities in both Houses of Congress, and on November 5, 1986, IRCA became law.

Immigration Law Journal 9, no. 757 (1995); Lee J. Teran, "Obtaining Remedies for INS Misconduct," *Immigration Briefings*, no. 96-5 (May 1996).

7. See generally Bach and Meissner, "Employment and Immigration Reform"; Fix and Hill, "Enforcing Employer Sanctions"; Maurice A. Roberts and Stephen Yale-Loehr, *Understanding the 1986 Immigration Law: A Practical Analysis* (Washington, D.C.: Federal Publications, 1987); United States Commission on Immigration Reform (CIR), *U.S. Immigration Policy: Restoring Credibility* (Washington, D.C.: U.S. CIR, 1994); Cecelia M. Espenoza, "The Illusory Provisions of Sanctions: The Immigration Reform and Control Act of 1986," *Georgetown Immigration Law Journal* 8, no. 343 (1994); Stanley Mailman, "The Employer as Immigration Inspector," *Bender's Immigration Bull* 1, no. 8 (July 1996): 20–25.

8. Fix and Hill, "Enforcing Employer Sanctions," p. 11; CIR, *U.S. Immigration Policy*, p. 51.

9. See American Enterprise Institute (AEI) for Public Policy Research, *Proposals to Prohibit Employment of Illegal Aliens* (Washington, D.C.: AEI, 1975), pp. 5–10 (citing bills introduced by Reps. Rodino and Sisk).

10. See 8 U.S.C. § 1324b; Roberts and Yale-Loehr, *Understanding the 1986 Immigration Law*, chap. 2.

11. See 8 U.S.C. § 1255a; Roberts and Yale-Loehr, *Understanding the 1986 Immigration Law*, chap. 3.

Under IRCA, it is an offense to hire, continue to employ, or recruit or refer for a fee any alien, knowing that the alien is not authorized to work in the United States.[12] It is also an offense to hire any person — citizen or alien — without performing certain prescribed paperwork designed to verify the applicant's identity and eligibility to work.[13] For the eligibility-to-work requirement, the law specifies a variety of documents that the employer may check.[14] The employer must fill out a standard form (I-9) attesting to having checked the required documents, keep that form for prescribed time periods, and make records available to government inspectors on request.[15] A grandfather provision insulates employers from liability with respect to personnel hired before enactment.[16] Violations are punishable by civil fines after administrative proceedings, and in certain extreme cases criminal sentences may be imposed.[17]

Even with the inclusion of new prohibitions on employment discrimination, there were widely held fears that employer sanctions would create new incentives to discriminate. Congress, therefore, required the comptroller general (in the General Accounting Office) to prepare a series of three annual reports assessing the impact of IRCA. If the final report concluded that "a widespread pattern of discrimination has resulted against citizens or nationals of the United States or against eligible workers seeking employment solely from the implementation of [employer sanctions]," then Congress would decide, on an expedited basis, whether to terminate the program.[18]

---

12. 8 U.S.C. §§ 1324a(a)(1)(A), 1324a(a)(2).
13. 8 U.S.C. § 1324a(a)(1)(B).
14. 8 U.S.C. § 1324a(b)(1). The list was winnowed slightly by IIRIRA; see note 1 above, § 412(a).
15. 8 U.S.C. §§ 1324a(b)(1)(A), 1324a(b)(3).
16. IRCA, § 101(a)(3).
17. 8 U.S.C. § 1324a(e,f,g).
18. 8 U.S.C. § 1324a(j–n).

In fact, the final report of the General Accounting Office (GAO), issued in March 1990, contained precisely such a finding.[19] Nonetheless, Congress declined to repeal employer sanctions.[20] Some people doubted the accuracy of the GAO's findings. Some believed that modifications could make the system both more effective and less discriminatory.[21]

The remaining sections of this chapter will suggest a framework for analyzing the impact of employer sanctions in greater depth. Those sections will consider both the benefits and the costs of employer sanctions and will note some of the modifications that others have proposed.

Benefits of Employer Sanctions

DETERRING ILLEGAL IMMIGRATION

Employer sanctions are built on three central premises: that illegal immigration is a serious social harm, that undocumented aliens would stop coming if people would stopped hiring them, and that employer sanctions discourage employers from hiring undocumented aliens.

As for the first premise, there can be little doubt that illegal immigration carries real social costs, as outlined earlier. Whether they outweigh the benefits that undocumented aliens bring (paying taxes, creating jobs by consuming goods and services, doing work that Americans won't do, working for lower pay, etc.) is another question. In this chapter I assume for discussion purposes that illegal immigration is a significant net detriment to the United States.

---

19. U.S. General Accounting Office (GAO), *Immigration Reform — Employer Sanctions and the Question of Discrimination* (Washington, D.C.: GAO, 1990), pp. 3–8.

20. Bills to repeal or modify employer sanctions in the wake of the GAO report are listed in Bach and Meissner, "Employment and Immigration Reform," p. 41 nn.2,3.

21. Ibid., pp. 16–17.

The last two premises can be collapsed into one: that employer sanctions deter illegal immigration. The accuracy of that assumption has been the subject of great debate. Opinion has ranged from (1) employer sanctions have apparently reduced illegal immigration[22] to (2) it is too early to tell[23] to (3) employer sanctions have been largely ineffective.[24] Several factors have limited the effectiveness of employer sanctions: the widespread use of fraudulent documents, employers' uneven awareness of what the law requires, and finite enforcement resources. These problems, and their proposed remedies, will be discussed later in the chapter.

In evaluating the effectiveness of employer sanctions, observing that the undocumented alien population has not shrunk since the enactment of sanctions is unhelpful. For one thing, it is hard to know what the undocumented population is, much less what it used to be. Border apprehension statistics are a notoriously unreliable indicator; how does one know whether increases in apprehensions mean that more people are coming or merely that more of the people who try to come are getting caught? Still, reasonable estimates are possible, as the chapter by Jeffrey Passel illustrates.

More problematic is that time comparisons reveal little about causation. Even if one concludes that the undocumented alien population has risen since the implementation of employer sanctions, no one can know for sure whether the increase would have been greater without employer sanctions. To cloud the picture further, let us assume that in the present political climate the repeal of employer sanctions would be unthinkable without the simultaneous adoption of alternative measures to stem illegal immigration. Let us assume further that Congress would be likely to adopt some of those alternatives whether or not it

---

22. GAO, *Immigration Reform*, pp. 3–8.

23. Bach and Meissner, "Employment and Immigration Reform," p. 25.

24. CIR, *U.S. Immigration Policy*, p. xii; Espenoza, "Illusory Provisions of Sanctions"; Andrew M. Strojny, "Papers, Papers . . . Please: A National ID or an Electronic Tattoo," *Interpreter Releases* 72, nos. 617, 618 (May 8, 1995).

retains employer sanctions, while others are unlikely to be adopted except to offset the repeal of employer sanctions. Under those assumptions, the question is not just whether repeal of employer sanctions would increase or decrease the undocumented alien population. Rather, the question is whether repeal, when combined with whatever alternatives Congress would adopt only in the event of repeal, would cause the undocumented population to increase or decrease.

More generally, in assessing the benefits of employer sanctions, the availability of alternative strategies is a crucial consideration. Thus, if the question is whether to retain employer sanctions, the relevant benefits are the marginal ones (i.e., those that would accrue over and above the benefits of existing enforcement strategies and over and above the benefits of any new strategies that are likely to be added).

These alternative and complementary strategies span a wide range, including

- Strengthening traditional law enforcement in the border area[25]

- Beefing up interior enforcement through more intensive workplace searches[26]

- Various criminal sanctions on aliens who violate the immigration laws and on those who assist them[27]

- Administrative fines on commercial carriers who bring undocumented passengers to U.S. ports of entry[28]

---

25. The INS has been moving in that direction. See *Interpreter Releases* 73, no. 101 (January 22, 1996). See also IIRIRA, §§ 101–03.

26. IIRIRA, §§ 131–32, takes this approach.

27. See generally Stephen H. Legomsky, *Immigration and Refugee Law and Policy*, 2d ed. (Westbury, N.Y.: Foundation Press, 1997), pp. 959–62 (discussing criminal penalties for illegal entry and for such other offenses as smuggling, transporting, or harboring unauthorized aliens). See now IIRIRA, §§ 201-03, 211-18, 334 (adding new offenses and stiffening penalties for existing offenses).

28. See generally INA §§ 271–73; Robert J. Jarvis, "Rusting in Drydock: Stowaways, Shipowners and the Administrative Penalty Provision of INA Section 273(d)," *Tulane Maritime Law Journal* 13 (1988): 25.

- Civil forfeitures of vehicles used to commit immigration offenses[29]

- Stricter enforcement of labor laws and occupational health and safety laws[30]

- The North American Free Trade Agreement (NAFTA) and other long-term projects designed to stimulate growth in source countries and thereby diminish the incentive to emigrate[31]

- State lawsuits against the federal government to recover costs associated with illegal immigration.[32]

More draconian measures, such as evicting undocumented children from public schools, are still live possibilities.[33]

---

29. See INA § 274(b); Robert Pauw and Greg Boos, "Conveyance Seizures and Forfeitures: Constitutional Limits on Agency Decision-Making," *Immigration Briefings* 96-4 (April 1996).

30. In addition to benefiting the United States labor force directly, some argue this would dampen the incentive for employers to hire undocumented aliens under exploitative conditions. See Bach and Meissner, "Employment and Immigration Reform," p. 7.

31. NAFTA went into effect on January 1, 1994. See North American Free Trade Agreement Implementation Act, Public Law 103-182, 107 Stat. 2057, 103d Cong., 1st sess., December 8, 1993. In the short term, many observers say, NAFTA's provisions for reduced farm subsidies will cause economic dislocations that might spur *higher* rates of illegal migration to the United States. In the long term, however, NAFTA is expected to stimulate the Mexican economy, thereby creating jobs, raising wages, and lessening the incentive for workers to go north. See *Interpreter Releases* 70, nos. 1472, 1473 (November 8, 1993); see also Kevin R. Johnson, "Free Trade and Closed Borders: NAFTA and Mexican Immigration to the United States," *University of California at Davis Law Review* 27 (1994): 937.

32. All such lawsuits have been dismissed for lack of a justiciable issue. See, for example, *New Jersey v. United States*, 91 F.3d 463 (3d Cir. 1996); *Padavan v. United States*, 82 F.3d 23 (2d Cir. 1996). The attention these lawsuits have generated, however, might well be contributing to the increased federal willingness to provide aid to states with large undocumented populations.

33. For now, California Proposition 187 is on hold. A federal district court, concluding that the proposition unconstitutionally usurps the federal power to regulate immigration, has issued a permanent injunction. *League of United Latin American*

In evaluating these and other tactical choices, one must also consider that not all the common alternatives or supplements to employer sanctions are equally effective with respect to all categories of undocumented aliens. Strengthening border enforcement, for example, does nothing to prevent people from entering lawfully and then overstaying. Common carrier sanctions are similarly ineffectual against overstayers. If employer sanctions were repealed, therefore, the question would be whether the other options outlined above are powerful enough to address the problem of visa overstayers.

HEADING OFF RADICAL RESPONSES

The discussion thus far has focused on the actual effectiveness of employer sanctions in minimizing illegal immigration. But sometimes perceptions are as important as realities. To whatever extent the public perceives employer sanctions as a bulwark against illegal immigration, there is the risk that their repeal could enhance the political prospects of more-radical measures.

Perhaps, however, that risk is small in marginal terms. Employer sanctions have been in force for ten years. They did not dissuade the voters of California from passing Proposition 187. They did not dissuade either House of Congress from passing the harshest immigration and asylum legislation in decades.[34] They did not discourage an election-year Congress from shutting even legal immigrants off from most

---

Citizens v. Wilson, 908 F. Supp. 755 (C.D. Cal. 1995). For a small sample of the many thoughtful articles that have been written on Proposition 187, see Kevin R. Johnson, "An Essay on Immigration Politics, Popular Democracy,and California's Proposition 187: The Political Relevance and Legal Irrelevance of Race," *Washington Law Review* 70 (1995): 629; Hiroshi Motomura, "Immigration and Alienage, Federalism and Proposition 187," *Virginia Journal of International Law* 35 (1994): 201; Gerald L. Neuman, "Aliens as Outlaws: Government Services, Proposition 187, and the Structure of Equal Protection Doctrine," *U.C.L.A. Law Review* 42, no. 1425 (1995); Peter H. Schuck, "The Message of Proposition 187," *Pacific Law Journal* 26, no. 989 (1995).

   34. IIRIRA, note 1 above.

major public benefit programs.[35] If employer sanctions have indeed been a safety valve against more radical alternatives, one shudders trying to imagine what kinds of measures employer sanctions have averted.

The Costs of Employer Sanctions

As with any government regulation, the first costs to consider are the internal costs (i.e., those incurred by the regulators and by the regulated). The government regulators must spend resources on education, enforcement, adjudication, and administration. The regulated employers can lose access to cheap labor and in any event incur administrative expenses.

But the most worrisome costs are the external ones that an employer sanctions regime shifts to at least two groups of individuals: those lawful workers who experience discrimination as a result of the sanctions program and any others who suffer invasions of privacy as a result of attempts to make the sanctions program more effective. The discussion that follows addresses these various costs.

COSTS TO EMPLOYERS

The cost analysis for employers cannot be reduced to slogans. Often we hear that employer sanctions are inherently wrong because they turn employers into immigration inspectors. If Congress believes that employers have been causing social harm by hiring undocumented aliens—and that belief cannot be dismissed as irrational—then there is nothing inherently wrong in prohibiting that practice. Our laws re-

---

35. Personal Responsibility and Work Opportunity Reconciliation Act of 1996, Public Law 104-193, 110 Stat. 2105, Title IV, 104th Congress, 1st sess., August 22, 1996.

quire employers to pay minimum wages and to maintain safe working conditions. Our laws prohibit employers from hiring young children and from engaging in certain forms of discrimination. Few question that the government may forbid what it regards as a socially or economically harmful labor practice. The true question is whether employee sanctions are fair and sensible, given the costs and burdens they impose.

One employer cost to consider is the loss of access to undocumented labor. Some industries, unable to find adequate numbers of American workers, depend on undocumented aliens.[36] To the extent that the employer is complying with all other labor, health, and safety regulations, it seems legitimate to take this cost into account in deciding whether to prohibit the employment of undocumented aliens.

Some will deny that there can be any such thing as a true labor shortage. When we have what looks like a labor shortage, they say, the true explanation is that the wages for that line of work are too low or the working conditions are too onerous or the amount of training one must invest to qualify for that occupation is too great to make entry into the occupation worthwhile. If undocumented aliens were not available, the argument runs, employers would be forced to bid up the prevailing wage to whatever levels would attract domestic workers.

There are, of course, economic costs to such an approach. These include the likelihood of higher consumer prices and the danger that employers will go out of business if the increased prices reduce the demand to a level below what the particular companies need to sustain the increased labor costs.

On balance, if Congress makes the economic and policy judgments that the social harm of exploitation and the economic harm of displacing or otherwise disadvantaging U.S. workers outweigh the employer and consumer benefits of hiring undocumented workers, then employers' loss of that opportunity cannot be counted as a cost of

---

36. See, for example, Fix and Hill, "Enforcing Employer Sanctions," p. 16.

employer sanctions. Under those circumstances, that "cost" would actually be a national benefit.

The administrative burden that the law places on employers is more clearly a cost. To comply with the law, employers must train employees to execute the legal requirements, stay abreast of changes to the law, fill out forms, make copies, maintain records, spend time accommodating government inspectors, and, sometimes, litigate.

Again, the fact that regulation entails paperwork for employers does not per se make it inappropriate. The issue is how burdensome that paperwork is in relation to the benefits. One study, conducted early on, concluded that the administrative burdens were not at a level that disturbed employers.[37] A later report by the Commission on Immigration Reform, however, says that "employers have found the [current] verification process time-consuming and confusing."[38]

COSTS TO THE GOVERNMENT

The main cost to the government is the creation and maintenance of a large bureaucracy. To implement the employer sanctions program, the government must disseminate information, respond to employer inquiries, investigate suspected violations, inspect work sites, prosecute alleged offenders, and adjudicate disputed cases (at hearings, administrative appeals, and judicial proceedings). All these costs are ongoing.

Those costs must be set off against the revenues collected in fines. In addition, to whatever extent employer sanctions reduce illegal immigration, they reduce the sums that the government must spend on law enforcement, prosecution of deportation hearings, and adjudication. Without empirical investigation, therefore, it is not clear whether employer sanctions feed or drain government coffers.

---

37. Bach and Meissner, "Employment and Immigration Reform," p. 14.
38. CIR, *U.S. Immigration Policy*, p. 53; accord, Fix and Hill, "Enforcing Employer Sanctions," p. 17.

COSTS TO VICTIMS OF DISCRIMINATION

From the beginning, ethnic groups and others feared that employer sanctions would induce employers to discriminate against applicants who looked or sounded "foreign." Some well-intentioned employers might discriminate out of a misplaced fear that they could be fined if they unwittingly hired someone who turned out to be undocumented. Others might use employer sanctions as an excuse to discriminate intentionally.

The congressionally mandated GAO study mentioned earlier found that widespread discrimination had in fact occurred and that employer sanctions were the cause. The GAO found two different forms of discrimination:

> An estimated 227,000 employers reported that they began a practice, as a result of IRCA, not to hire job applicants whose foreign appearance or accent led them to suspect that they might be unauthorized aliens. Also, contrary to IRCA, an estimated 346,000 employers said that they applied IRCA's verification system only to persons who had a "foreign" appearance or accent. Some employers began both practices.[39]

Although some have questioned the validity of the GAO's findings,[40] several studies conducted during roughly the same period reached similar conclusions.[41] More recently, the United States Com-

---

39. GAO, *Immigration Reform*, pp. 3–8.

40. See Bach and Meissner, "Employment and Immigration Reform," p. 16 (describing reaction of sanctions supporter Senator Alan Simpson [Rep.-Wyo.]).

41. For example, U.S. Commission on Civil Rights (CCR), *The Immigration Reform and Control Act: Assessing the Evaluation Process* (Washington, D.C.: U.S. CCR, 1989); New York State Inter-Agency Task Force on Immigration Affairs (IATFIA), *Workplace Discrimination under the Immigration Reform and Control Act of 1986: A Study of Impacts on New Yorkers* (New York: IATFIA, 1988); Martha F. Davis, Lucas Guttentag, and Allan H. Wernick, "Report of the Committee on Immigration and

mission on Immigration Reform, a strong supporter of employer sanctions, acknowledged the problem.[42]

Deciding how much weight to place on the discriminatory impact of employer sanctions requires both empirical fact-finding and subjective judgment. One must decide, first, how harmful an individual instance of discrimination is, which probably varies with the type of discrimination involved. A discriminatory demand for more-extensive documentation is bad; a substantive decision not to hire a person because of a foreign appearance or accent is worse. Second is the empirical question of how widespread each type of discrimination is (as a result of employer sanctions). The combined empirical and value question is to what extent each form of discrimination can be reduced through procedural changes that will not unacceptably sacrifice effectiveness or impose undue affirmative costs.

COSTS TO PRIVACY

Early on, civil liberties organizations warned that employer sanctions would eventually spur calls for a national computerized registry of authorized workers or possibly even a national identity card.[43] Either development would have serious privacy implications.

Those warnings have proved prophetic. As fraudulent documents and other problems continue to hamper the effectiveness of employer sanctions, key players have begun to advocate a national registry. Employers would be required to telephone the registry to verify applicants' eligibility to work. This issue is considered below.

Nationality Law of the Association of the Bar of the City of New York: An Analysis of Discrimination Resulting from Employer Sanctions and a Call for Repeal," *San Diego Law Review* 26, no. 711 (1989).

42. CIR, *U.S. Immigration Policy*, p. 54.

43. See, e.g., Fix and Hill, "Enforcing Employer Sanctions," p. 17 (citing the ACLU).

Proposals to Modify
the Employer Sanctions Program

In recent years, the movement to repeal employer sanctions has died down. Instead, calls to reform the program have emanated from various quarters. Such proposals have generally focused on three areas: improved educational efforts, stronger and more consistent enforcement, and a more secure documentation system (which could include a national registry).

EDUCATION

When IRCA was first adopted, the Immigration and Naturalization Service (INS) and the Office of Special Counsel (OSC) for Immigration-Related Unfair Employment Practices[44] worked hard to inform employers of their new responsibilities. The transition strategy prioritized education over enforcement.[45] Since then, however, enforcement has clearly commanded higher priority. Educational efforts, understandably, are not as intensive as they once were.[46] As a result, employer awareness of their legal obligations is uneven; large employers with professional personnel directors tend to understand what is required, whereas many smaller employers do not.[47]

To remedy those deficiencies, many authorities advocate increased attention to employer education (but not at the expense of enforcement, as discussed below).[48] Educational efforts would focus, presum-

---

44. This office, located within the Department of Justice, investigates and prosecutes violations of the antidiscrimination provisions of IRCA. See INA § 274B(c).

45. The statutory scheme contemplated precisely such a strategy. See INA § 274A(i).

46. CIR, *U.S. Immigration Policy*, p. 107.

47. Bach and Meissner, "Employment and Immigration Reform," p. 19.

48. CIR, *U.S. Immigration Policy*, pp. 106–9; GAO, *Immigration Reform*, pp. 3–8; Bach and Meissner, "Employment and Immigration Reform," pp. 23–24.

ably, both on complying with the employer sanctions provisions and on avoiding accidental discrimination.

ENFORCEMENT

With respect to enforcement, at least three kinds of concerns have emerged. They relate to overall magnitude, tactical specifics, and consistency.

Both in the early years of employer sanctions and in more recent years, authorities have suggested that enforcement was unnecessarily lax.[49] In February 1996, however, the Justice Department stepped up its enforcement efforts, doubling the number of employer sanctions investigators.[50]

More-detailed suggestions have been made for tactical changes in enforcement methods. These recommendations have ranged from prioritizing the probability of detection over the sizes of the fines[51] to making the Labor Department the primary enforcement agency[52] to targeting industries historically dependent on undocumented labor.[53] In February 1996, President Clinton issued an executive order prohibiting federal government agencies from contracting with companies who violate the employer sanctions provisions.[54]

Finally, critics point to inconsistent enforcement and inconsistent

---

49. CIR, *U.S. Immigration Policy*, pp. 91–94 (discussing both employment of undocumented aliens and other labor violations); Bach and Meissner, "Employment and Immigration Reform," p. 10; Fix and Hill, "Enforcing Employer Sanctions," p. 108.

50. Mailman, "Employer as Immigration Inspector," p. 21.

51. Bach and Meissner, "Employment and Immigration Reform," p. 20 (noting disagreement).

52. This suggestion has been advanced by Senator Ted Kennedy (Dem.-Mass.), who believes that employers would be more prone to cooperate with the Labor Department. See Bach and Meissner, "Employment and Immigration Reform," pp. 22–23.

53. CIR, *U.S. Immigration Policy*, pp. 97–101.

54. Executive Order 12989, 61 Fed. Reg. 6091 (February 13, 1996).

fines.[55] Some recommend increased central oversight, including better coordination of local district and border patrol operations, to achieve consistency.[56]

DOCUMENTS AND DATABASES

By far the greatest impediment to the success of employer sanctions has been the inevitable proliferation of counterfeit and fraudulently obtained documents.[57] False Social Security cards and false INS documents have been especially problematic. In addition, the sheer number of different documents that applicants may use to establish identity and work authorization can bewilder employers. Consequently, many have recommended that the relevant documents be both fewer and more counterfeit resistant.[58] Greater security is especially vital for so-called breeder documents, which are those used to acquire other documents (e.g., birth certificates used to obtain drivers' licenses, Social Security cards, passports, etc.).

But the most controversial proposals for curing the fraudulent document problem call for a national computerized registry of authorized workers with telephone employer access. The Commission on Immigration Reform proposed such a system in 1994. Under the commission's proposal, a centralized data bank would contain the name and Social Security number of every authorized worker in the United States—citizen and alien alike. The employer would be required to call this registry to verify that a job applicant's Social Security number is valid and that it matches the applicant's name. The system would

---

55. For example, Bach and Meissner, "Employment and Immigration Reform," p. 21; Fix and Hill, "Enforcing Employer Sanctions," p. 106.

56. Ibid., p. 108.

57. CIR, *U.S. Immigration Policy*, p. 54; GAO, *Immigration Reform*, pp. 3–8.

58. Ibid. See also CIR, *U.S. Immigration Policy*, pp. 54–55; Bach and Meissner, "Employment and Immigration," pp. 31–32. For a modest move in this direction, see IIRIRA, § 412(a).

then either confirm the match or tell the employer that the match cannot be confirmed and that the employer should therefore contact the Social Security Administration. Special conditions on work authorization (duration, hours per week, particular employer) would also be communicated. The commission recommended a pilot program as a first step,[59] and Congress has recently obliged.[60]

The commission believes that a national registry would bring several improvements. First, the commission argues, a registry would all but eliminate document fraud. Second, it would be less discriminatory since the employer would merely phone in a name and a number rather than have to distinguish citizens from aliens. Third, less paperwork would be required.[61]

But the concerns about an employer-accessed national registry are ably voiced by Andrew Strojny, the former acting special counsel for Immigration-Related Unfair Employment Practices, Department of Justice.[62] First, he argues, there are practical implementation concerns. These include the expense of starting and maintaining the system (more than $2 billion), the expense of using the registry once it is functioning (employers' card readers and phone lines), the harm to individuals victimized by erroneous information, the reliability of procedures for correcting faulty information, and the complications associated with temporary and otherwise restricted work authorization. Second, there is always the danger that more-personal information will be added as lawmakers invent new uses for the database and that government officials will access the information for improper purposes. Third, Strojny argues, leaks pose great danger to personal privacy.[63]

---

59. CIR, *U.S. Immigration Policy*, pp. 60–62. The INS has proposed a similar program. 59 Fed. Reg. 24472–73 (May 11, 1994).

60. IIRIRA, §§ 401–05.

61. CIR, *U.S. Immigration Policy*, p. 63.

62. Strojny, "Papers, Papers."

63. Ibid., pp. 619–22.

Conclusion

The case for employer sanctions is not an obvious one. Reducing illegal immigration is a legitimate goal, but one has to examine the importance of the goal, the likelihood that employer sanctions can meaningfully address the goal, and the economic and human costs of employer sanctions. For me, the single most compelling argument for employer sanctions is rooted in practical politics—that they might help blunt the danger of more-radical measures against legal immigrants. To date, however, there is little to suggest that employer sanctions have done even that.

Employer sanctions proponents have clearly been right on one score: Employer sanctions have created jobs for Americans. Unfortunately, those jobs have been in the fraudulent documents industry. I suspect this is not what the proponents had in mind.

At the same time, employer sanctions have come at a price. Up to now, the costs have included the expenses of running the system, the administrative burdens on the employers, and the resulting "widespread discrimination" against job applicants who look or sound foreign. The Commission on Immigration Reform and other respected groups have made serious proposals to improve the effectiveness of employer sanctions and reduce the various costs. Some of the recommendations, including those that relate to education and enforcement, seem eminently reasonable and might well produce marginal gains. But the proposals with the greatest potential impact—those that entail a national computerized registry—spell large economic costs and even larger risks of error, abuse, and invasion of privacy.

Sometimes it is best to leave well enough alone.

Jeffrey S. Passel

CHAPTER SEVEN

Undocumented Immigration

Undocumented immigration remains an issue about which a great deal of misinformation abounds. Although it has been a focus of political and social debate for more than two decades, little agreement can be found on its causes, impacts, or successful modes of control. Virtually the only widely supported principles in the often fractious debates over undocumented immigration are that it must be brought under control and that the United States has the sovereign right to control its own borders. The solution to the illegal immigration "problem" was supposed to be the Immigration Reform and Control Act (IRCA) passed in 1986 after several years of debate. Now, more than a decade after IRCA's passage, it has become apparent that it did not reduce illegal immigration and that other solutions must be sought.

Although the exact magnitude of both the flow of undocumented

Initially presented at a conference on contemporary immigration at the Hoover Institution, Stanford, California, October 17–18, 1996. The views expressed are attributable to the author and do not necessarily reflect those of other staff members, officers, trustees of the Urban Institute, The Ford Foundation, or any organizations that provide financial support to the Urban Institute's Program for Research on Immigration Policy.

immigrants into the United States and the number living here remain unknown, there is sound evidence that both currently surpass pre-IRCA levels. Of the myriad issues relating to undocumented immigration, this chapter attempts to address three major questions on undocumented immigration and its control. First, what is the magnitude of undocumented immigration and what does it mean to say that we've "lost control of our borders"? Second, how successful have been efforts at control—mainly border interdiction and employer sanctions? And, finally, will the reforms put in place by recent legislation lead to significant reductions in illegal immigration?

Magnitude of Undocumented Immigration

It is essential to place undocumented immigration in the larger demographic context of the United States. The United States is in the midst of a profound demographic transition: in slightly more than one generation, the population has been transformed from one consisting of almost entirely whites of European descent and native blacks to one with significant percentages of other "visible" minorities with roots in Latin America, Asia, and the Middle East. In this contemporary situation, there is an unfortunate tendency to equate "nonwhite" with "immigrant" and "Hispanic" with "undocumented immigrant." Many myths abound about the numbers relating to undocumented immigration. In particular, the general public and even many immigration specialists have a tendency to confuse illegal immigration and its impacts with the much larger aspects of *legal immigration.*

NUMBER AND DISTRIBUTION OF UNDOCUMENTED ALIENS

The actual size of the undocumented population has been a matter of some dispute for more than twenty years. (See Passel et al. 1990 and Passel 1995 for reviews of estimates of undocumented immigration.) During this time, we've seen an interesting phenomenon—as the number of undocumented immigrants has gotten larger, the range of estimates has narrowed and estimates have actually gotten smaller to the point where reality and rhetoric have converged. Over the last several years, a rough consensus across the political spectrum has emerged on the number of undocumented immigrants living in the country and the annual increase in this clandestine population.

According to the best available estimates there are some four to five million undocumented aliens currently living in the United States (Passel 1996; Warren 1997). This is almost surely the largest number ever, even more than the number in the country on the eve of the passage of IRCA ten years ago—the previous peak. Although four and a half million (the midpoint of the range) is clearly a large number, it needs to be placed in demographic perspective as representing about one-sixth of the foreign-born population, or *only slightly more than 1.5 percent of the U.S. population* of more than 260 million.

Were the undocumented population spread evenly across the country, much less attention would be focused on the group. But the numbers and percentages vary significantly across the country. Five states—California, Texas, New York, Florida, and Illinois—have much larger numbers than the remaining states, accounting for more than three-quarters of the U.S. total in both the 1980s and the 1990s (Warren 1994; Passel and Woodrow 1984). Within this group, *California's situation is unique*. It has perhaps 40 to 50 percent of the country's illegal aliens—a figure that gives the state both absolute numbers (about two million) and concentrations much higher than anywhere else. Perhaps 5–7 percent of California's population is undocumented versus 1 percent in the rest of the country.

Even in California, this distribution is far from uniform. In Los Angeles County, 10–15 percent of the population consists of undocumented aliens; nowhere else is remotely similar. Unfortunately, these large numbers and concentrations seem to be behind much of the *national* reaction to illegal immigration since popular and political opinion in California seems to drive much of our immigration policy or at least the rhetoric surrounding it.[1] And, although the numbers might be considered to be of crisis proportions in parts of California, the same cannot be said for the rest of the country.

GROWTH OF THE UNDOCUMENTED POPULATION

What about annual changes? The consensus on the basis of current empirical research is that the undocumented population is increasing annually by roughly 200,000 to 300,000. Is this number big? Is it small? Clearly, it is not insignificant, particularly since it cumulates steadily. In any case, there are almost three times as many legal immigrants every year. What does this figure mean in terms of control of immigration? Does it mean that we have "lost control of our borders"? To answer these questions, it is necessary to examine in detail the different modes of entry into the United States.

About 40–50 percent of the annual increase, or some 120,000 to 150,000 illegal aliens a year, are "visa abusers"—that is, persons who enter the United States with legal entry visas but stay beyond their expiration date. The annual increment represents a "net" increase consisting of new visa overstays less the number of persons who previously overstayed but eventually either leave the country or convert from an illegal status to a legal one. According to Warren's (1990) estimates, the number of *new* overstays is roughly double the net figure.

Even this analysis does not fully inform an assessment of the rela-

---

1. Contrast, for example, the politics of California with those of New York and Texas. Mayor Rudolph Giuliani of New York was extremely critical of his Republican Party's negative view of immigration (even illegal immigration) in the 1996 presidential campaign. In the 1994 gubernatorial race in Texas, immigration, either legal or illegal, was not a central issue for either party. In contrast, Pete Wilson's successful campaign for governor of California in 1994 treated illegal immigration as the main issue. In his unsuccessful bid for the Republican presidential nomination in 1996, the same approach failed to resonate with voters outside his home state.

tive magnitude of visa overstays. A more complete assessment requires that the estimate of overstays be compared with the annual number of nonimmigrants coming to the United States, a group consisting primarily of tourists, businesspeople, students, and so on. In fiscal 1994, more than twenty-two million nonimmigrants came to the United States and this number has been increasing steadily (Immigration and Naturalization Service [INS] 1996). Thus, net visa overstays amounted to only about 1 percent of the total number of nonimmigrant admissions. This level of "abuse" can hardly be termed a crisis of control; rather, it could be deemed a successful enforcement effort.

The remaining undocumented immigrants are what INS quaintly calls EWIs (standing for "entries without inspection"). These are persons who sneak across the border, mainly from Mexico. The net annual increase from these clandestine entries is about 150,000 to 200,000 a year. By way of comparison, there are more than 300 million legal crossings (INS 1996) and more than 2 million illegal ones (e.g., Espenshade 1990, 1994). Again, the *net* impact of these illegal entrants is only a small fraction of the total.

Thus, the undocumented population apparently continues to grow by one million persons every three to five years. Clearly then, control efforts are not completely successful. This net impact is only a small percentage of the potential growth, however, given the much larger numbers of both legal and illegal entries into the United States. This pattern suggests that some factors are at work to keep down the total increase.

Border Enforcement Strategies

Over the years, the INS has tried a variety of strategies to deter illegal immigration, to turn back the flow of undocumented immigrants into the country, and to reduce the numbers already here. In the 1990s, there have been a number of innovations in this area and new legislation attempts to improve enforcement. The next section describes a number of current and proposed enforcement strategies and addresses their effectiveness, with particular attention to their potential for sharply reducing the scale of undocumented immigration beyond current levels.

BORDER INTERDICTION

Border interdiction has always been the most popular enforcement strategy politically. Since 1990, the enforcement effort along our southern border has more than doubled (in terms of person-hours). *There is little evidence, however, that border interdiction at current or historic levels has deterred potential immigrants from setting forth to enter the United States.* Surveys in both the United States and Mexico show that the probability of an individual setting out to enter the United States illegally has hardly changed at all over the last two decades (Donato et al. 1992; Kossoudji 1992). Even multiple apprehensions (catching the same person more than once as they attempt to enter the United States) seem to have little deterrent effect because the penalty for getting caught is merely a return trip to Mexico—right across the border—and the chance to try again the next day (or even the same day).

The large and intensive new interdiction efforts have not succeeded in reducing the flow but apparently have managed to divert the permanent flow to less well-fortified sectors of the border. Operation Hold the Line in El Paso stationed border patrol agents "shoulder to shoulder" along the border to put up a barrier for illegal aliens and to deter attempts at crossing. This strategy apparently did effectively stop many short-term crossers into El Paso but seemed to have little effect on illegal immigration to other parts of the country (Bean et al. 1994). Those bound for the U.S. interior simply went around the city and continued on their way.

The San Diego sector of the U.S.-Mexico border is the busiest in terms of legal crossings and apprehensions of undocumented aliens.

Twenty-five percent of all apprehensions along the 2,500-mile border occur within a 5-mile segment of this sector, where a variety of enforcement strategies have been tried. In October 1994, Operation Gatekeeper was initiated as a multifaceted approach to controlling illegal migration through the San Diego sector. The operation included infrastructure improvements (better fences, other barriers, sensors, night-vision goggles, and the like) plus increased personnel, particularly support personnel, and automation of forms processing and fingerprinting.

Initially under Operation Gatekeeper crossings appeared to drop, but the severe devaluation of the Mexican peso in December 1994 and the attendant economic disruptions in Mexico pushed many new Mexican migrants northward. Gatekeeper did enable the border patrol to control areas previously used as entry points and disrupt historical migration patterns, as many of the crossers were pushed inland, even to Arizona and New Mexico. Although this has undoubtedly improved the quality of life for many residents of San Diego neighborhoods, it has not led to major reductions in the undocumented flow. And there are now charges of serious environmental impacts in more remote parts of the border and complaints from different groups of border residents.

These interdiction efforts do appear to have had an unintended but consequential effect. Several streams of research over the past two decades have shown that if crossings are made more expensive (either in time through multiple apprehensions or in money paid to smugglers), then the illegal immigrants tend to stay longer in the United States. But because illegal immigrants are essentially always successful in eventually getting into the United States, the expanded interdiction efforts have tended to convert temporary migration to more permanent immigration.

The Illegal Immigration Reform and Immigrant Responsibility Act of 1996 continues to pursue interdiction strategies in a vigorous manner. The act will double the size of the border patrol, adding another five thousand agents over the next five years. It also authorizes money for expanding and strengthening the San Diego fence. Perhaps these increased barriers of matériel and personnel will succeed in deterring potential crossers. More likely, however, is further conversion of temporary to permanent migration.

EMPLOYER SANCTIONS

Before the passage of IRCA in 1986, undocumented aliens were violating federal law by entering the United States and working but their employers were not. Employer sanctions corrected this asymmetry and made the knowing hire of illegal aliens a violation of federal labor law for the first time. In addition, employers were now required to verify the status of their new hires by examining a variety of documents and keeping records of their examinations.

The INS implemented employer sanctions slowly, beginning with an extensive effort to educate employers about the new standards, the need for compliance, and how to comply. Fines were not assessed until at least one "education" visit or warning or both. This "go slow" approach was a deliberate decision by INS to establish and sustain the legitimacy of both the law and the agency. It was also consistent with Congress's intent and the generally probusiness attitudes prevalent in the United States (Fix and Hill 1990). In some respects, this implementation strategy was successful; few employers complained, and virtually all employers were made aware of the law.

The enforcement was less successful, however, in the two major areas of concern: (1) reduction of illegal immigration and the employment of undocumented aliens and (2) discrimination. Some four to five years after IRCA's passage, there were a number of efforts to assess the impacts of employer sanctions (e.g., Fix 1991a; Papademetriou et al. 1991; Bach and Meissner 1990; Fraser 1994). The general consensus of these various studies was that IRCA was not having a significant impact on the employment of illegal aliens in the U.S. labor market but that discrimination against foreign-looking or -sounding persons had apparently increased as a result of IRCA's paperwork requirements. Employment patterns changed little. The ready availability of fraudulent documents eased the impact of the law on both employers and undocumented aliens.

Initially, there did appear to be a reduction in the flow of undocumented aliens from Mexico. The consensus of many studies was, however, that virtually all the reduction could be attributed to the removal of almost two million newly legalized aliens from the flow (see Passel et al. 1990). New undocumented aliens soon replaced the now legal group. Current estimates confirm this result, as flows in the first half of the 1990s were even higher than those of a decade earlier.

RECENT LEGISLATIVE INITIATIVES

The Illegal Immigration Reform and Immigrant Responsibility Act of 1996 includes several provisions to designed to address deficiencies of employer sanctions and to attempt to control visa overstays (besides the aforementioned doubling of enforcement personnel). It introduces penalties for visa overstayers by limiting their subsequent access to the United States as either nonimmigrants or immigrants. This provision may meet with some success, but it requires much better data systems than the INS currently has. For example, almost 10 percent of nonimmigrant arrival forms cannot be matched to departure forms because of what INS calls "system error" (Warren 1990). This far too common phenomenon is well documented and will render such exclusions open to easy challenge.

The law tries to attack the problem of false documents in several ways. It increases penalties for production and use of fraudulent documents and encourages states to tighten controls on so-called breeder documents, such as birth certificates. Employers still have little incentive to challenge fraudulent-looking documents, however, since they are not held liable for accepting them.

The key to solving this dilemma is supposedly a computerized database that would include the names and identities of *all* persons eligible to work in the United States. The new law sets up several pilot programs to test such computerized worker verification systems. With these new systems, employers would query the system for each new hire via the person's name and Social Security number. The system would then report back on whether the person was authorized to work.

These systems, however, still leave a number of critical issues unresolved. First, how does the employer know that the person presenting the documents is the correct person? Then, leaving aside the intrusions into private lives necessitated by such a system as well as its expense, the success of a computerized identification system requires the active cooperation of employers and a high degree of accuracy. Even a system that is 99 percent accurate will result in *hundreds of thousands* of U.S. citizens and legal aliens being denied legitimate employment every year; less-accurate systems could harm millions of legal residents (National Council of La Raza 1995; Miller and Moore 1995). Problems in implementing these systems could thus lead to substantial expansion of government databases without developing a serious deterrent to employment of undocumented aliens.

It is instructive to consider what the recent Congress did *not* do in attempting to control illegal immigration. It is widely accepted that control of illegal immigration, and especially visa overstays, must involve cutting off the lifeblood of illegal immigrants: their access to jobs (i.e., the so-called jobs magnet). Other methods, such as limiting access to social services such as schools for children and welfare, have been deemed less effective or counterproductive.

Employer sanctions' lack of success has been attributed mainly to ineffective enforcement and the proliferation of fraudulent documents, the area mainly attacked by the new law. Much current employment of undocumented immigrants appears to be consensual; the employer knows the employee is undocumented but either doesn't care, can't do anything about it, or even prefers undocumented employees. (They are often characterized as "hard workers who don't complain.") Yet the new legislation still does not deal effectively with employers. Drafts of the legislation included provisions to add enforcement personnel in INS to try to locate and apprehend visa overstayers and, more important, to increase workplace enforcement by adding labor inspectors to the Department of Labor. These provisions were eventually either dropped from the bill or not funded.

Conclusion

So what is the future of undocumented immigration? Clearly, no level of enforcement tolerable in a democratic society can eliminate undocumented migration completely. The best that can be done is to "control or manage" illegal immigration. Current enforcement efforts do not stop this migration; they may deter some undocumented migration, but we do not know how much. As a fraction of the flow of legal migrants to the United States, undocumented migration is actually quite small. Steeply increased enforcement has not reduced levels significantly and may not be able to.

Even though there is general agreement among researchers that jobs bring illegals to the United States, control measures are not being directed at economic factors or employers. In this regard, there have been few identifiable attempts to focus public attention on the employers of undocumented labor. Nor does the recent legislation attempt to target employers directly. Neither the public nor legislators perceive violations of employer sanctions to be as serious as violations of other labor standards.

At some point, the cost of reducing illegal immigration outweighs the benefits. Expansion of sanctions through a worker verification system and increasing border interdiction efforts will be expensive and may not be particularly effective. What hasn't happened yet is a sustained effort against employers of illegal immigrants through either enforcement or negative public reactions. Without such reactions, it is unlikely that any tolerable enforcement regime will succeed in making a substantial reduction in illegal immigration below current levels.

References

Bach, Robert L. and Doris Meissner. 1990. *Employment and Immigration Reform: Employer Sanctions Four Years Later.* Immigration Policy Project. Washington, D.C.: Carnegie Endowment for International Peace.

Bean, Frank D., Roland Chanove, Robert G. Cushing, Rodolfo de la Garza, Gary Freeman, Charles W. Haynes, and David Spener. 1994. "Illegal Mexican Migration and the United States/Mexico Border: The Effects of Operation Hold-the-Line on El Paso/Juarez." Report for the U.S. Commission on Immigration Reform, Population Research Center, University of Texas at Austin, July 15.

Bean, Frank D., Barry Edmonston, and Jeffrey S. Passel, eds. 1990. *Undocumented Migration to the United States: IRCA and the Experience of the 1980s.* Washington, D.C.: Urban Institute Press.

Donato, Katherine M., Jorge Durand, and Douglas S. Massey. 1992. "Stemming the Tide? Assessing the Deterrent Effects of the Immigration Reform and Control Act." *Demography* 29, no. 2 (May): 139–57.

Espenshade, Thomas J. 1990. "Undocumented Migration to the United States: Evidence from a Repeated Trials Model." In Frank D. Bean, Barry Edmonston, and Jeffrey S. Passel, eds., *Undocumented Migration to the United States: IRCA and the Experience of the 1980s.* Washington, D.C.: Urban Institute Press.

——. 1994. "Does the Threat of Border Apprehension Deter Undocumented US Immigration?" *Population and Development Review* 20, no. 4 (December): 871–92.

Fix, Michael. 1991a. "IRCA-Related Discrimination: What Do We Know and What Should We Do? In Fix, ed., *The Paper Curtain: Employer Sanctions' Implementation, Impact, and Reform.* Washington, D.C.: Urban Institute Press.

Fix, Michael, ed. 1991b. *The Paper Curtain: Employer Sanctions' Implementation, Impact, and Reform.* Washington, D.C.: Urban Institute Press.

Fix, Michael, and Paul T. Hill. 1990. *Enforcing Employer Sanctions: Challenges and Strategies.* Urban Institute Report 90-6. Washington, D.C.: Program for Research on Immigration Policy, Urban Institute.

Fraser, John R. 1994. "Illegal Immigration in the United States and the Limits of Sanctions against Employers." In *Migration and Development: New Partnerships for Cooperation.* Paris: Organization for Economic Cooperation and Development.

Immigration and Naturalization Service. 1996. *Statistical Yearbook of the Immigration and Naturalization Service: 1994.* Washington, D.C.: U.S. Government Printing Office.

Kossoudji, Sherrie A. 1992. "Playing Cat and Mouse at the U.S.-Mexican Border." *Demography* 29: 159–80.

Miller, John J., and Stephen Moore. 1995. "A National ID System: Big Brother's Solution to Illegal Immigration." Policy Analysis No. 237, Cato Institute, Washington, D.C.

National Council of La Raza. 1995. *Racing toward "Big Brother": Computer Verification, National ID Cards, and Immigration Control. State of Hispanic America, 1995.* Washington, D.C.: National Council of La Raza.

Papademetriou, Demetrios G., et al. 1991. *Employer Sanctions and U.S. Labor Markets: Second Report.* Washington, D.C.: U.S. Department of Labor.

Passel, Jeffrey S. 1995. "Characteristics and Impacts of Undocumented Immigrants in the United States." Paper presented at CEPR workshop on "The Political Economy of Illegal Immigration," Halkidiki, Greece, September 14–16.

———. 1996. "Recent Efforts to Control Illegal Immigration to the United States." Report to the Working Party on Migration of the Organization for Economic Cooperation and Development, Urban Institute, Washington, D.C.

Passel, Jeffrey S., Frank D. Bean, and Barry Edmonston. (1990). "Undocumented Migration since IRCA: An Overall Assessment." In Frank D. Bean, Barry Edmonston, and Jeffrey S. Passel, eds., *Undocumented Migration to the United States: IRCA and the Experience of the 1980s.* Washington, D.C.: Urban Institute Press.

Passel, Jeffrey S., and Karen A. Woodrow. 1984. "Geographic Distribution of Undocumented Immigrants: Estimates of Undocumented Aliens Counted in the 1980 Census by State." *International Migration Review* 18: 642–71.

Warren, Robert. 1990. "Annual Estimates of Nonimmigrant Overstays in the United States: 1985 to 1988." In Frank D. Bean, Barry Edmonston, and Jeffrey S. Passel, eds., *Undocumented Migration to the United States: IRCA and the Experience of the 1980s.* Washington, D.C.: Urban Institute Press.

———. 1994. "Estimates of the Unauthorized Immigrant Population Residing in the United States, by Country of Origin and State of Residence: October 1992." U.S. Immigration and Naturalization Service, Washington, D.C.

———. 1997. "Estimates of the Unauthorized Immigrant Population Residing in the United States: October 1996." *Backgrounder* (Office of Policy and Planning, U.S. Immigration and Naturalization Service, Washington, D.C., January.)

PART THREE

Education
and
Employment

Peter Skerry

CHAPTER EIGHT

Immigrants, Bureaucrats, and Life Choices

As the United States experiences the largest influx of immigrants in a century, it is simultaneously approaching a crossroads in its social policy. Yet amid all the speculation about the record number of newcomers arriving here, little if any attention is being paid to the implications of this influx for social policy innovation. Nor are policy analysts, pundits, or politicians giving much thought to the effects of such innovation on immigrants and their families.

It is still too soon to discern the outlines of tomorrow's social policy, but two distinct approaches are clear. One of these entails our moving away from social welfare entitlements and rights and toward benefits conditioned by obligations and demands on those receiving them. Moreover, this balancing of benefits against responsibilities is not depicted as reciprocity between equals. Particularly in the work of Lawrence Mead, one of the foremost architects of this new direction in social policy, the emphasis is on the need for social programs to be more authoritative, to provide guidance and direction to recipients who cannot simply make it on their own. Mead argues that the poor are "dutiful but defeated"[1] and that, as a result, "the poor as they now are need help."[2] More broadly, Mead argues that "the main problem with the welfare state is that it lacks authority, not that it is too large or too small."[3] Critics of Mead's approach have, perhaps not surprisingly, dubbed it "the new authoritarianism."[4] Mead himself prefers "the new paternalism."[5]

Yet as the new paternalism has gained currency and is being tested in various states, an alternative approach has persisted and gained a wider audience. I refer to the various proposals to build more choice into our social policies. Whether the topic is public housing, education, or social security, we hear more and more about the need to get out from under large government bureaucracies that make decisions for individuals and to allow them to make their own choices.

How will the unfolding of these two divergent policy approaches affect immigrants? And, conversely, what are the social policy implications of what may prove to be the largest influx of immigrants in our history? Ironically, the bureaucracies now perceived as the problem were once the solution, particularly as many of them were established in response to the last great influx of immigrants. Does this mean that today's immigrants will evoke similar hierarchical, bureaucratic policy responses? Will immigrants stymie contemporary efforts to rely on market mechanisms and individual choice? More broadly still, will today's immigrants prove to be constituents for the welfare state?

1. Lawence M. Mead, *The New Politics of Poverty: The Nonworking Poor in America* (New York: Basic Books, 1992), p. 24.

2. Ibid., p. 13.

3. Lawrence M. Mead, *Beyond Entitlement: The Social Obligations of Citizenship* (New York: Free Press, 1986), p. 265.

4. Margaret Weir, Ann Shola Orloff, and Theda Skocpol, "Epilogue: The Future of Social Policy in the United States: Political Constraints and Possibilities," in Margaret Weir, Ann Shola Orloff, and Theda Skocpol, eds., *The Politics of Social Policy in the United States* (Princeton, N.J.: Princeton University Press, 1988), p. 438.

5. Lawrence M. Mead, *The New Paternalism: Supervisory Approaches to Poverty* (Washington, D.C.: Brookings Institution, forthcoming).

For some immigration enthusiasts, the answer to each of these questions is no. Indeed, for Ron Unz, the computer software entrepreneur who was the 1994 Republican challenger to California governor Pete Wilson, immigrants will help bring about the end of the welfare state:

> Under the right circumstances, this [immigration] can be the issue that sparks a massive rollback of the welfare state and the ethnic group policies of the past 20 or 30 years, with these dramatic changes being backed by a dominant political alliance of Asians, Hispanics, and conservative Anglos.[6]

If recently enacted measures denying various social welfare benefits to noncitizen legal immigrants (in addition to efforts to clamp down on illegal immigrants receiving benefits) prevail, then Unz might prove at least partially correct. Under such conditions immigrants will emerge as a reserve army of the unentitled competing against citizens with entitlements, thereby undermining the welfare state.

But this is only one possible scenario. It is just as plausible to argue that poorly educated, unsophisticated immigrants who come here from group-oriented, hierarchical societies will not prosper under policies designed to maximize choice for individuals. After all, choice programs are predicated on the individual's ability to make the "right" choices. Yet we don't know that immigrants will do so. Indeed, there is evidence indicating they will not.

I cannot offer definitive answers to the questions asked here. But I can shed some light on a set of concerns—the social policy implications of contemporary immigration—that has received remarkably little attention.

---

6. Ron Unz, "Immigration or the Welfare State: Which Is Our Real Enemy?" *Policy Review*, no. 70 (fall 1994): 37.

Building the Bureaucracies

It is not generally disputed that the last great immigrant wave at the turn of the century led to a transformation of the nation's public schools. Lorraine McDonnell and Paul Hill write in a recent RAND study, *Newcomers in American Schools*, that "there is general consensus among historians that this influx of immigrants into the public schools, while not the sole reason, was a major impetus for the transformation of schooling from a localistic enterprise to a more uniform, professional, and bureaucratic undertaking."[7] This same picture emerges from divergent sources: neoconservative historian and Bush administration appointee Diane Ravitch writes of the role of immigrants in New York City's "great school wars";[8] revisionist Michael Katz critiques the emergence of bureaucratic urban school systems as part of the effort of "improving poor people";[9] and education historian David Tyack offers a middle-of-the-road interpretation of the creation of "the one best system."[10] From each of these perspectives the view is similar: past waves of immigration have resulted in increased bureaucratization and professionalization of what had been decentralized and politician-dominated neighborhood schools.

Moreover, these developments in the schools paralleled what was occurring in municipal government and politics generally. During the late nineteenth and early twentieth century, local government was streamlined and rationalized. Typically sprawling, bicameral munici-

---

7. Lorraine M. McDonnell and Paul T. Hill, *Newcomers in American Schools: Meeting the Educational Needs of Immigrant Youth* (Santa Monica, Calif.: RAND, 1993), p. 5.

8. Diane Ravitch, *The Great School Wars: New York City, 1805–1973* (New York: Basic Books, 1974).

9. Michael B. Katz, *Improving Poor People: The Welfare State, The "Underclass," and Urban Schools as History* (Princeton, N.J.: Princeton University Press, 1995).

10. David B. Tyack, *The One Best System: A History of American Urban Education* (Cambridge, Mass.: Harvard University Press, 1974).

pal legislatures were trimmed to single, relatively small legislative bodies. Scores of minor elective posts that had provided opportunities for neighborhood-based candidates to enter politics were eventually replaced, by means of the short ballot, with a handful of contested posts. The remaining offices became appointive positions on the theory that these would be less subject to the passions of politics. In the same vein, local government agencies became more bureaucratic, with less reliance on patronage employees and more on professionally trained experts.[11]

In the Progressive era in particular, this emphasis on expertise led to the creation of nonpartisan municipal electoral systems designed to be insulated from the partisan conflicts of state and national politics. In many cities district-based elective offices were replaced by at-large offices with citywide constituencies, making it more difficult for neighborhood-based candidates representing immigrant interests to prevail. At the same time, big cities became even bigger as state legislatures expanded municipal boundaries to create metropolitanwide jurisdictions. One result, clearly intended by reformers, was to dilute the political clout of immigrant-dominated urban cores.

The standard explanation of such developments is that they were the machinations of embattled, antidemocratic elites attempting to hold on to their power in the face of increasing challenges from newly arrived immigrant populations. With counties and municipalities spending about 60 percent of all public funds in the nation as late as the 1920s,[12] the raw political stakes at the local level were high. And although the various reforms were not uniformly successful, they did tend to weaken the neighborhood-based power of immigrants, whose

11. A recent treatment of this theme can be found in Kenneth Finegold, *Experts and Politicians: Reform Challenges to Machine Politics in New York, Cleveland, and Chicago* (Princeton, N.J.: Princeton University Press, 1995).

12. Dennis R. Judd and Todd Swanstrom, *City Politics: Private Power and Public Policy* (New York: HarperCollins College Publishers, 1994), p. 121.

participation in politics—before the reforms at least—was much greater than that of immigrants today.

Yet there is more to this story than political power. These elites were also motivated by substantive purpose and to some extent by civic-mindedness. Immigrant-dominated political institutions were typically corrupt, incompetent, and inefficient. Quite aside from any self-interested economic or political motives, elites had legitimate reasons to be concerned about the condition of the urban infrastructure necessary to maintain economic growth and social order. Those in positions of power and authority had understandable concerns, as do their counterparts today, as to whether immigrants and their children were adopting the appropriate attitudes and values.

It is not surprising that elites in the past focused on the public schools. Accounting for a large proportion of public-sector jobs in any jurisdiction, schools have long been important political bases—and therefore sites of political contest and conflict. (It is surely no accident that Lyndon Johnson, one of this nation's master politicians, started out as a schoolteacher in Cotulla, Texas.) Yet there are also substantive issues at stake. Charged with the formation of the next generation, schools are important institutions in their own right. With regard to newcomers specifically, the public schools inescapably institutionalize the conviction that immigrant children and their parents need help and guidance as to how to become Americans

The Evidence on Immigrant Choice

This history is important because it reminds us that the school bureaucracies criticized by many Americans were created at least partially in response to the arrival of earlier immigrants. To be sure, these bureaucracies have over the decades also grown in response to court decisions and federal categorical grants. But precisely because of their historical origins, the question arises, How will today's immigrants fare if these bureaucracies are dismantled or weakened? If choice proposals are implemented, what kinds of choices will immigrant families make?

We don't have an abundance of direct evidence on how poorly educated immigrant families would exercise greater choice, but there is some compelling indirect evidence, including a study of how black Americans in one large city have made educational decisions under a choice plan. Amy Stuart Wells interviewed a sample of black parents and their high school–age children in Saint Louis, where a federal court's desegregation order permits all black school children to transfer to predominantly white suburban schools. The court order provides for reimbursement to the suburban schools of the costs of educating the students who transfer, while requiring those schools to increase their black enrollments and not allowing them to reject prospective transfers on the basis of prior school achievement. Black families in Saint Louis are provided with extensive information about their options, and transferring students are provided with free transportation to the suburbs. Amy Stuart Wells concludes that "black students in the city of Saint Louis have more real choice under this desegregation plan than they would under a voucher plan."[13]

How have the black residents of Saint Louis responded to this opportunity? Some have seized it and, in Wells's words, "pushed their children onto buses heading for the suburbs."[14] But most families have apparently chosen not to transfer out of the Saint Louis schools. Among this large group of nontransferees, Wells reports that the parents typically "absolved themselves of the school choice responsibility, leaving the decision to their adolescent children."[15] Not surprisingly, these youngsters tended to decide on the basis of their activities and friends in their present all-black schools. As one young woman said, "I wanted

---

13. Amy Stuart Wells, "African-American Students' View of School Choice," in Bruce Fuller and Richard F. Elmore, eds., *Who Chooses? Who Loses?* (New York and London: Teachers College Press, 1996), p. 29.

14. Ibid., p. 32.

15. Ibid.

to go, but I didn't. I don't know why . . . I didn't want to leave the pom squad . . . I didn't want to go that far."[16]

Even when the parents of nontransferees got involved in the decision, it tended to be based on the school's proximity or on their discomfort over sending their children to an unfamiliar and potentially hostile racial environment. Nontransferees also tended to downplay the difference between inner-city and suburban schools. As one student put it, "It doesn't really matter where you go . . . if you want to learn—you got the ability—you will."[17]

Overall, Wells confirms what other studies of choice plans have found: disadvantaged students tend to exercise choice options less than their more advantaged classmates, and disadvantaged families tend to opt for the relative security of the nearby and familiar neighborhood school.[18] Even among those who chose to participate in the suburban transfer program, Wells reports that their decisions were not well informed. Many participating families were not aware of basic information about the various suburban schools they had to choose among, even though they had been provided with such information. Such families tended to base their decision on the status or popularity of a suburban school rather than on any hard evidence about, for example, school outcomes. In general, these families acted as though *any* suburban school would be preferable to the likely inner-city alternative. In this regard they were undoubtedly correct, but their decisions were nevertheless not those of scrupulous, inquisitive consumers. Perhaps most revealing is the fact that none of the parents or students opting for a suburban transfer whom Wells talked to had visited the school of their choice in advance. (It should be added that, despite this, these

---

16. Ibid., p. 34.

17. Ibid., p. 35.

18. Jeffrey R. Henig, "The Local Dynamics of Choice: Ethnic Preferences and Institutional Responses," in Fuller and Elmore, *Who Chooses? Who Loses?* p. 114.

transfer students were highly motivated and enthusiastic about their participation in the program.)[19]

Now it is true, as Wells reports, that these black families are burdened by racial anxieties and prejudices—their own as well as those of white suburbanites. Immigrants presumably carry less racial baggage. But because the decisions of inner-city blacks are also shaped by social class, their behavior can to some extent be taken as indicative of how struggling immigrants would respond to educational choice plans.

As I have already indicated, direct evidence on this point is limited. Nevertheless, the evidence that does exist is not encouraging for choice advocates. To be sure, evidence from the Milwaukee choice program indicates that Hispanics are overrepresented (based on their population) among participants in that effort.[20]

But Milwaukee may well be the exception. A recent national survey of magnet schools reported that limited- or non-English-proficient students were less likely than other students to be enrolled in them.[21] It is not obvious how to interpret such a finding, but one explanation may be that immigrant parents are not well informed about their options—a not surprising possibility, given the language barrier and other obstacles facing immigrants. This interpretation is borne out by research on the Montgomery County (Maryland) magnet school program, which reveals that while many parents of all backgrounds have never heard the terms *magnet school* or *magnet program*, even fewer Hispanic parents have.[22] Similarly, an ethnographic study of school-family relations in the principal barrio of Austin, Texas, revealed that Mexican-origin parents who were U.S. born, as well as those who were

19. Wells, "African-American Students' View of School Choice," p. 36.

20. John F. Witte, "Who Benefits from the Milwaukee Choice Program," in Fuller and Elmore, *Who Chooses? Who Loses?* p. 122.

21. Rolf K. Blank, Roger E. Levine, and Lauri Steel, "After 15 Years: Magnet Schools in Urban Education," in Fuller and Elmore, *Who Chooses? Who Loses?* p. 168.

22. Henig, "Local Dynamics of Choice," p. 110.

recent immigrants, typically did not understand what school personnel told them about their children's academic problems or progress and did not understand how educational decisions about their children were made.[23]

Still other evidence indicates that immigrants are not well situated to take advantage of market-oriented choice schemes. Again, the evidence available is limited to Hispanics and draws from reseach not on schools but on social service and child care programs.

A recent survey of exemplary social service programs for Hispanics emphasizes repeatedly that, quite aside from not knowing English, Hispanic immigrant families simply do not understand how the system works and therefore need a good deal of help negotiating it. In fact, service providers complain that they often provide this kind of help more than they do the specific services they were trained to deliver.[24]

Perhaps the most provocative finding comes from a research project at the Harvard Graduate School of Education that has been looking at Hispanics' use of child care programs. Bruce Fuller and his colleagues report that 59 percent of all Latino families with children between the ages of three and five use some form of nonparental child care, compared with 75 percent of African American and 69 percent of white famiies. Even among families who do rely on some form of nonparental care, Latino families stand out: only 39 percent of them choose a formal center or preschool (the rest rely on some informal, nonparental arrangement), compared with 58 percent of black and 54 percent of white families.[25]

Such differences may reflect any number of factors, of course, including income, education, family structure, and parental employ-

23. Harriett Romo, "The Mexican Origin Population's Differing Perceptions of Their Children's Schooling," *Social Science Quarterly* 65, no. 2 (June 1984): 648.

24. Angela Shartrand, *Supporting Latino Families: Lessons from Exemplary Programs*, vol. 1 (Cambridge, Mass.: Harvard Family Research Project, 1996), pp. 13–14.

25. Bruce Fuller et al., "Rich Culture, Poor Markets: Why Do Latino Parents Forgo Preschooling?" *Teachers College Record* 97, no. 3 (spring 1996): 402.

ment outside the home. But even after controlling for such variables, Fuller and his colleagues conclude that "Latino parents are not buying into the burgeoning preschool market to the same extent as white and African-American families."[26] Their research thus confirms what a drive through any large metropolitan area reveals: black neighborhoods have child care centers and preschool programs seemingly on every block, and certainly attached to most churches, whereas Latino neighborhoods display little evidence of such programs.

The important question, as Fuller and company ask, is, "Why do Latino families select preschools less frequently than white and black families?"[27] One factor that comes to mind are the dense social networks that provide Latinos with all manner of social supports, including babysitting, ride-sharing and carpools, and job and housing referrals. Some research indicates that Latinos have an abundance of such supports relative to inner-city blacks certainly and probably to most Anglos as well.[28] One reason these networks may be so strong among Hispanics is that, as immigrants, they depend on such face-to-face relationships to negotiate the obstacles and hazards of getting here in the first place.[29] My point here, however, is that Latino families may rely on preschools less than blacks and whites in part because they have other options close at hand.

To explain the child care choices of Latinos, Fuller emphasizes an alternative factor: the clash of values between Latino parents and Anglo child care providers, which results in unease or outright disaffection

26. Ibid., p. 400.

27. Ibid., p. 405.

28. Martha Van Haitsma, "Attitudes, Social Context, and Labor Force Attachment: Blacks and Immigrant Mexicans in Chicago Poverty Areas," paper prepared for the Chicago Urban Poverty and Family Life Conference, sponsored by the University of Chicago and the Social Science Research Council of New York, 1991. See also Philip Kasinitz and Jan Rosenberg, "Missing the Connection: Social Isolation and Employment on the Brooklyn Waterfront," *Social Problems* 43, no. 2 (May 1996).

29. Douglas Massey et al., *Return to Aztlan: The Social Process of International Migration from Western Mexico* (Berkeley: University of California Press, 1987).

on the part of the parents. Indeed, Fuller reports that Latino parents worry about losing their children to an irreverent and individualistic Anglo way of looking at the world.[30] Latino parents use words like *cold* and *rough* to describe the Americans who staff child care programs and complain that they lack *cariñosa* (warmth and caring) when dealing with their children.[31]

Such factors add up to a distinctive cultural dynamic among Latino parents that, Fuller argues, exerts an independent effect on child care choices quite apart from economic or social structural constraints. He concludes that "the ongoing rationalization of early childhood—now endorsed by most policymakers and professional groups—has not penetrated as deeply into the consciousness of Latino families as it has into that of white middle-class and black families."[32] In the context of early childhood, the traditional, nonrationalized tenor of Latino family life may of course have considerable appeal. Yet, to the extent that early childhood programs such as Head Start may contribute to positive developmental gains for participants, the appealing cultural ethos that Fuller highlights is more problematic.

There is, in fact, evidence that these traditional Latino family dynamics have less than benign consequences. One obvious such consequence among poor, uneducated immigrants is the expectation that young people in their teens will abandon school in order to assume adult responsibilities. For example, an ethnographic study of illegal aliens in Texas observes that

> Families fortunate enough to have teenage children often encouraged them to enter the labor force full time, simply skipping school. . . .

---

30. Fuller et al., "Rich Culture, Poor Markets," pp. 412–17; and Susan D. Holloway, Bruce Fuller, Marylee F. Rambaud, and Costanza Eggers-Piérola, *Through My Own Eyes: Women's Views of Child Rearing and Work within Diverse Cultures of Poverty* (Cambridge, Mass.: Harvard University Press, forthcoming), chap. 5.

31. Fuller et al., "Rich Culture, Poor Markets," p. 414; and Holloway et al., *Through My Own Eyes*, chap. 8.

32. Fuller et al., "Rich Culture, Poor Markets," p. 417.

Even young children, especially girls, were given major responsibility for the care of infants and younger children while the mother worked outside the home.[33]

Similarly, anthropologist Maria Eugenia Matute-Bianchi reports from her field research on Mexican-descent students in a California high school that although many academically successful young women get encouragement from their immigrant parents, some do not. Indeed, several Mexican-American women reported that their parents did not want them to leave home and go off to a college or university. As one stated,

> I think the real reason my parents don't want me going away to college is that they are afraid I might get pregnant or something. That plus they want me to work in the restaurant like my older sister.[34]

Colleges and universities complain that, despite strong educational aspirations, Latino families are reluctant to send young men as well as women off to college. Recruiters echo the story told above and offer some of their own. One Notre Dame Latina alumna involved in recruitment observed, "The problem I have to deal with is parents think their son or daughter won't care for them or their family as much when they go away to school."[35]

---

33. Harley L. Browning and Nestor Rodriguez, "The Migration of Mexican Indocumentados as a Settlement Process: Implications for Work," in George J. Borjas and Marta Tienda, eds., *Hispanics in the U.S. Economy* (Orlando, Fla.: Academic Press, 1985), p. 291. For a similar finding, see also McDonnell and Hill, *Newcomers in American Schools*, pp. 72–75.

34. Maria Eugenia Matute-Bianchi, "Situational Ethnicity and Patterns of School Peformance among Immigrant and Nonimmigrant Mexican-Descent Students," in Margaret A. Gibson and John U. Ogbu, eds., *Minority Status and Schooling: A Comparative Study of Immigrant and Involuntary Minorities* (New York: Garland Publishing, 1991), p. 231.

35. William Celis 3d, "Colleges Battle Culture and Poverty to Swell Hispanic Enrollments," *New York Times*, February 24, 1993, p. A17.

Sociologist Rubén Rumbaut has observed that family ties can be liabilities as well as assets. Citing his own finding of a negative relationship between strong, family-oriented attitudes and educational outcomes, Rumbaut concludes, "Family ties bind, but sometimes those bonds may constrain rather than facilitate particular outcomes."[36]

Trade-Offs and Expectations

Explanations of social phenomena that emphasize cultural factors are controversial because they have been used, particularly by clumsy observers, to deny or at least deemphasize human agency and choice. But in the hands of more subtle analysts, due consideration of cultural factors need not crowd out appreciation of how individuals do make choices.

Yet what if Latinos make the "wrong" choices? What if their choices result in diminished educational outcomes for the second or third generation? Some might regard this as a reasonable trade-off: lessened individual achievement and mobility in return for stronger, more cohesive families. Some might also point out that this is essentially the choice that Italian immigrant families made earlier this century.

This is not, however, an easy position to defend—especially at this point in our history. For example, most individuals reading this chapter would probably find the choice I have described Latino families making as unwise or at least inadvisable. As a society we are not tolerant of unequal group outcomes, whether or not they reflect the diversity we so strenuously claim to tolerate. More to the point, we interpret unequal outcomes, regardless of cause, as the result of prejudice and

---

36. Rubén G. Rumbaut, "Ties That Bind: Immigration and Immigrant Families in the United States," paper presented to the National Symposium on International Migration and Family Change, Pennsylvania State University, November 2–3, 1995, p. 27.

discrimination. Many immigrants and their leaders, especially Latinos and to a lesser extent Asians, attribute any and all divergent group outcomes to the racism of society's dominant groups and institutions.

This focus on racism soon leads to demands for programs to equalize outcomes across groups. Such efforts begin by seeking to eliminate discriminatory barriers and obstacles, but they invariably move in the direction of seeking to provide better social services—for example, child care, education, or job training—to the discriminated against and disadvantaged. The very term *social service* helps obscure the fact that what is being provided is not a consumer commodity but, to varying degrees, authoritative direction and guidance. We seldom own up to it, but the so-called social services inevitably entail an element of social control. When it comes to social policy, Mead's paternalism is difficult to avoid.

A good example is the above-mentioned RAND study, which documents the cultural problems that immigrant children bring to the schools from home. But instead of squarely addressing the need for authoritative guidance of immigrant families, the RAND researchers opt for service-oriented consumer language, arguing that schools should become "general resources for [immigrant] parents" in need of enhanced "educational opportunies."[37]

We have not always been so convoluted about these matters. Back in the 1960s, Head Start began with an explicit "cultural deficit model" that assumed the disadvantaged lacked cultural as well as material resources. What was needed, therefore, were various social policy "interventions" (to use the revealing phrase that is revealingly no longer used). Head Start programs were to provide help with both deficits: disadvantaged kids' teeth were to be fixed but so were their—and their parents'—outlooks on life.

Such a stance is difficult to maintain in a modern democratic society, particularly one like ours with its strong antielitist, antiexpert

---

37. McDonnell and Hill, *Newcomers in American Schools*, pp. 76, 105.

populist strain. (Appropriately enough, Head Start has since changed its tune and no longer talks about remedying the cultural deficits of its clients.) Liberals don't want to appear elitist, of course. But neither do conservatives, for whom antielitism and fiscal conservatism have fired the romance of family values.[38] As a result, conservatives now argue that the poor and disadvantaged don't need special guidance or authority. All they need is to be freed from government bureaucrats and given . . . *choice*.

Conclusion

My own sense, as should be evident by now, is that if immigrants are to prosper and become full participants in American society, then they will need authoritative help and guidance. Yet it is not at all clear that we as a society know how to undertake such efforts—even when we acknowledge the paternalism inherent in them. In fact, the evidence is that we don't. But the issue of our collective know-how and ability is separate from that of immigrants' needs.

At the beginning of this century labor leader Samuel Gompers supported immigration restriction because he feared that masses of docile, dependent workers would undermine the American Federation of Labor's antistatist, voluntarist philosophy by weakening the ties between individual workers and local unions and replacing them with direct ties between workers and a centralized state.[39] The picture he painted was perhaps overly stark. But it reveals aspects of the situation facing us today.

---

38. The most original exposition of this perspective of which I am aware is Ferdinand Mount, *The Subversive Family: An Alternative History of Love and Marriage* (New York: Free Press, 1992).

39. See Gwendolyn Mink, *Old Labor and New Immigrants in American Political Development: Union, Party, and State, 1875–1920* (Ithaca, N.Y.: Cornell University Press, 1986), pp. 241–57.

What we are contemplating is the future of the welfare state in an age of virtually unrestricted immigration. If proimmigrant advocates such as Ron Unz are to be believed, then the immigrant population will in effect constitute a reserve army of the unentitled who will bring down the welfare state by competing with citizens who are dependent on entitlements. Apart from being socially divisive, this scenario is highly unlikely. As the evidence here suggests, most immigrants do not arrive in America prepared to make the "right" choices—that is, the choices that lead to maximum individual mobility. Therefore, many immigrants are likely to become, in the short if not in the long term, constituents of the existing welfare state. Those who advocate open immigration while at the same time pushing for the choice approach to social policy will sooner or later have to face up to this likelihood.

Stuart Anderson

CHAPTER NINE

The Effect of Immigrant Scientists and Engineers on Wages and Employment in High Technology

Immigrants are "cheap labor" and "steal" American jobs. That is an article of faith among those who want tighter restrictions or even a moratorium on all types of immigration. The most prominent critic of U.S. employment-based immigration policy, Senator Alan Simpson (R-Wyo.), contends that immigrant scientists and engineers are willing to work for one-third less pay just so they can get green cards.[1] Another immigration critic promotes a conspiracy theory whereby an American "establishment" has designed our current immigration policy to pay scientists and engineers less so it can pay lawyers and MBAs

A version of this paper originally appeared in *International Educator* (fall 1996).

1. "Borderline," National Empowerment Television, January 22, 1996. Senator Simpson said, "The computer industry is saying my bill will deny them the opportunity to get these highly skilled people to come to the United States. . . . They bring them here on temporary visas and who wouldn't work for one-third less as long as they knew at the end of the tunnel was a green card."

more.[2] Some claim that colleges and universities are hiring cheap for-eign-born faculty to undercut the wages of American-born professors. There's at least one major problem with those and other theories about employment-based immigration—they're wrong.

The evidence is clear and persuasive on two crucial points. First, the typical immigrant professional in science and engineering earns *more* than his or her native-born counterpart, not less, evidence that the foreign born are not bidding down wage rates by being willing to work for far less than the native born. Second, there is no correlation between the unemployment rates among Ph.D.s and the presence of foreign-born Ph.D.s in their fields. Some of the lowest unemployment rates are in the fields with the highest concentrations of foreign born. Both those points, along with a basic understanding of how labor mar-kets function, illustrate why immigrant professionals do not harm the employment prospects of their native counterparts. In fact, by expand-ing the total output of the nation's economy and by creating new jobs through a variety of means, including innovation and entrepreneur-ship, immigrants provide economic benefits both to their native col-leagues and to all Americans as a whole.

The data presented here tell us about the quality of the people who immigrate since no one believes American employers are prejudiced in favor of immigrants. (In fact, other things held constant, one would expect to find that immigrants are paid less than the native born be-cause of the obvious advantage of the native born in language and culture.) Wages are a function of productivity. We thus conclude from

---

2. David S. North, "On the Use of Nonimmigrant Visas in the U.S. Labor Market, Notably by Scientists and Engineers," testimony before the Subcommittee on Immi-gration, Judiciary Committee, U.S. Senate, September 28, 1995. In his testimony, North stated that "the presence of large numbers of bright, hard-working overseas candidates for these PhDs has soothed the American Establishment to the extent that it need not pay its lawyers and MBAs a little less so that it can pay its scientists and engineers a little more."

the data that the foreign born who work in America are exceptionally productive.

As the data in table 1 show, the annual median earnings of foreign-born engineers and scientists are $1,100 *more* than those of the native born one to five years after they complete their master's degrees, $2,000 more eleven to fifteen years after, and $4,000 more sixteen to twenty years after.

At the Ph.D. level, the data are even stronger (see table 2). Foreign-born Ph.D. scientists and engineers one to six years out of school earn $44,000 compared with $40,000 earned by the native born. Foreign-born science and engineering Ph.D.'s six to ten years out earn $6,200 more annually. After eleven to fifteen years, the advantage is $8,000 a year, and it increases to $10,000 after sixteen to twenty years.

Although the data shown here are for 1993, the same data hold for 1991 as well. In 1993, with the sole exception of older recipients of master's degrees in science and engineering (twenty-one years or more), the data are consistent. Since the "twenty-one years or more category" does not include five-year increments, it could include native-born master's degree recipients disproportionately older than the foreign born, which would explain the difference.

Table 1   Median Salaries of Recipients of Master's Degrees
           in Science and Engineering:
           Foreign Born vs. Native Born, 1993

Years after Earning Degree	Foreign Born	Native Born
One to five	$41,400	$40,300
Six to ten	$48,000	$47,900
Eleven to fifteen	$52,000	$50,000
Sixteen to twenty	$56,000	$52,000
Twenty-one or more	$55,000	$58,200

SOURCE: Unpublished National Science Foundation tabulation of the 1993 National Survey of College Graduates. Foreign born includes naturalized U.S. citizens, permanent residents, and workers on temporary visas (including H-1B visas). Those in the category "one to five years" after degree received their degree between 1988 and 1992.

Table 2   Median Salaries of U.S. Recipients of Ph.D.'s in Science and
               Engineering: Foreign Born versus Native Born, 1993

Years after Earning Degree	Foreign Born	Native Born
One to five	$44,400	$40,000
Six to ten	$55,400	$49,200
Eleven to fifteen	$64,000	$56,000
Sixteen to twenty	$70,000	$60,000
Twenty-one or more	$70,200	$68,000

SOURCE: Unpublished National Science Foundation tabulation of the 1993 Survey of Doctoral Recipients. Foreign born includes naturalized U.S. citizens, permanent residents, and workers on temporary visas (including H-1B visas). Those in the category "one to five years" after degree received their degrees between 1988 and 1992.

To produce tables 1 and 2, I asked Mark Regets of the National Science Foundation to extract the necessary data on native- and foreign-born recipients of master's degrees and Ph.D.'s in the science and engineering disciplines. The data are on people who completed their degrees in the same year, which is important since, all things being equal, an individual fifteen years in the field will earn more than someone relatively new. To prevent distortions of the data, naturalized U.S. citizens, permanent residents, and workers on temporary visas, such as H-1B visas, are all included under foreign born.

The data also hold true for a particular occupation, as is the case with university and college professors. As table 3 shows, for all science and engineering faculty the median earnings of a foreign-born full professor are $65,000 versus $64,000 for a native-born colleague. At the associate professor level the foreign born earn $51,000 compared with $49,700 earned by natives. For an assistant professor the median salary for the foreign born is $42,000, whereas for natives it is $41,300.

The data hold for life sciences, math and computer sciences, physical sciences, and social sciences at all three faculty levels (with a tie between natives and foreign born in two places). Engineering presents the only exception, which may be explained by the fact that the many of the best foreign-born engineers find it relatively easy to obtain high-

Table 3   Median Salaries of College and University Faculty
               by Nativity and Rank, 1993

	FIELD OF PH.D.					
	All Science and Engineering	*Engineering*	*Life Sciences*	*Math and Computer Sciences*	*Physical Sciences*	*Social Sciences*
FULL PROFESSOR						
Native born	$64,000	$75,000	$65,000	$60,800	$65,000	$60,000
Foreign born	$65,000	$71,000	$72,000	$61,000	$67,000	$61,000
ASSOCIATE PROFESSOR						
Native born	$49,700	$58,000	$52,000	$46,000	$45,700	$46,600
Foreign born	$51,000	$55,000	$52,000	$49,300	$47,000	$48,000
ASSISTANT PROFESSOR						
Native born	$41,300	$49,200	$44,000	$40,000	$38,000	$38,000
Foreign born	$42,000	$47,000	$45,500	$41,500	$40,000	$38,000

SOURCE: National Science Foundation, 1993 Survey of Doctoral Recipients. Data for recipients of degrees at U.S. institutions.

paying jobs outside academia. According to the National Science Foundation, 25.7 percent of native Ph.D.'s in engineering go into academia, whereas only 17.5 percent of foreign-born engineering Ph.D.'s do so.[3]

The data used here are the best available on science and engineering salaries. The National Science Foundation uses surveys, with telephone and personal visit follow-up, that go beyond data from the Census Bureau or the Bureau of Labor Statistics. Mark Regets, senior analyst, the National Science Foundation, extracted the data based on the parameters outlined for this study.

A study by Paul Ong at the University of California at Los Angeles and doctoral candidate Evelyn Blumenberg uses different data but reaches a similar conclusion: "There are no differences in the wages between the U.S.-born and foreign-born employees with a U.S. edu-

---

3. National Science Foundation.

cation after controlling for other factors." (Paul Ong and Evelyn Blu-menberg, "Scientists and Engineers," in Paul Ong, ed., *The State of Asian Pacific America: Economic Diversity, Issues & Policies* [Los Angeles, Calif.: LEAP, 1994], p. 180.) Their study finds that those who receive their degrees abroad do earn "about 10 percent less than those with a U.S. education," but this only tells us that foreign degrees are less highly valued in the U.S. labor market than degrees earned at American universities, not that employers are seeking "cheap" labor. Most important, employers typically hire a foreign student who has received a degree in the United States.

Ong and Blumenberg found that, without controlling for place of education, newer Asian Pacific immigrants as opposed to all immigrants in engineering earned about one-third less than their U.S.-born counterparts but that the "lower earnings of recent immigrants may reflect unobserved differences in the quality and type of education among immigrant cohorts." They note, however, that this gap disappears with time in the United States. Since individual pay is based primarily on productive capacity, what Ong and Blumenberg found does not have to do with "cheap" immigrant labor but with how U.S. employers evaluate the relative importance of a U.S.-based education.

These findings on salaries do not mean that the foreign born are taking away high-paying jobs from Americans or doing well at the expense of the native born. Neither the total number of jobs available in the U.S. economy nor the amount of compensation paid to workers is static and fixed. Both grow based on several factors, including labor force growth, technology, education, entrepreneurship, and research and development.

The higher salaries for immigrants can be explained by several factors. The people who immigrate are not picked randomly but are carefully selected by employers. Companies say that some of the foreign nationals they recruit not only attend leading universities but are near the top of their classes. And the immigrants are self-selected, meaning that those who gamble on success in a new country are highly motivated individuals. "If you made all the immigrants go away tomorrow you would decimate this company, my group within this company, and most companies in this industry," says John Q. Torode, president of Cypress IC Designs, a division of Cypress Semiconductor.[4] New York native Rich Martinez in Cypress's human resources department is more direct: "Without immigrants this company would not exist."[5]

Can we find stories of people being exploited because they are immigrants? Undoubtedly, but there is no evidence that this is widespread in science and engineering. Pay scales at companies and on university campuses do not differentiate by national origin or immigration status. Salaries are in the end determined by ability, experience, and education.

Three other factors are worth noting. First, under Department of Labor regulations it is unlawful to pay a foreign-born individual less than a similarly skilled native. Second, it is unlawful for an employer to even ask a job applicant his or her immigration status. Third, employers can typically spend $10,000 to sponsor a foreign national for permanent residence; thus any "savings" on salaries would have to be substantial to be worthwhile, and there is no evidence that this is the case. Ike McDonald, director of business operations and controller at Rockwell International says, "Foreign nationals are critical to our research because some of them are among the best to come out of school." Rockwell's research lab in Ventura County, California, has four hundred employees, a significant portion of whom are foreign born. "The rate of development in technology is spectacular," says McDonald. "It's not a question of native or immigrant. You pay top dollar because you want to be competitive."[6]

The issue of whether foreign-born professionals are paid less than American-born professionals is best summed up by Ehud Yuhjtman,

---

4. Interview with the author, December 12, 1995.
5. Interview with the author, December 12, 1995.
6. Ike McDonald, Rockwell International, October 8, 1996.

an Israeli-born engineer at Chip Express who often interviews prospective hires. "You cannot pay foreign-born engineers less. These are smart people, if you try to fool with them, then they will go someplace else."[7] Indeed even a foreign national on an H-1B visa can change firms by obtaining a new petition. Some companies even "raid" other firms' H-1B employees, which indicates how competitive the marketplace is for talent in America today.

Unemployment

If immigrant professionals cost Americans jobs, one would expect the evidence to show that the higher the proportion of foreign born in a field, the higher the unemployment rate in that field. Yet, if anything, the opposite appears to be true. The two Ph.D. fields with the highest concentrations of foreign born—engineering and computer science— have much lower unemployment rates than the two fields with the lowest concentration of foreign born—the geosciences and social sciences.

Using data from the National Science Foundation, I calculated the percentage of foreign-born Ph.D.'s employed in eight fields and compared the unemployment rates in those fields (see table 4). As can be seen, *no correlation exists between the percentage of foreign born and the unemployment rate within a field,* except to the extent that those disciplines with a higher percentage of foreign born tend actually to have *lower* unemployment rates than the fields with a low percentage of foreign-born Ph.D.'s.

More than 39 percent of computer science Ph.D.'s are foreign born, and the unemployment rate for Ph.D.'s in that discipline was 1.0 percent in 1993. In engineering, 40.3 percent were foreign born and the unemployment rate was 1.7 percent. The geosciences (geology and

---

7. Interview with the author, December 13, 1995.

Table 4   Unemployment Rates (1993) among U.S. Science and
                 Engineering Ph.D.'s: All Graduation Years

Percentage Foreign Born in Field	Ph.D. Field	Unemployment Rate among All Ph.D.'s in Field
40.3%	Engineering	1.7%
39.4%	Computer Science	1.0%
31.1%	Math and Science	1.2%
30.6%	Physics/Astronomy	2.3%
25.7%	Chemistry	1.8%
21.3%	Life Sciences	1.5%
16.8%	Geosciences	2.8%
13.1%	Social Sciences	2.3%

SOURCE: Mark Regets, "Preparing the U.S. Scientist for the 21st Century," National Science Foundation and Data Brief NSF/SRS Data Brief 95-340.

related disciplines), which had less than half the proportion of foreign born that engineering did, had an unemployment rate almost twice as high, at 2.8 percent. Of the three fields with the highest unemployment rates among Ph.D.'s, only physics/astronomy (2.3 percent unemployment) has a notable percentage of foreign born (30.6 percent). The data are essentially the same for those who graduated between 1988 and 1992, except that the unemployment rate is higher for physics/astronomy (4.0 percent) and lower among more recent Ph.D. graduates in engineering (1.5 percent).

According to the National Academy of Sciences, "unemployment rates for Ph.D. scientists and engineers have remained steady and low for the last decade, compared with those in other segments of the economy."[8] In the 1980s, surveys showed the unemployment rates for Ph.D. scientists and engineers at about 1 percent. In the 1990s, the figure is approximately 1.5 percent. Although the unemployment rate did rise to 2 percent in the 1993 academy survey, its report notes that

8. National Academy of Sciences, *Reshaping the Graduate Education of Scientists and Engineers* (Washington, D.C.: National Academy Press, 1995), p. 26.

"it is not known how much of this increase in unemployment rates should be attributed to a change in survey methods."[9] Still, by any measure, a 2 percent rate is not only low but, given frictions in the labor market (i.e., people change jobs), one would not expect it to be significantly lower. The unemployment rate for all professionals during this period was 3 percent, and it hovered around 7 percent for all workers nationally.

The engineering and sciences market has shifted in the past few years. A major conclusion of a 1995 National Academy of Sciences study is that "Ph.D.'s are increasingly finding employment outside universities and more and more are in types of positions that they had not expected to occupy."[10] That shift in itself could account for a longer wait for jobs, which statistically increases the unemployment rate. Information on employment opportunities may be more diffuse and, therefore, harder to come by in companies than in the centralized apparatus of the federal government or in the close networks established within and among universities. But the data show that immigration has not led to high unemployment rates in any of the fields in which the foreign born make up a significant percentage of Ph.D.'s. The data should also dispel the myth that America has "too many" Ph.D.'s. If, for example, an English literature Ph.D. is having difficulty finding a job, it has no bearing on fields like engineering or computer science.

We must remember that the years leading up to 1993 saw a *sharp increase* in the number of foreign born entering these fields, yet still we have not seen serious negative employment effects on native-born scientists and engineers. Those data should be kept in mind when reading news reports that cite individuals who complain that immi-

9. Ibid. Dan Pasquini, research associate, Office of Science and Engineering Personnel, said in an interview, November 30, 1995, "The way the questions were asked may have impacted comparability with data for previous years."

10. National Academy of Sciences, *Reshaping the Graduate Education of Scientists and Engineers*.

grant professionals are hurting natives job prospects in their fields. In a *Wall Street Journal* article entitled "Math Ph.D.'s Add to Anti-Foreigner Wave; Scholars Facing High Jobless Rates Seek Immigration Curbs," the writer quotes some recent math Ph.D.'s complaining that foreign-born mathematicians are responsible for their inability to land better jobs.[11]

The article, however, contained several factual errors. The writer based the article primarily on a report by the American Mathematical Society (AMS) that said 10.7 percent of new math Ph.D.'s were unemployed. Yet many of those surveyed by the AMS had completed their doctorates only three months before answering the survey, so one would be surprised to find a 100 percent employment rate among such recent graduates. One could say that it is actually positive that 90 percent of new doctoral recipients had found a job within three to twelve months of completing a degree, although in the past the number has been above 95 percent. An estimated one-half of mathematics Ph.D.'s receive their degrees in April, May or June; the AMS, however, starts surveying departments in June and July, and among those individuals who respond to follow-up surveys, three-quarters answer by the end of September. The National Academy of Sciences waits at least a year after completion of the Ph.D. before including "new" Ph.D.'s in its unemployment totals.

James Maxwell, associate executive director of the AMS and the man who oversaw the employment study cited in the *Wall Street Journal*, says that the reporter "egregiously misused" AMS data.[12] He points out that the math society's data on unemployment among new math Ph.D.'s are useful primarily as a trend indicator specifically for new Ph.D.'s—comparing information on the current year with that on prior

---

11. "Math Ph.D.'s Add to Anti-Foreigner Wave; Scholars Facing High Jobless Rates Seek Immigration Curbs," *Wall Street Journal*, September 4, 1996, p. A2.

12. Interview with the author, September 6, 1996.

years. The AMS survey does not attempt to describe the economic climate of the overall field.

The trend is that it takes new Ph.D.'s longer to find their first job. The reporter's cardinal mistake was to use the AMS data to generalize about *all* math Ph.D.'s, which produced a misleading impression. In fact, although the math society's 1993 survey showed nearly a 9 percent unemployment rate among the new doctoral recipients responding to its survey, among all math Ph.D.'s the unemployment rate was only *1.2 percent*, which would hardly be classified as a crisis. Such a strikingly low unemployment rate, based on the best available data, contradicts the newspaper article's premise that math Ph.D.'s generally are experiencing a high degree of joblessness. Once the 1995 figures become available, James Maxwell does not expect the overall unemployment rate in the field to have risen significantly. In 1993 among math Ph.D.'s one to three years out of school the unemployment rate was only *0.7 percent*, according to the National Academy of Sciences.

A Closer Look at Foreign-Born Faculty

Immigrants' contributions to the American workforce are *in addition to* those of the native born, not at their expense. Even in fields where one may hear complaints about competition, natives still dominate overall employment. For example, among U.S. higher education faculty, 85 percent in the natural sciences and math/computer sciences are native born, as are 70 percent in engineering and 89 percent in the social sciences (see table 5).

One way to hurt the employment prospects of professors would be to enact sharp restrictions on family and employment-based immigration or on the availability of nonimmigrant visas for foreign students. If the number of students declines, there will be fewer faculty positions since the fewer students there are to teach, the fewer faculty are

Table 5   Native-Born Faculty in U.S. Higher Education (in percent)

	Native-Born Faculty
Social sciences	89%
Natural sciences	85
Math/computer sciences	85
Engineering	70

SOURCE: National Science Foundation

needed. Family immigration boosts the supply of college students—both now and in the future—particularly since so many immigrant families stress the value of education. And if a change in U.S. immigration policy prevented foreign students from obtaining employment here after completing their advanced degrees, a certain percentage would no longer attend American universities and colleges. Moreover, further restricting the ability of universities to hire foreign-born professors would diminish the pool of teaching talent and could encourage more foreign *and* American graduate students to study outside the United States. The impact of restrictive immigration legislation would be profound on universities.

Those who complain about immigrants "taking" jobs, on university campuses or elsewhere, need to view immigration more generally as a dynamic phenomenon. In 1995, 12 percent of the *Inc. 500*—a compilation of the fastest-growing corporations in America—were companies started by immigrants. Many leading high-tech companies were started by immigrants. By starting businesses and spending their money on products made by Americans and immigrants alike, immigrants create at least as many jobs as they fill. Simply put, immigrants increase the supply of labor, but they also increase the *demand* for labor. That is why economists Rachel M. Friedberg of Brown University and Jennifer Hunt of Yale University wrote recently in the *Journal of Economic Perspectives* that "despite the popular belief that immigrants have a large adverse impact on the wages and employment opportunities of the native-born population, the literature on this question does not provide much support for this conclusion."[13]

The number of jobs in the U.S. economy, even in academia, is not fixed. Between 1976 and 1993, the number of full- and part-time faculty in institutions of higher education increased by nearly 45 percent, rising from 633,210 to 915,474, according to the National Center for Education Statistics. What has increased anxiety on university campuses, says George Aiyetty, a Ghana-born economics professor at American University in Washington, D.C., is that an economics department that years ago had fifteen of twenty faculty teaching full-time may have only ten of twenty faculty doing so today. The proportion of part-time faculty nearly doubled, from 22 percent to 40 percent, between 1970 and 1993, according to the National Center for Education Statistics.

Many part-time faculty positions do not include benefits, and typical jobs pay $3,000 to $4,000 a course. There is no evidence that universities pay part-time foreign-born faculty less than part-time natives. "These jobs are not attractive to the average American, they're looking for something better," says Aiyetty.[14]

If the foreign-born faculty weren't available as adjuncts, wouldn't universities have to hire more full-time faculty? That is only one scenario and perhaps the least likely one. It is more plausible that universities would simply offer fewer classes or be forced to hire faculty of lesser quality to fill the part-time positions. Either way, the losers would be the students and society overall.

Conclusion

In theory, if American companies and universities were prohibited from hiring skilled foreign nationals on H-1B petitions and prevented

---

13. Rachel M. Friedberg and Jennifer Hunt, *Journal of Economic Perspectives*, spring 1995, p. 42.

14. Interview with the author, September 5, 1996.

from sponsoring such foreign-born employees for permanent status, wages could be higher for some employees in some areas of competition. It is important, however, to keep in mind the two facts presented here. First, on balance, immigrant scientists and engineers are not paid less than their native-born counterparts. In other words, they are not being hired because they are cheap. They are hired because they are productive. Second, there is no correlation between the presence of foreign-born Ph.D.'s and the unemployment rate in a field. Although it is difficult to isolate the wage effects on natives, these facts certainly suggest that there is no significant wage effect of immigrants on natives in the high-tech fields.

The American economy overall benefits significantly from the immigration of foreign-born scientists and engineers. A significant number of foreign nationals who come to the United States help foster the creation of more jobs and better products for consumers. As noted, many large and successful companies, such as Intel, Lam Research, Computer Associates, and AST Computer, were started by immigrants. Two foreign nationals, both graduate students at Stanford University, founded Sun Microsystems. But it was two other foreign-born engineers who created that innovation in chip design called SPARC, on which Sun Microsystems today bases much of its $6 billion in annual revenues and employs eleven thousand people in America. When Sun hired Indian-born Anant Agrawal, one of the creators of SPARC, the company employed fewer than three hundred people. We cannot assume that the demand for labor at high-tech firms would be constant whether or not employers were able to hire foreign nationals.

Changes in the U.S. economy, whether in industry or in academia, produce winners and those who, at least for the time being, are not doing as well. Predictably, that brings forth calls to limit the international flow of labor as well as goods. Yet among the least effective approaches to coping with modernity is to turn the clock back to when America shut the door tighter against those who sought lawful entry to the United States. America's history has proven immigration to be a positive force that adds people with talent, drive, and energy to our economy and culture. Yet, despite that, the concern is as old as the Republic that immigrants hurt the employment opportunities of those born here. The evidence shows that that concern continues to be misplaced.

Joseph B. Costello,
Nicholas Imparato, and
Lance Director Nagel

CHAPTER TEN | # Ensuring Continued High-Tech Leadership with a Rational Immigration Policy

Immigration is often a divisive and emotional issue today, placed at the top of the American agenda by politicians and the media. The topic now occupies premium space in public affairs forums everywhere. More often than not immigration is presented as a threat to America's economy and social services. Images of unskilled laborers wading across shallow portions of the Rio Grande and into the United States in search of a day's wage below the legal minimum affect the attitudes of many Americans. These images, however, unfairly taint the discussion surrounding legal immigration and the positive effect it has had on America's high-tech economy.

Legal immigration consists of two categories: family based and employment based. The form of immigration most directly affecting American companies and their global competitiveness is employment-based immigration, the practice of allowing foreign nationals into the United States to fill specialty jobs on either a temporary or permanent basis. Ironically, today's heightened public pressure to stave off illegal immigration comes at a time when key sectors of the U.S. economy need to rely more heavily than ever on legal, employment-based immigration. The danger is that negative attitudes about one domain unduly shape negative attitudes about another.

To put the point bluntly, American high-tech companies have experienced such rapid growth that they have collectively outpaced the ability of America's educational system to produce a sufficient number of technically knowledgeable workers. The gap between America's besieged educational system and the acute labor needs of high-tech industries creates a situation where American companies feel compelled to hire foreign nationals to fill many strategic, technically demanding positions.

Keeping the United States globally competitive with properly skilled workers requires thoughtful immigration policies that honor both the needs of American business and the prosperity of the American worker. By enlisting global talent, American high-tech companies position themselves to maintain global leadership, create new jobs for American workers, and contribute to the long-term growth of the American economy.

The overarching importance of the immigration question means that it needs to be taken out of the arena of special-interest politics and partisan maneuvering. In a climate hostile to immigration, nativist language can be seductive to politicians running for reelection. Thus, establishing productive guidelines for legal immigration requires the attention and input of business leaders and academics, as well as politicians and regulators. Any change in immigration policy that threatens to further restrict businesses' ability to enlist talent should undergo heightened scrutiny. Otherwise, America's position in the global high-tech market will suffer, as will its capacity to prosper in the emerging, new economy.

High Tech and the New Economy

Business everywhere has been experiencing a major transformation over the past decade. Technology, particularly communications technology, has been a major driver in the process, meaning that most organizations today are primarily in the "knowledge business." The market capitalization of firms such as Intel and Microsoft demonstrates the confidence that investors have in businesses that trade in knowledge and expertise more than in the scale of brick and mortar investments: manufacturing plants, warehouses, and transportation equipment. Indeed, when Walt Disney, a creator and distributor of entertainment product (primarily the result of knowledge work) replaced U.S. Steel in the Dow Jones Index, one chapter in American industry was prepared to close.

For companies that make the organizational backbone (read hardware) and the nervous system (read software) in this environment, the demand for technical expertise has been accentuated. The value of what is produced is ultimately found in the ideas and technical knowhow of the workforce. The firms with the more imaginative and skilled workforces will generally prevail in competitive contests. Good marketing and management and financial wherewithal are also necessary, but these too are knowledge-based functions.

Thus, getting access to skilled workers is no longer just a human resources task or an operational issue but a strategic concern. Brain power is what produces intellectual capital, which is what organizations need to compete successfully. In the rawest terms, the fate of a high-tech company rests primarily on the technical knowledge of the employees and, by extension, its capacity to garner the best and brightest available for hire. Intel chairman Andy Grove, often quoted in discussions of the issue, says that watching his workers leave the office every day at five o'clock is the scariest moment of his work day. That's when all the company's assets get into a car and drive onto a crowded freeway.

Where the profit formulas for other industrial segments are often driven by the cost of raw materials and the careful pricing of products, high-tech companies typically compete on innovation. Companies like Cadence Design Systems are measured by their ability—and their success in increasing the ability of their customers—to get a new, conceptually complex product to market in a timely fashion, in order to capture market share before another engineering company releases a comparable product. Whereas many companies fight for 2 or 3 percent growth in market shares (think, for example, of the cola wars, auto rebate programs, or competition among the fast-food operators), high technology primarily competes in a world of huge leaps and bounds and hyperfast growth. The telling success factor in this competitive environment is not the slow and steady improvement in procedures or the sharpening over time of marketing plans but the "big idea" or the "killer application" or the "revolutionary platform." Each of these depends on the skills and talents of the organization's workforce in a way that has not been seen before. Imagination and technical know-how, in addition to the commonly accepted demands of "process improvement," spell the difference between companies that are successful and those that are not.

Furthermore, as leading representatives of the new economy, high-technology firms are in a fluid, global market, where skills and revenues flow from one company to another regardless of international borders. As evidence, U.S. high-tech companies are experiencing enormous growth in sales to overseas customers, in many cases after the domestic market for a product has become saturated. In the knowledge-based model of today's high-tech industry, technology itself breaks down geographic borders. The explosive growth and acceptance of the Internet as a communication vehicle means that information and knowledge can be shared instantaneously from anywhere in the world.

An engineer in Singapore can readily communicate in real time with his counterpart in the United States. No longer is the productivity of a company based on how many warm bodies it can place in a factory. Technology has allowed companies to assemble virtual teams that operate remotely and report to supervisors across town or across oceans.

This element of geographic independence is especially characteristic of high-tech companies, where the product is a technical concept or the knowledge of its employees and can be transferred easily via modern communication devices. Indeed, the rise of "cybercommunities" questions the traditional notion of immigration. The engineer who is offshore but delivers his work by the Internet is, in terms of the work that he has done, an "electronic immigrant." Yet few discussions of the immigration issue deal with this reality of the high-technology workplace.

Finally, the high-tech industry is driven to invest in research and development overseas. In many cases, foreign research and development (R&D) investments are for the purpose of localizing products to specific international markets. Operating a facility in Taiwan allows a company such as Cadence to tailor its products to the technical and cultural requirements of the Taiwanese market, something that could not be accomplished as effectively from within the United States. With so much real and potential revenue growth derived from international markets, foreign R&D investments are a key strategy for high-tech companies. The ability of a technology to be quickly adopted overseas makes meeting these global R&D requirements a market pressure in the high-tech industry. As a result, Cadence employs almost one-fourth of its workforce in sites outside the United States. Investing in global R&D is a practice that transcends national borders and is increasingly common in high tech. The influence throughout the high-tech sector of immigrant talent in guiding this and related processes is probably unprecedented in its scope and authority.

Silicon Valley: A Global Workforce Producing Global Technologies

In short, the United States has captured an early lead in high tech because of its encouragement of technical innovation and entrepreneurial spirit. There is no better example of success in the high-tech industry than Silicon Valley. Along fifty miles of highway between San Jose and San Francisco, Silicon Valley has given birth to more of the world's recent technological innovations than any other geographic region. Companies such as Cadence lead the world in providing highly technical products and services to customers worldwide. The companies of Silicon Valley, many no more than ten years old, contribute to a fast-growing sector of the American economy that is globally competitive and entrepreneurial by nature. High tech has quickly become one of America's model industries because the government has created a regulatory climate that encourages—or at least avoids discouraging—companies to innovate and grow.

Contributing to the global technology incubator of Silicon Valley is a high proportion of foreign nationals working for American companies. In 1996, twenty-three of *Forbes* magazine's two hundred best small companies were immigrant run. Silicon Valley powerhouses such as Intel, Sun Microsystems, Oracle, Cirrus Logic, Solectron, and Lam Research were all either founded or cofounded by immigrants. In fact, almost all high-tech companies, including Cadence Design Systems, rely on foreign nationals in key positions. At Cadence, roughly 30 percent of its U.S.-based employees are not U.S. citizens.

Legal, employment-based immigration has helped fuel the explosive growth of Silicon Valley companies. The H-1B visa was established to allow foreign nationals to be hired into U.S. companies for a period of three to six years on the basis of their exceptional education, training, or experience. The H-1B program recognizes that foreigners provide an important perspective in developing and marketing products for global markets. In addition to temporary H-1B workers, American companies can sponsor foreign nationals in their applications for permanent U.S. residency. Although the United States boasts of its leadership in technology, restrictive immigration policies now threaten to cut off one of the most crucial arteries of high-tech companies: the ability to enlist global talent.

Wanted: The Best Talent Money Can Buy

Politicians and regulators involved in the debate over legal immigration need to recognize and understand not only the new characteristics of the knowledge-based economy but also how high-tech companies are forced to operate by intense recruiting and time-to-market pressures. High tech has become a leading sector of the global economy in just a few decades; it is not unusual for a Silicon Valley company to experience year-over-year doubling of revenues and employee count. As suggested earlier, the mantra of all high-tech companies is growth — steady growth to survive and explosive growth to become a leader. In an industry where employees are far and away the number one asset, high-tech companies need to fill job openings quickly to stay in business. The narrow window of opportunity to market a high-tech product drives the pace at which companies hire. If a company can't find enough good engineers to turn a concept into a shipping product within a reasonable time frame, another company will likely dominate that market area.

Not only do high-tech companies like Cadence need to fill job openings quickly, but they need to hire the best and brightest personnel in order to develop and sell the best products. American high-tech companies are competing both against one another and against a growing number of foreign-based companies for revenue and market share. This also means competing for a global pool of human resources. The explosive growth of high tech has created a global demand for technically knowledgeable employees that exceeds the current supply, especially for positions requiring specialized education.

This labor shortage is evidenced each week by pages of high-tech job openings listed in the *San Jose Mercury News*, Silicon Valley's leading newspaper. Cadence, a company of roughly thirty-two hundred employees, typically has more than three hundred job openings to fill at any given time. Still, even with that many positions available, it takes Cadence an average of four to six weeks to fill each opening. The situation is the same at other successful Silicon Valley companies—they can't hire talented employees quickly enough to keep up with their enormous growth potential.

A change in strategic direction of a number of Asian companies is likely to exacerbate the imbalance between supply and demand for highly skilled labor. Many firms have become successful by means of efficient manufacturing processes; they have been able to produce high-quality technology goods cheaply and quickly. In fact their prowess in this arena has caused an array of products to be treated as commodities. Now, however, firms such as Taiwan-based Acer are moving from manufacturing to design. The new emphasis on the design of technology products (increasingly recognized as a primary source of added value) by a large number of firms will put an even greater premium on technical skill and expertise.

With the high-tech industry's growth outpacing that of the knowledge labor supply, companies are driven to operate by color-blind recruiting practices. In virtually all cases, high-tech companies recruit only on the basis of the company's needs and the applicant's merits. Cadence recruiters are prohibited from inquiring about the race or citizenship of a candidate until they decide that that candidate is worth pursuing based on his or her qualifications. To overlook global talent would be a costly mistake for any high-tech company and one that no successful company has opted to make.

American Education:
Underproducing for the High-Tech Industry

Adding to the recruiting difficulties of American high-tech companies is the fact that the United States lags dangerously behind other countries in contributing to the global pool of knowledge workers. The Third International Mathematics and Science Study, released in November 1996 by the U.S. Department of Education, measures the educational progress of eighth graders in forty-one countries. The United States ranked only twenty-eighth in math and seventeenth in science, whereas Singapore, Japan, and Korea all scored in the top four in both categories. The study suggests that, although American students cover many different topics in math and science, not enough attention and depth are given to the most important topics.

In addition, of nineteen countries recently surveyed by the American Federation of Teachers, the United States pays its high school educators a smaller proportion of its gross domestic product than does any other technologically advanced nation except Italy and Norway. Until the United States dramatically improves its primary and secondary school education in math and science, American high-tech companies will see a growing proportion of qualified job candidates coming from other countries.

Many Americans think that the United States makes up for its struggling secondary school system by having the best universities in the world, offering superior programs in math, science, and engineering. America's universities are indeed among the leading institutions worldwide, but *foreign* students are earning a high proportion of the advanced degrees in fields directly relevant to the fast-growing high-tech industry. According to a 1993 study by the National Science Foundation, among Ph.D. candidates at U.S. universities, 40 percent are foreign born in the engineering and computer science fields and 31 percent are foreign born in mathematical science. By the year 2000,

50 percent of all science and engineering Ph.D. degrees awarded by U.S. universities could go to foreign graduate students by default because not enough American students are enrolled. In addition to the many foreign students in these fields, many professors in engineering and the sciences are foreign born as well.

Compounding the sheer numbers of foreign students receiving engineering and science degrees are cultural differences that influence how recipients apply those degrees. American students are much more likely to apply engineering and science degrees to employment in business and other nonscience fields than are foreign-born students, who lean toward the practice of math and science disciplines. Even among engineering graduates, Americans are more motivated to take "creative" engineering jobs in specialties such as Internet and multimedia development, whereas foreign nationals are more likely to engage in "hard" engineering disciplines like semiconductor or circuit design. In this setting it is inevitable that the labor needs of Cadence and other companies for leading engineers and other knowledge workers are in many cases being filled by qualified and readily available foreign nationals. U.S. politicians and regulators need to realize—and give voice to the idea—that most American high-tech companies are making use of employment-based immigration programs not to undercut the American worker but rather to fill strategic positions critical to the company's success.

American High-Tech Companies Rely on Foreign Nationals to Succeed

Consider the case of Cadence Design Systems as a successful, responsible Silicon Valley company. Cadence has grown to lead the global electronic design and automation market by hiring the best talent available to fill a growing number of job openings. Its growth has been exponential, rising out of near obscurity ten years ago to become the market leader in its industry segment. Today the company ranks among the top ten software companies worldwide, with 1996 revenues surpassing $700 million.

Currently, out of approximately 3,200 total employees at Cadence, only 159 (or 5 percent) hold H-1B temporary employment visas. Those 159 employees all fill positions crucial to Cadence's success. Fifty percent work in product development, 30 percent work in consulting engineering, and 20 percent occupy other roles. These employees are paid at least prevailing wages and oftentimes even higher salaries as the market demands. Their employment creates jobs for other developers and consultants, many of whom are American workers.

The notion that Cadence hires foreign nationals to undercut qualified American candidates is absurd considering the high average wage and increased procedural time and cost associated with recruiting H-1B visa holders. In the high-tech industry, where employees and knowledge are among a company's most critical assets, hiring cheap labor simply does not pay. Cadence lives by a color-blind recruiting practice whereby job candidates are evaluated on their ability to fill company needs. Nationality is never an issue. Other successful high-tech companies adhere to the same color-blind hiring policy, not because it serves any existing cultural biases but rather because it effectively increases a company's global competitiveness.

And the task is not as easy as some proponents of stiffer immigration policy might think. For example, the belief of some that the United States is the ultimate lure for foreign workers in high-tech industries is a naive proposition. To combat America's early lead in the global high-tech market, many countries have implemented probusiness regulatory environments aimed at increasing their share of that market. These countries, many of which are in Asia where a high number of qualified job candidates originate, are seeking to keep their own citizens from filling job openings in the United States. Infrastructure investments, benign tax treatments, and research and development assistance are all part of the mix. Instead of establishing anti-immigration policies aimed at keeping foreign nationals out of American companies, U.S. policymakers should be concerned with keeping the talent we currently employ within U.S. borders. This is not a call for heavy-handed government interference in commerce, à la the corporatist schemes that have worked so poorly in the past. It is, however, a plea for a commonsense immigration policy.

Restricting Employment-Based Immigration: A Misguided Policy

The observation is simple enough: The xenophobia underlying today's immigration reform movements threatens to erase America's early lead in high tech. In their misguided attempts to protect the American worker, politicians and regulators who propose cuts in legal, employment-based immigration would do immeasurable harm to both American companies and the American worker. By further restricting the number of H-1B holders who can enter the United States to fill key positions, the government threatens to place the United States at a disadvantage in its ability to attract and retain valuable knowledge workers. Even placing increased bureaucracy and regulation on the process of recruiting H-1B workers can jeopardize the ability of American high-tech companies to meet intense time-to-market pressures for delivering products. If a company has a product concept and needs key engineering or other technical personnel to make that concept a reality, it is in the interest of both the company and the nation for that company to be able to hire the best person for the job in the most timely manner.

If American companies are denied the opportunity to hire as many foreign nationals as they need into key positions, the consequences will be shared by both business and government. When American companies cannot fulfill their needs on American soil, they will undoubtedly shift operations to other countries to meet demand. An exodus of American high-tech operations to other countries would damage the U.S. economy, sending valuable tax dollars and other expenditures outside the United States. Policymakers must recognize the risk of losing American business to foreign lands if companies cease to enjoy the same growth opportunities historically afforded in the United States.

Restricting employment-based immigration would have serious repercussions for the American worker. In sports, athletes improve most when given the opportunity to play on a team alongside the best in the world. This is true in business as well. In the high-tech arena, American workers have enjoyed an advantage in recent years because they have been able to work alongside the best and brightest from whatever country. The numerous instances of immigrants founding successful Silicon Valley companies, as mentioned, offer perhaps the best example. The American employees hired to help those immigrants launch their companies and products undoubtedly benefited from the opportunity to work alongside some of the best entrepreneurs in high tech. In the majority of cases, the hiring of H-1B workers to fill key positions in American high-tech companies creates jobs for American workers that might not have existed otherwise.

If regulators truly want to crack down on abuses of the employment-based immigration program, they could target H-1B-dependent operations where more than 20 percent of employees are temporary visa holders. These companies are suspected of ignoring prevailing wage standards and hiring foreign nationals to fill numerous job openings quickly and cheaply. A few companies that meet this H-1B-dependent profile have tarnished high-tech's reputation and created negative exposure in the press for the high-tech industry in general. Targeting these companies for investigation, and leaving responsible companies like Cadence to selectively utilize productive, employment-based immigration programs, are the best options for America.

A Balanced Immigration Policy Fosters American High-Tech Growth

Rather than further restrict legal, employment-based immigration—the form of immigration most beneficial to America—politicians and regulators must implement a rational immigration policy that balances the market realities facing American companies with the needs of our society and workers. Simply placing artificial hiring restrictions on businesses ignores the fluidity of global markets and deprives American companies of their right to compete. A rational and productive immigration policy, in contrast, examines the immediate and future needs of American companies along with the effect any policy would have on American workers. By carefully weighing the benefits and drawbacks—both economic and cultural—of employment-based immigration, politicians and regulators can implement immigration laws that continue to encourage growth and leadership for American companies in global markets.

At a time when high technology is revolutionizing the planet and contributing billions of dollars and thousands of jobs to the American economy, keeping American high-tech companies globally competitive should be a national priority. The high-tech industry, just some thirty years old, is still in its infancy. Although some of the companies in this sector have already grown to be among the biggest in the world, the enormous potential for future growth in high tech makes most other industrial sectors green with envy. Not since the industrial revolution has America been so well poised to lead the world into a new era. Other nations, however, realize this and will fight tooth and nail to climb into the upper echelon of twenty-first-century high-tech leadership. Opportunity knocks, and now it is up to American policymakers to create the regulatory climate that will allow American business to answer resoundingly. U.S. law concerning employment-based immigration has a huge impact on the future of high tech.

Today's reality is that, with a shortage of highly skilled, technical workers to fill key positions, foreign nationals provide a critical knowledge injection that allows American high-tech companies to prosper and grow. Regulators should leave the doors open for responsible companies to recruit the best talent in the world. Affording American companies that opportunity will boost the nation's economy, position the United States for continued global leadership, and create new jobs for American workers. It is difficult to fathom why these would not be the goals of American government.

American High Tech at the Crossroads

In many ways, the American high-tech industry is at a critical, formative juncture, much like that of a family-operated business in its third generation. The founder had a great idea, rounded up some capital, and in his lifetime grew the business to be a profitable leader in its niche. Perhaps a son or daughter was intimately involved in the business as well and took over the reins when the founder retired. That second-generation family member continued to grow the business and maintain leadership based on family support and additional hired labor. But, as is often the case with growing family businesses, the third-generation leader lacked the interest, talent, or capacity to take an already prospering business to the next level of success. At this point, the family has a big decision to make. Do they compromise the growth of the company and the prosperity of its employees by keeping the reins in family hands, or do they hire a CEO from outside the family to guide the third generation in growing the business to new proportions, becoming more profitable and employing more workers in the process?

This is the crossroads American high-tech business has reached. Much like that family-operated company, the United States must decide whether it is willing to look outside its borders for the critical knowledge and talent to help drive its continued growth and leadership in high tech. If it hires the outside CEO—allowing companies to recruit top engineers and other professionals through the H-1B program—America has the potential to increase its lead over other nations in the burgeoning global high-tech market. If America elects to ignore its growth potential by placing greater restrictions on foreign talent entering the country, it must be willing to lose its precious share of the fastest-growing industry to other countries willing to enlist the best.

Making the right decision requires the attention and input of business leaders, academics, politicians, and regulators. Although illegal immigration has become a red-hot item on the American agenda and occupies the thoughts of preeminent thinkers, legal, employment-based immigration has kept a low profile in corporate human resource departments and concerned government agencies. By recognizing its profound effect on America's future, and by committing time and resources to the employment-based immigration debate, business and public affairs leaders can elevate the issue to the level where big decisions are made. Only then will the United States be capable of implementing a policy that empowers both our economy and our society.

Peter Duignan and
L. H. Gann

CONCLUSION

The Immigration Workshop held October 17–18, 1996, at the Hoover Institution brought together prominent researchers, Silicon Valley executives, and advocates and opponents of immigration. Immigration advocates called for increasing the flow of highly skilled workers while decreasing the flow of unskilled people. They argued that, overall, immigrants did not take jobs from Americans or create unemployment but instead added wealth to the United States and created jobs and businesses. George Borjas of the John F. Kennedy School of Government at Harvard University claimed that most recent unskilled immigrants (in the last thirty years) were less well educated relative to contemporary natives than were past immigrants. He also contended that they added less than 1 percent to the GNP or to economic productivity. Julian Simon of the University of Maryland disagreed that recent immigrants were less well educated than previous ones, and he opposed the suggestion by Norman Matloff of the University of California at Davis (UC-Davis) that the United States limit the number of foreign students educated in American graduate schools. Education was one of our best exports, Simon said, and many of these foreign students stayed and added to American productivity.

Restrictionists such as Peter Brimelow, senior editor of *Forbes* and *National Review*, and Roy Beck, editor of the *Social Contract*, argued that the large numbers of immigrants would make whites a minority by 2050 and would disunite us, breed multiculturalism, harm the environment, and impoverish native unskilled workers and African Americans. Whereas Stuart Anderson of the Cato Institute said it was a myth that America had too many foreign people with doctoral degrees in science and engineering, Norman Matloff of UC-Davis said there were too many foreigners keeping jobs out of the hands of native-born American engineers and lowering their wages. Silicon Valley executives not only denied Matloff's charges but contended that foreign engineers and software experts filled a shortage and helped the American economy grow. If we could not import skilled people because of shortages in the United States, we would have to go offshore, maintained Joseph Costello, CEO of Cadence Design Systems of San Jose.

George Borjas and Ron Unz, cofounders of the Palo Alto–based Wall Street Analytics, conceded that some people became unemployed and were hurt by job competition from immigrants but said that was true of every progressive economic policy in a free market society. But, overall, Unz (and others at the workshop) claimed that immigration benefited Americans and the economy and eventually even those temporarily hurt. Like many other scholars of immigration, Simons, Unz, and Borjas claimed that the negative consequences affected only a few people while most benefited—as they had from free trade—from falling consumer costs and rising productivity, which resulted in job growth.

Even though the debate over immigration had been intense in Congress, congressional reform has failed to address the major issue—how many and who? Stephen Moore of the Cato Institute wondered why we made it so difficult for skilled, talented people to come to the United States. The restrictionists countered by insisting we had too many coming in and that they were hurting the native-born skilled and the environment.

Annelise Anderson, a Hoover senior research fellow who chaired a panel, said that the nation as a whole had no long-term model that looked at how much immigration would be good for the United States in a global economy with competition for capital that flowed easily across borders to places with low wages and lenient regulations. The Silicon Valley problem of finding and keeping skilled labor was, Anderson concluded, a bellwether of a gradual U.S. adjustment to world labor markets.

Although President Clinton signed a law against illegal immigrants in September 1996, the debate over immigration has been renewed. The issue will be legal immigration and the number of people who should be admitted into this country.[1] Both Democrats and Republicans seem ready to reduce legal immigration as recommended by the Jordan Commission in 1994. But there will be stiff opposition to such legislation from ethnic and immigrants' rights lobbies and from businesses. The Immigration and Naturalization Service (INS) reckons about one million people entered the United States in 1996, an increase of 250,000 from 1995. The sharp rise in legal immigration is blamed on the 1986 amnesty law that legalized 2.6 million illegal aliens, many of whom became citizens and then brought in family members, for whom there is no numerical limit.

Congress has become concerned about the long-term impact of immigration on the country's population growth, the social costs of the system, and the loss of control over further immigrants to the United States through family reunification. At present that "chain migration" allows waves of immigrants to bring in their relatives, many of whom are old, unskilled, speak no English, and become a charge on the welfare system. Cuts in immigration would reduce family reunification or the intake of political refugees and could prevent businesses from recruiting skilled foreigners. No consensus has been reached yet on

---

1. William Branigin, "Immigration Issues Await New Congress," *Washington Post*, 18 November 1996.

the size of cuts in immigration numbers or where to cut—on family reunification, on employment-related immigrants, or on refugees. The problem will not go away, and the influx grows each year and not just from legal immigration.

On February 7, 1997, the INS reported an illegal immigrant population of five million, which increases by about 300,000 people a year. Since about one million legals and asylum seekers come in each year, minus the 200,000 or so a year who emigrate, this leaves an annual addition of about 1.1 million immigrants. Another 650,000 people a year come in for three to ten years under various "nonimmigrant" visa categories, perhaps half of whom stay on. As a result of all these immigrant streams, the Census Bureau estimates that about one-third of the current U.S. population growth derives from immigration. If U.S.-born children of recent immigrants are excluded, more than half the population growth comes through immigration. Levels of immigration are double what they were twenty years ago; hence the Census Bureau has significantly revised its population growth projections for the twenty-first century. The bureau now projects a U.S. population in 2050 of 400 million (not 300 million). Some argue it will be even higher—more than half a billion. This population growth by 2050 will be generated mostly (93 percent) by immigrants who arrived after 1991.

Instead of pushing a lower number of immigrants (from 1.1 million a year to say 500,000 or so), Senator Edward M. Kennedy favors only a slight reduction in legal immigration but a sharp crackdown on employers who hire illegals, in order to protect American workers. Other Democrats would roll back the 1996 welfare restrictions on legal immigrants. Republicans, in contrast, will try again to allow states to deny free public education to illegal children and to end citizenship for children born in the United States to illegal immigrant parents.

What's to Be Done?

Who then has the better case—the advocates of immigration or the anti-immigrationists? An answer is hard to give because there are all too many unknowns. How many aliens reside illegally in the United States? What is their average income? How much do they pay in the way of taxes? How much do they use taxpayer-funded services? How many, in particular, manage to live on welfare? What exactly is the role of immigrant entrepreneurship? How will any individual immigrant succeed once he or she arrives in the United States? No expert can be sure. No immigrant selection board could have predicted that Andrew Carnegie, a youthful Scottish immigrant employed in a U.S. cotton factory, would ever become a rich man. Yet Carnegie turned into one of the United States' greatest industrial magnates, a man who gave employment to a huge army of workers.

Nevertheless, agreement can be reached, perhaps, on a number of specific issues. Under international as well as domestic law, the United States, as a sovereign power, has the right to control its own frontiers. Most Americans feel somewhat ambivalent—their own forebears may, after all, have come from abroad. But respondents in public opinion polls (61 percent in 1994) wish to restrict immigration[2] and believe that the present influx (estimated to exceed 900,000 legal immigrants in 1996) is too high. This view is shared by most Hispanics, who support limits on immigration and welfare—much to the Hispanic opinion leaders' disapproval.[3]

In the past fifteen years the U.S. labor market has been transformed—the demand for skilled labor has increased while the demand for unskilled labor has diminished. High tech and the export trade have

---

2. "Immigration," *American Enterprise*, January–February 1994, p. 97.

3. Jonathan Tilove, "Poll of Four States' Hispanic Americans Yields Surprise," *Jersey Journal* (New Jersey), 4 March 1996, p. 12.

transformed the American workplace—with stark implications for U.S. immigration policies. The United States will find jobs for skilled people. However, the United States does not require many unskilled workers and in future will need even fewer. Current studies show a lack of job opportunities and declining wages for the least-skilled workers and for those who do not have a command of English. Yet the INS still lets in mostly unskilled or semiskilled people and the old. (The great majority of Mexican immigrants in the United States have less than nine years of schooling.) Reuniting families is not a sufficient reason to burden the U.S. economy and welfare system with elderly, unskilled, semiliterate, non-English speakers.

Americans are particularly opposed to illegal immigration, though not to undocumented aliens as individuals. (The ordinary citizen will not report an illegal alien to the police or the INS unless the citizen has a personal quarrel with that particular newcomer.)[4] Illegal immigration is opposed not only by whites but also by minority groups and even by legal immigrants. (California's Proposition 187, directed against publicly funded social benefits for illegal immigrants, enjoyed support among 54 percent of all immigrants, 56 percent of black Americans, 57 percent of Asians, and 59 percent of the general population.)[5] The general public's dislike for illegal immigration is fully justified, for the undocumented alien's very presence in this country offends against its laws. Every sovereign country in the world claims the right to control its own borders—including Mexico, which treats its own illegal immigrants harshly while lecturing the United States on the subject. Mexico called the new U.S. laws, in effect in 1997, anti-immigrant, discriminatory, xenophobic, and damaging to U.S.-Mexican relations. Mexican lawmakers fear the United States will deport hundreds of thousands of Mexican illegal aliens. Central American leaders also raised this fear

---

4. See Edwin Harwood, *In Liberty's Shadow* (Stanford: Hoover Institution Press, 1986).

5. *Sacramento Bee*, 13 November 1994.

during Clinton's tour of Central America in May 1997. Nor do we have any patience with those Chicano nationalists who claim for Mexican immigrants a special privilege on the grounds that the southwestern states of the United States once belonged to Mexico. The Southwest was conquered by the United States, developed by the United States, and will stay American.

The Illegal Immigration Reform and Immigrant Responsibility Act of 1996 (IIRIRA) went into effect on April 1, 1997. IIRIRA has a new "expedited removal" process at ports of entry, new grounds of inadmissibility, and a new removal system to replace the old deportation and exclusion systems. The 1996 act toughens penalties on illegal immigrants and threatens immediate deportation if illegals do not turn themselves in. Under the new law, illegals who overstay for more than 180 days will be denied an entry visa for three years; if they overstay for 365 days, they are barred for ten years. Under IIRIRA, it is more difficult for aliens to avoid removal from the United States. The INS has gotten court approval to give an alien two choices: to leave voluntarily at his expense and not be barred from returning to the United States or to be removed at government expense and be barred from the United States for ten years.

The 1996 law makes it difficult for class actions to be filed against the INS; in the past such class actions have led to court decisions favoring Central Americans and Haitians. In June 1997, however, a Florida judge stopped the deportation of forty thousand Central Americans despite IIRIRA.

The sponsorship requirements of IIRIRA have been challenged by advocacy goups claiming that Mexican and Salvadoreans have insufficient income to sponsor their relatives for admission. Under IIRIRA all family reunification must have U.S. sponsors who are legally bound to support the immigrant(s) at 125 percent of the U.S. poverty line, and the sponsor must prove that he has an income of at least 125 percent of the U.S. poverty line for himself, his dependents, and the sponsored immigrants. These provisions were intended to slow down family reunification of impoverished people who might become dependent on U.S. welfare programs. As of January 1995, more than 3.7 million foreigners who applied to immigrate are waiting to enter the United States. Almost all the backlog is for the family reunification category: 1.6 million adult brothers and sisters, 1.1 million spouses and children, and 500,000 unmarried adult children. Over one-fourth of this backlog are Mexicans, and they must wait at least four or five years.

The INS in fiscal year 1996 increased its apprehensions and sanctions to 1.6 million aliens in the United States, up from 1.3 million in 1995. Most returned voluntarily; 72,500 fought their return to Mexico. The Border Patrol caught 380,000 aliens in the first four months of fiscal year 1997, down from 435,000 in the first four months of fiscal year 1995. (Total number of apprehensions in 1996 was 1,507,020.)

Last year's immigration act restricted many deportees' access to appeals and barred suits by people placed into new "expedited removal" proceedings at airports and borders. Also prohibited were class-action complaints against INS policies. In San Francisco, a three-judge panel in May 1997 ruled that Congress acted legally in 1996 in restricting court reviews for some 400,000 late amnesty applications for the 1986 amnesty law. In ten years 2.7 million illegals received legal status under IRCA at a cost of $78.7 billion, or $29,148 per illegal.[6]

The INS is lax in finding and deporting illegal aliens who defraud the United States by obtaining documents from corrupt officials and even commit crimes in the United States. The INS seldom deports criminals after they are released from prison. In one INS office 4,100 work permits were issued to ineligible aliens.[7] The INS defends its poor record in finding and deporting illegals by claiming lack of detention space, work overload, the deportation system, and underfunding. There are, at present, almost 500,000 illegal aliens tied up in deportation hearings.

---

6. See the *Los Angeles Times*, 1 May 1997.
7. Walter Branigin, *Washington Post*, 24 October 1996.

Georges Vernez, in a 1996 report of the Rand Corporation, "National Security Migration: How Strong the Link?" argues that there are two immigration-related threats to national security. One is potential loss of credibility in the federal government's ability to protect its citizens from such unwanted elements as illegal immigrants, drug traffickers, terrorists. Inaction or ineffectiveness in reestablishing and maintaining this credibility could become a serious threat to internal stability and confidence in the government. The second threat is the possibility of a massive, uncontrolled flow of migrants across the Mexican border. (An estimated one million people cross the Mexican border illegally each year and are caught, but about 300,000 get through.) If Mexico's relatively peaceful political transition were to be interrupted, and its economy were to collapse, the flight from Mexico to the United States might become uncontrollable. Moreover, the ongoing concentration of migrants in the western regions of the United States might lead to a divergence of interests between the eastern and western parts of the country. In the East, English would continue to dominate, as the East would still see its future tied to Europe's. In the West, by contrast, English and Spanish would compete for dominance, while the region as a whole would see its future linked to the Pacific Rim. This divergence would grow over time as an ever-increasing share of the population would have its roots in Mexico, Central and South America, the Philippines, Japan, Korea, and China. Already the great majority of the 6.5 million immigrants into California are from Latino and Asian countries. The children of these immigrants account for almost two-thirds of the growth in the population of California.

We are in general agreement with the Personal Responsibility and Work Opportunity Reconciliation Act (1996), which imposes serious restrictions on welfare assistance for certain legal immigrants as well as illegal aliens. Aid should not be available to newcomers unless they have lived in the United States and paid taxes in the United States for a reasonable period. But, in our opinion, some allowance should be made for children, including the children of illegal immigrants. They should be admitted to public schools, lest they become part of a juvenile illiterate and unskilled underclass. We need more skilled workers for the future, not uneducated alienated ones. The same exception should be made for emergency treatment in hospitals. We do not expect a physician or a nurse about to give emergency treatment to a sick person to ask for that patient's passport. Public health of the entire population should be protected; legals and illegals cannot be separated for health services.

The August 22, 1996, welfare law cut off many federal benefits from noncitizens. Ever since, the Clinton administration has been trying to restore some of those benefits. The Congressional Budget Office noted that 500,000 legal immigrants will lose SSI benefits this summer under the 1996 welfare law. (Indigent elderly and the disabled get up to $484 a month, $726 a month for a couple.)

During 1997 numerous suggested changes worked their way through Congress. The Clinton administration and congressional leaders agreed to restore disability and health benefits to several hundred thousand legal immigrants as part of a deal on the five-year balanced budget plan. (The House passed one such resolution on May 20, 1997 [333 to 99].) The amount of money to be spent was $14 million. Republicans are less supportive than Democrats, but some benefits are likely to be restored, that is, SSI and Medicaid benefits for old and disabled legal immigrants.

The Democrats want to restore SSI and Medicaid not only to all disabled legal immigrants but also to those who became disabled after August 1996. The Republicans, in contrast, would only restore benefits to those getting them up to August 22, not to those who became disabled after that date. The Republican bill would also deny legal immigrants SSI benefits if the individual who sponsored them earns more than 150 percent of the federal poverty level (about $20,000 a year). The Shaw Bill would make new immigrants sign legal documents swearing that they will not become public charges while they are noncitizens and making them subject to deportation if in their first three years they receive welfare for more than twelve months.

How should illegal aliens be traced? We welcome the Clinton administration's recent moves to strengthen the INS and increase its personnel. We reject, however, employer sanctions. As Stephen H. Legomsky, a distinguished U.S. legal scholar points out in this book, employer sanctions have indeed created new jobs for Americans; unfortunately, these are in a burgeoning industry that manufactures those fraudulent documents that are now presented en masse by undocumented job seekers to employers. It should not be an employer's responsibility to act as an unpaid immigration inspector. Employer sanctions seem to us just another form of an unfunded mandate. Nor have we any trust in projects designed to set up a central, nationwide registry to create a national identification card. Such systems smack of a police state and would not be acceptable to the majority of U.S. citizens. Such systems, moreover, take no account of the unreliable nature of computer storage. Computerized systems face the ever-present dangers of human error, electronic breakdown, and even sabotage through the introduction of "viruses." American citizens seeking jobs should not be exposed to the vagaries of any such systems. Nor should Hispanic Americans have to "prove" they are legal! To deal with illegal aliens is the task of the INS. This agency deserves to be well financed and well staffed. It also merits support by the courts—that is, quick hearings to determine legality—and then rapid deportation. Coordination, moreover, must improve among government agencies. Welfare officers, police officers, and immigration officers should be encouraged and empowered to exchange information efficiently on who is, or is not, a legal resident in the United States.

Should children born to illegal aliens in the United States be entitled to U.S. citizenship? At present they are thus entitled under the U.S. Constitution. Conservative critics thus call for an amendment to take away this right. We sympathize with them when they argue that those who violate U.S. law should not thereby gain benefits for their child or children. But the Constitution should only be amended for reasons of extreme urgency. This is not one of them.

What of the economic benefits of immigration? In the olden days, immigration remained unregulated by the state; immigrants came when jobs were plentiful, and they ceased to come or left when times were hard. The federal government provided no benefits to newcomers who relied for assistance on their kinfolk, neighbors, churches, self-help societies, or at best on local authorities controlled by organizations such as Tammany Hall. Now—by contrast—the United States has an elaborate welfare structure operating alike on a federal, a state, and a local level. Immigrants naturally make use of such assistance. As poor immigrants qualify for citizenship, they are likely to go on supporting the welfare state. This preference is understandable in terms of their own interests but does not serve the interests of taxpayers at large.

What of the poor and unqualified who wish to come to the United States? Emma Lazarus expressed admirable sentiments in her sonnet, engraved on a memorial tablet on the Statue of Liberty in New York: "Give me your tired, your poor, / Your huddled masses yearning to breathe free." Unfortunately the sonnet is a poor guide to present policy. We ourselves would rather bid the world's huddled masses to stay at home and send us the educated and skilled. The great majority of the world's population is desperately poor and uneducated by U.S. standards. If the United States were to follow a truly nondiscriminatory admissions policy, it would have to admit every newcomer who chooses to come to these shores. The United States' own poor and unskilled would be the first to object. Public opinion overwhelmingly demands a more restrictive policy that also applies to the admission of immigrants' family members. Family members are now so broadly defined that it is the immigrants themselves who decide who should, or should not, be accepted. The system needs to be altered in such a way that only members of a citizen's immediate nuclear family are eligible for admission and that once admitted the new entrants must not be allowed to become charges on the U.S. taxpayer for at least ten years.

We once again emphasize, therefore, that the United States should cease to be a welfare agency for poor and aged foreigners. (To give just one example, between 1982 and 1994 the percentage of senior immigrants receiving supplemental security income [SSI] went from 6 percent to 30 percent.) Social benefits such as Medicare, Medicaid, and SSI should be restricted to means-tested U.S. citizens; longtime taxpaying legal immigrants were excluded in 1996. Recent legal immigrants who rushed to become citizens in 1996 (1.2 million) should have had to wait ten years before qualifying for welfare benefits.

Between September and October 1996, more than 310,000 immigrants became citizens, at least partly to avoid losing state and federal benefits. (They would have lost Aid to Families with Dependent Children, SSI, and food stamp benefits.) According to Michael Fix of the Urban Institute, recent U.S. policy induced people to become citizens in order to keep or get benefits, not to accept American values and institutions. The welfare bill has inadvertently helped produce profound changes in the meaning of citizenship. In addition, the INS had been carrying out an active campaign for naturalization and had organized mass swearing-in ceremonies, never mind whether the prospective citizens spoke or read English or knew much about American history and government. (Democratic Party zealots were observed signing up the new citizens to vote—80–85 percent were expected to vote for the Democratic Party, especially in California.) By forcing people to choose citizenship or lose their benefits, the government has inadvertently forced many legal immigrants to stay in the United States.

In more general terms, courts and legislatures alike should be discouraged from further diminishing the difference in status between resident aliens and citizens. The public should likewise insist that U.S. law be upheld—no further amnesties for illegal aliens, which naturally raise the expectation that illegal conduct will once more be rewarded in future. Stop the reuniting of families with elderly relatives; let in only the immediate family members and the skilled and educated; lower the immigration quota from 1.0 million to 0.5 million or less for a period of years.

The United States, in our opinion, should also restrict the right of asylum. Most professed asylum seekers are, in fact, economic refugees. Moreover, spokespersons for asylum rights keep trying to extend the criteria according to which asylum seekers ought to be admitted. Many foreign governments discriminate against homosexuals, persecute feminists, imprison abortionists. Ought the United States then to admit all foreign homosexuals, feminists, and abortionists? How about victims of ritual genital mutilation of women in Africa? Should they enjoy asylum rights as well? As Mark Krikorian, an immigration expert, puts it, for many U.S. advocates of asylum rights "the battle over asylum seems to have far less to do with giving shelter to persecuted individuals than with some larger quest to remake the American legal norms and establish victim status for a number of officially recognized groups."[8]

What of immigration's economic benefits and economic burdens? As we have said before, a definitive answer is hard to give, as opponents and proponents of immigration alike must make do with inadequate statistics. Overall immigrants make a positive contribution to the United States, and their economic contributions are great. Common sense, however, suggests that the United States should not admit so many unskilled workers at a time when the United States' own unskilled poor are increasingly hard to employ as industrial jobs diminish in number and when the United States increasingly depends on high-tech and information industries requiring a well-qualified workforce. Unskilled Americans are the most vulnerable people within the U.S. army of labor; for political, though not for economic, reasons, they merit protection in the struggle for scarce jobs. To admit more poor people to the United States, moreover, widens the growing numerical disproportion between the poor and the rich—another reason for keep-

8. Mark Krikorian, "Who Deserves Asylum?" *Commentary*, June 1996, p. 54,

ing out poor aliens—except as guest workers on limited contracts. Even in agriculture, does the United States really need 500,000 or so braceros each year? If wages were doubled, native labor would go to the fields, according to Philip Martin, an agricultural economist at the University of California at Davis. Doubling wages would have little effect on the prices of food in the markets because labor costs are less than 6 percent of total costs.

U.S. policy, therefore, should favor immigrants with special educational skills, money, or proven entrepreneurial talent. Highly qualified immigrants do compete with highly qualified natives. But natives enjoy natural advantages: they know the country, they know the language, they know conditions. Recruitment costs for foreigners are higher than for natives; to recruit a foreigner entails more paperwork. To recruit a foreigner also may entail extra costs in moving the foreigner's family to this country. Particularly valuable are those highly qualified foreign postgraduates already in this country. (Half the Ph.D.'s in computer science awarded in the United States go to foreign students who then mostly stay in the United States—to this country's advantage.) The present ceiling on skilled immigrants is 140,000 a year. This should be raised and the process made easier, quicker, and less expensive.

REFUGEES

The global flow of asylum seekers, political refugees, and displaced people declined in 1996 to thirty-four million people—a seven-year low—as a result of Western nations discouraging people from seeking safe havens in the United States, Germany, France, and Britain. All in all, the World Refugee Survey lists fifteen countries where guarantees of political asylum have deteriorated. Repatriations have also caused the lower figure of refugees; for example, nearly two million people were sent back to Rwanda and other African countries. Although the United States gives the most money to refugee relief agencies ($389 million in 1996), it is ninth on a per capita basis. The Rwanda refugees appear to be the worst off, as Zaire's new rulers have been accused of letting Tutsi soldiers kill tens of thousands of Rwanda Hutu refugees in Zaire and forcing more than one million to return.

The U.S. asylum law, which went into effect in April 1997, has made it harder to apply for asylum by summarily deporting people arriving at airports and ports with false documents. German authorities have been denying asylum to thousands of so-called refugees since 1994 and are withdrawing asylum for Bosnians and sending them back to an unstable, dangerous Bosnia.[9]

On June 6, 1997, the bipartisan commission on immigration released a report on reforming refugee policy in the post–cold war era by having the White House take charge of refugee affairs through a new office in the National Security Council to coordinate all aspects of the problem. The nine-member Commission on Immigration Reform was established in 1990 and in 1995 issued a controversial report that called for major cuts in legal immigration. In this recently issued study the commission sought to end abuses of the asylum system whereby thousands of people are admitted on false claims of persecution in their homelands. Most were not political refugees at all but were fleeing because of economics, their homosexuality, or fear of cultural practices such as clitoral surgery, common in some African societies. The report called for rapid hearing and speedy deportation of rejected asylum seekers. Chairwoman Shirley M. Hufstedler insists that the United States needs "a comprehensive and coherent refugee policy" but did not mention the number of refugees to be admitted. (A 1995 report set a target of fifty thousand refugee admissions a year—about half of recent levels.) The report set a floor, not a ceiling, for future admissions and proposed a new system of priorities—at the top those who need urgent rescue down to those who are "safe" but need resettlement. Unaccountably, the commission did not deal with the growing num-

---

9. Associated Press, "Global Refugee Flow Declining," 19 May 1997.

bers of people who claim refugee status on grounds of homosexuality, female genital mutilation, forced birth control, or spousal abuse. Restrictionists were disappointed that the commission did not take up this disturbing definition of persecution. After all, as Mark Krikorian, director of the Center for Immigration Studies, noted, the world is full of refugees, and the United States has to carefully decide who should be let in.[10] The 1996 law calls for the quick deportation of illegals or refugees from Central America and Mexico. As a result arrests and deportation of illegals were stepped up during 1997. But judges in various states have been delaying deportations of thousands. The issue is a major concern to Central American nations and Mexico, which fear the return of hundreds of thousands of people who fled the wars in El Salvador and Nicaragua or the economic decline of Mexico. A judge in Florida stopped the deportation of forty thousand Central Americans in June 1997.

HIV victims have similarly claimed and been granted asylum. To many observers, asylum on the grounds of persecution for sexuality or gender is an abuse of the law and could open the immigration floodgates to gay and lesbian HIV positives around the world. The Clinton administration in January 1996 decided to allow HIV infection as a basis for asylum in response to a recommendation of an HIV AIDS advisory council. This in opposition to a 1996 law whereby Congress had barred aliens with HIV or AIDS from being admitted to the United States. The result is that the president is saying that if you manage to sneak into the United States we will give asylum even though HIV has made you excludable. As a result, more gay and lesbian people are applying for asylum.

The immigration problem is then complicated by the refugee problem. Few wish for any more waves of refugees now that the cold war is over and flight from Indo-China has slowed. Many in the United

---

10. William Branigan, "White House Leadership Sought on Refugee Matters," *Washington Post*, 7 January 1997.

States not only want fewer immigrants but also fewer refugees. Why not settle people persecuted because of their race, religion, nationality, or class near the country from which they flee, in regions which are likely to have similar cultural and linguistic values? Caring for political refugees in their regions is less expensive and may be more humane than uprooting them and admitting them to the United States.

Refugees are only about one-tenth of the total immigrant population; the other nine-tenths come to the United States for economic opportunities and for political reasons or to join family members. Nevertheless, refugees represent more than 100,000 new immigrants a year, and elderly refugees are heavy users of welfare benefits. In 1994 the U.S. ceiling for refugees was 121,000, but only 112,500 were accepted, mostly from Russia and Eastern Europe but also from East Asia, Latin America, the Middle East, and Africa. In 1995 the ceiling was set at 112,000, and in our opinion this figure is still too high. U.N. authorities estimate that fifty million people are exposed to political persecution, that perhaps twenty-three million refugees have left their countries, and that another twenty-five million are displaced within their own countries in U.N. "safe havens." The United States can admit but a small fraction.

Carnegie Endowment for International Peace scholar Kathleen Newland cites three reasons the United States is turning against refugees. Refugees were welcomed during the cold war because they were voting with their feet and discrediting communism. Now, however, political refugees are no longer popular in Afghanistan, Thailand, Indonesia, Germany, Switzerland, or Canada. (Germany, once one of the world's most generous countries, has amended its constitution to limit the right to seek asylum.) The "right to leave" is no longer a principle acclaimed worldwide. After all, if people have a right to leave, they have a right to go somewhere, and the choice is usually the wealthy West. Second, the United States is understandably reluctant to take on regimes whose oppressive practices cause refugees to leave. Humanitarian interventionism has been costly and ineffectual. U.S.

intervention may have helped in Haiti but not in Somalia and probably not in Bosnia.

Legitimate political refugees should still be admitted to the United States but in smaller numbers now that the cold war is over. Studies show that most refugees in time become economically self-sufficient but that the old and disabled do not. Nevertheless, refugees in general stay on welfare longer and use it more than native borns. (Some groups, for example, the Hmong people from the Laotian highlands, have had more problems in adapting to life in a modern society than others.)

Standards are now being tightened on asylum seekers (although one federal judge has stopped the INS officials at airports from deporting them without a trial). Refugee advocates claim this would mean the persecuted will not be able to seek asylum in the United States. To us, interdiction at the airports, harbors, or borders seems the best solution. (Most refugees and some legals and illegals probably come in through airports and harbors, as do tourists, students, and businesspeople.) The United States is far away for most people and costly and difficult to assimilate into for the old, unskilled, and backward who make up the great number of refugees in the world. Rather than come to the United States and be supported at great cost, refugees should settle down near their mother country.

The Swiss Academy for Development (SAD) has devised a plan that would integrate refugees into the host country where they have settled if there is little or no chance of their returning to their homeland. Four pilot projects along the Iran/Iraq border (among the world leaders in displaced persons, with 2.5 million in border camps) were given financial help to build housing and to create training programs for local business. So far this approach has been successful and appears superior to the United Nations High Commission for Refugees' (UNHCR's) approach of treating refugees as temporary problems. Better to treat displacement as permanent and to provide funds for skills training and citizenship in the adopted country. According to journalist Lyn Shepard, the primary SAD guideline "is . . . to resettle refugees

Table 1   Alternative Projections of the U.S. Population,
                 by Race/Ethnicity, 2000–2040 (in millions)

| | WHITE | | | | | | |
Year	Total	Non-Hispanic	Asian	Black	Hispanic	Other	Total
2000	224.6	196.7	12.3	35.5	30.6	2.4	274.8
2020	250.6	206.2	23.1	45.7	49.0	3.2	322.6
2040	268.6	205.6	35.0	56.4	69.8	4.1	364.3

SOURCE: Edmonston and Passel, eds., *Immigration and Ethnicity*, p. 345.

permanently in their 'land of first reception'—countries usually similar in culture to their abandoned homelands."[11]

Resettlement programs such as SAD's are humane and relatively inexpensive. A refugee can be resettled, retrained, and made self-reliant for a tenth of the costs of establishing his or her asylum in the United States or a European country.[12] It was therefore irresponsible of the Central Intelligence Agency to offer asylum to more than two thousand Kurds who worked for the agency in northern Iraq; the Kurds should have beens resettled in the region and not brought to the United States.

Discussions concerning immigration raise the wider question— what kind of a United States do Americans want for the future? Statisticians in the Census Bureau forecast that, by 2050, whites will barely form a majority and that Hispanics will be the largest minority in the country, exceeding black Americans (see table 1). We ourselves do not think much of such forecasts. For instance, such predictions take little or no account of lower birthrates for immigrants or of intermarriage with other social groups. The intermarriage rate is high both for Latin and Asian people in the United States; the rate, moreover, goes up from one generation to the next. The United States will certainly be more ethnically and racially mixed in future than at present. None can

---

11. See the *Christian Science Monitor*, 1 March 1995, p. 11.
12. Ibid.

be sure, however, how this amalgam will be composed, especially as future immigration patterns may change in an unexpected manner. If the number of immigrants is reduced, bilingualism stopped, and Americanization encouraged, there will be no danger to U.S. unity.

In all probability, the United States will not, in decades to come, stick to the present arbitrary system of racial classification. To give an imagined example: Juan Gomez, a blonde Castilian from the Argentine, is accounted a Hispanic and hence eligible for affirmative action privileges. By contrast, João Gomes, a dark-haired Brazilian of mixed Portuguese, African, and American Indian descent, is *not* classified as a Hispanic. Gomes describes himself as "white" in the census form and is *not* therefore eligible for affirmative action benefits. To pass from imagined people to a real person, the king of Spanish-language entertainment in the United States is Don Francisco (whose variety show, *Sábado Gigante*, is the longest running in TV history). Don Francisco's real name is Mario Kreutzberger. As a Hispanic, Don Francisco could claim affirmative action privileges, were he inclined to do so— but his forebears, from whom he inherits his German name, could not have done so were they alive today. Political lobbies no more agree on what should be a proper classification system than do demographers. (For instance, the National Council of La Raza believes that Hispanics should be considered a race. Other Hispanic activists, by contrast, reject such a simplistic classification. Some Americans of multiple origin now call for a "multiracial" category, a request rejected by bodies such as the NAACP, which fear a reduction in their clientele.)

Bilingual Education: Yes or No?

Bilingual education has failed to achieve its original objective of teaching children English; now the education bureaucracy wants to teach Hispanic-surnamed children Spanish. The Center for Equal Opportunity's president and CEO accuses bilingual education advocates of being politicized and taken over by cultural activists. The result is that bilingual education has failed and has undermined the future of the Hispanic children it was meant to help.[13] The guiding principle of bilingualism is "cultural maintenance," and some enthusiasts want Spanish to be a second national language. Yet the evidence is clear that Hispanics taught in bilingual programs test behind peers taught in English-only classrooms.

The problem began in 1976 when the Supreme Court, in *Lau v. Nichols*, ignored two hundred years of English-only instruction in America's schools and said that students who did not speak English must receive special treatment from local schools. This allowed an enormous expansion of bilingual education, from $7.5 million to $8 billion a year. In 1968 the U.S. Office for Civil Rights bilingual education advocates had begun a small program to educate Mexican American children; by 1996 it had expanded enormously, to $8 billion a year. The initial objective to teach English to Spanish speakers for one or two years was perverted into a program to Hispanicize the Latinos, not to Americanize them. The federal program insists that 75 percent of tax dollars be spent on bilingual education, that is, long-term native-language programs, not English as a second language. Asians, Africans, and Europeans are in mainstream classes all the time and receive extra training in English as a second languge programs for a few hours a day. Hispanic students, in contrast, are taught in Spanish for 70 to 80 percent of the time. New York is especially irresponsible in this regard, forcing children with Spanish surnames, even those who speak no Spanish at home, to take Spanish and at least 40 percent to stay in Spanish classes.

Some critics of bilingualism claim that the vast majority of Spanish speakers want their children to be taught in English, not Spanish, and do not want the U.S. government to keep up Hispanic culture and

---

13. See Jorge Amselle, ed., *The Failure of Bilingual Education, 1966* (Washington, D.C.: Center for Equal Opportunity, 1997).

language. The bilingual bureaucracy at local and federal levels wants to Hispanicize and capture federal funds for schools. Meanwhile, African, Asian, and European students achieve higher academic scores, in part because they are not wasting time on Spanish language and culture and failing to master the language of the marketplace and higher education—English. Since there are seldom enough bilingual teachers, Asians and Arabs and Europeans go right into classes with English-speaking students. They score higher and graduate more often than bilingually taught Hispanics. The Center for Equal Opportunity's book shows the dangers of bilingual education and demands its reform. Otherwise the United States will become deeply divided linguistically and be stuck with an Hispanic underclass who cannot meet the needs of a high-tech workplace because their English is poor.

Recent Mexican immigrants have lower educational attainments than earlier immigrants, on average, by about two years of schooling (i.e., eight years to less than six years). The recent immigrants are also older. Mexican Americans on average have a lower educational level than non-Hispanic whites and have a higher proportion of high school dropouts and a lower proportion of college attendees. Still, both percentages have improved somewhat in recent years. The low level of Latino educational attainments is an indication of their lower level of social incorporation and economic success.

Since Latino immigration is likely to continue in the future and since Latino fertility levels are high, the Hispanic population will grow. The economic costs of not adequately educating Hispanics will be great, and their economic well-being will be lower than if they were to stay in school longer and focus on English, not on bilingualism, according to Edward Lazear.[14] Lazear argues that much of the anti-immigrant rhetoric in America is generated by government policies that reduce the incentives to become assimilated and emphasize the differ-

---

14. Edward P. Lazear, *Culture Wars in America*, Essays in Public Policy series (Stanford: Hoover Institution Press, 1996).

ences among ethnic groups in the population. Examples are bilingual education and unbalanced immigration policies that bring in large numbers of Asians and Hispanics, who move into large and stable ghettos.

Rosalie Pedalino Porter, a bilingual education teacher for more than twenty years, is convinced that all limited-English-proficiency students can learn English well enough for regular classroom work in one to three years, if given some help. The old total immersion system still works best; the longer students stay in segregated bilingual programs, the less successful they are in school. Even after twenty-eight years of bilingual programs, the dropout rate for Latinos is the highest in the country. In Los Angeles the Latino students dropped out at double the state average (44 percent over four years of high school). Special English-language instruction from day one gets better results than Spanish-language instruction for most of the day.

Hispanic activists now call for limited recognition to be accorded to Spanish—*inglés y más* (English and more) runs the slogan. (Official documents of various kinds are now printed in Spanish and other languages as well as English. At the Democratic convention of 1996 speeches were given in Spanish as well as English.) If this course continues, the demand for recognition of Spanish will inevitably change into a demand for recognition of Spanish as an official language. Such a transformation would give great benefits to Spanish speakers in public employment but leave Anglo-Saxons at a disadvantage. Bilingualism, or multilingualism, imposes economic transaction costs. The political costs are even higher. We do not wish, therefore, the United States to become a bilingual country such as Canada or Belgium, which both suffer from divisiveness occasioned by the language issue.

We also insist on a higher degree of proficiency in English than is at present required by applicants for naturalization in the United States. A citizen should be able to read all electoral literature in English—no more foreign-language ballots! For similar reasons, we oppose those educators in publicly funded high schools who regard as their task maintaining the immigrants' cultural heritage. Such endeavors should be left to parents, churches, "Saturday schools," the extended family. The public school's teacher is to instruct students in American culture. English plays a crucial role in cultural assimilation, a proposition evident also to minority people. (In Brooklyn, for example, the Bushwick Parents Organization went to court in 1996 to oppose the imposed Spanish-English education of Hispanics in the local public schools, arguing that this instruction would leave their children badly disadvantaged when they graduated.) As Ruth Wisse, herself a distinguished educator, puts it, before we encourage ethnic language revivals in the European manner, "we should recall what millions of immigrants instinctively grasped: that English is the most fundamental pathway to America's equal opportunities."[15] (The European experience is likewise clear. "In general, mother-tongue education is unrealistic and unsuccessful. The children of immigrant parents rapidly acquire the language of their country of residence, and are often less comfortable and successful in their parents' mother-tongue.")[16]

A Center for Immigration Studies *Backgrounder* (April 1996) asks the question, "Are immigration preferences for English speakers racist?" The center answers in the negative because one-third of humanity has some knowledge of the English language and most of these people are nonwhite. Although the immigration bill in the House and Senate had an English requirement for certain employee-based categories of immigrants, it was removed lest it discriminate against nonwhites.

Knowledge of English is an acquired, not an inherent skill—any-

---

15. Ruth Wisse, "Shul Daze," *New Republic*, 27 May 1996, p. 19. According to the 1990 U.S. census, the U.S. population stood at 253,451,585. In 1975 the total number of legal immigrants amounted to 386,194. By 1993 this figure had more than doubled, to 904,922 (not counting illegals). An annual immigration rate of two per thousand would still let in more than half a million every year. Reduced immigration would facilitate the assimilation of immigrants in this country. In case of need, the number of legally admitted newcomers could be increased.

16. Zig Layton-Henry, *The Politics of Immigration: Immigration, 'Race' and 'Race' Relations in Post-war Britain* (Oxford, Eng.: Basil Blackwell, 1992), pp. 223–24.

one, white, black, or brown, can learn English. Immigrants line up to learn English because they believe that learning English will improve their prospects—and it does, significantly. English is the most widely used language in history. English is the language of science, technology, diplomacy, international trade, and commerce. Half of Europe's business deals are carried out in English, and more than 66 percent of the world's scientists read English. The world's electronically stored information is 80 percent in English. The world's forty million Internet users mostly communicate in English. Experts conclude that one-third of mankind speaks or understands some English. Selecting immigrants on the basis of some command of the language therefore cannot be discriminatory.

No economist, no social planner, can tell with confidence the ideal number of immigrants that the U.S. economy should accept each year. But if it is the United States' political aim to assimilate immigrants into a single nation, annual immigration must be kept in bounds; we suggest not more than two per thousand of the population during any one year (ca. 500,000 a year). For political reasons, the United States should also ensure a diversity of immigrants—not too many (perhaps not more than 10 percent of the total) from any one country in every single year. Regular immigration could be supplemented once again by a bracero or guest-worker program to assist agribusiness in the Southwest if a real labor shortage were to occur.

In conclusion, we reiterate our preference for an immigration policy designed to attract newcomers with skills, technical qualifications, and capital. We wish to preserve the United States as a free market society based on the rule of law, a Western, not a "world," nation. We reiterate that assimilation should be the United States' national object—not the ethnicization of America. We reject race as a criterion for admission to the United States—better Nelson Mandela black than Joseph Stalin white! We observe with pleasure that assimilation and intermarriage are ongoing processes. We are pleased that ethnic separatists at U.S. universities have not had much success in converting to their own viewpoints those popular masses for whom the ethnic elites profess to speak. Compared to any other multinational state on this globe—be it Nigeria, Russia, Cyprus, Sri Lanka, Ethiopia, Bosnia, or whatever—the United States has been the most successful society. The United States can rightly demand that immigrants be loyal to its language its laws, its flag, its constitution. Only those who accept this proposition merit welcome. The biggest challenge facing the United States and the new immigrants is adaptation because they are so different from previous immigrants, who came from Europe. The acceptance of immigrants by native-born Americans is crucial to their adaptation. The current rise of an immigrant-baiting mood does not bode well for a quick, peaceful integration of the new immigrants.

The new immigration bill strengthens enforcement measures at the border, but more enforcement authority is needed in the workplace and to stop illegal entry at airports, smuggling, and document fraud. The INS should process political asylum seekers and illegals more quickly. All ports of entry must also be strictly watched, and the abuse of claims for political asylum at these ports of entry should be better controlled. Heavy penalties for illegal immigrants who arrive as students, tourists, or businesspeople but stay on should also be enforced. Employer sanctions should be repealed as unenforceable. Those who come in illegally should be caught, punished, and deported quickly. The computer verification system is expensive and unworkable and could lead to a national identification card. There should be generous quotas for the admission of skilled immigrants but smaller quotas for refugees and unskilled non-English speakers. Sponsors of immigrants should face tough financial requirements and should not be able to use welfare benefits for ten years.

In 1997 Congress should reform the policy for legal immigrants, as Congress has already done for illegals. No more amnesties for illegal immigrants! Family reunification only for youthful members of a nuclear family, not for adult members! Legal immigration should be cut to 400,000 to 500,000 newcomers a year (still a generous quota). This number should include refugees and skilled immigrants. Affirmative action programs should be terminated. Welfare should be denied to immigrants for the first ten years of their residence in this country. Census categories such as "Hispanic" and "Asian" should be replaced by national origin classifications. The time for legal residence for naturalization should be extended to ten years. The children of illegal immigrants born in this country should no longer be automatically entitled to U.S. citizenship. English only should be required in the law, in government, in schools, and in the political system. No long-term bilingual education programs should be mandated; a transition year or two can be provided for those who do not speak English. Then English only in all academic courses but foreign languages should be studied. "Becoming proficient in the language of America is a price that any immigrant should want to pay."[17]

To conclude: overall, most contributors to this volume see immigration as a positive force that throughout American history has brought men and women of talent, drive, and energy into our country. These immigrants have enriched our economy and culture. Since 1965 immigrant flow has shifted from Europe to Latin America and Asia; with the legalization of undocumented immigrants in 1986 and then two laws in 1996 forcing citizenship on legal immigrants in order to preserve their welfare benefits, Congress has dramatically changed the dynamics of immigration and citizenship with as yet unknown consequences for the United States. In addition, the drying up of jobs for the unskilled reduces America's needs for uneducated immigrants while increasing the need for skilled, legal immigrants.

---

17. *Issues '96*, p. 355; for reforms of the U.S. immigration, see chap. 11, pp. 333–57.

Conference Agenda and Participants

HOOVER INSTITUTION CONFERENCE
The Debate over U.S. Immigration

Stauffer Auditorium
Herbert Hoover Memorial Building
Stanford University
October 17–18, 1996

Agenda

Thursday, October 17

1:30 P.M. **Welcome**
John Raisian, Director, Hoover Institution
Introduction
L. H. Gann, "Current Crisis in Immigration and Refugees"

1:45 P.M. **Benefits and Costs of Immigrants in the United States**
Moderator: Thomas Gale Moore
Panel: Frank D. Bean, "Hispanic Experience"
Bill Ong Hing, "Asian American
Experience"
Philip Martin, "Mexican Experience"
Julian Simon, "Benefits of Immigrants"
Georges Vernez, "The California
Experience"

3:45 P.M. **Arguments for Limiting Immigration**
Moderator: Annelise Anderson
Panel: Peter Brimelow, "Case for Limiting
Immigration"
Peter Skerry, "Immigrants, Bureaucracies,
and Life Choices"
Comments: Norman Matloff

Friday, October 18

8:30 A.M. **Overview of Federal Immigration Laws and Policies**
Moderator: Edward Lazear
Panel: Stuart Anderson, "Immigration in the
High-Tech Industry"
Michael Fix, "Immigrant vs. Immigration
Policy"
Stephen Legomsky, "Employer Sanctions:
Past and Future"
Stephen Moore, "Immigration and the Rise
and Decline of American Cities"
Jeffrey Passel, "Undocumented Immigrants"

10:15 A.M. **Costs of Immigration**
Moderator: Kenneth Judd
Panel: Roy Beck, "The High Cost of Cheap
Foreign Labor"
George Borjas, "Welfare Costs"
Thomas MaCurdy, "Welfare"
Harry Pachon, "Costs in California"

1:15 P.M. **Silicon Valley and the Immigration Debate**
Moderator: Nicholas Imparato
Presenter: Joseph Costello, "Technology, Immigration,
and Global Leadership"
Comments: Dado Banatao
Norman Matloff
Ronald Unz
Phil White

Conference Participants

ANNELISE ANDERSON—Senior Research Fellow, Hoover Institution,
Stanford University

STUART ANDERSON—Former Director of Trade and Immigration
Studies, Cato Institute, Washington, D.C.

DADO BANATAO—Chairman, S3 Incorporated, Santa Clara,
California

FRANK D. BEAN—Population Center, University of Texas, Austin

ROY BECK—Washington Editor, the *Social Contract*, Washington,
D.C.

GEORGE J. BORJAS—Professor of Public Policy, John F. Kennedy School of Government, Harvard University

PETER BRIMELOW—Senior Editor, *Forbes* and *National Review*

JOSEPH B. COSTELLO—President and Chief Executive Officer, Cadence Design Systems, San Jose, California

PETER DUIGNAN—Senior Fellow, Hoover Institution, Stanford University

MICHAEL FIX—Urban Institute, Washington, D.C.

LEWIS H. GANN—Senior Fellow, Hoover Institution, Stanford University

BILL ONG HING—Visiting Professor, Boalt Hall School of Law, University of California, Berkeley

NICHOLAS IMPARATO—Research Fellow, Hoover Institution, Stanford University; Professor of Marketing and Management, McLaren School of Business, University of San Francisco

KENNETH JUDD—Senior Fellow, Hoover Institution, Stanford University

EDWARD LAZEAR—Senior Fellow, Hoover Institution, and Jack Steele Parker Professor, Graduate School of Business, Stanford University

STEPHEN H. LEGOMSKY—Charles Nagel Professor of International and Comparative Law, Washington University School of Law, Saint Louis, Missouri

THOMAS MACURDY—Senior Fellow, Hoover Institution, and Professor, Department of Economics, Stanford University

PHILIP MARTIN—Professor of Agricultural Economics, University of California, Davis

NORMAN MATLOFF—Professor, Department of Computer Science, University of California, Davis

STEPHEN J. MOORE—Director of Fiscal Policy Studies, Cato Institute, Washington, D.C.

THOMAS GALE MOORE—Senior Fellow, Hoover Institution, Stanford University

HARRY PACHON—Thomas Rivera Center, Pitzer College, Claremont, California

JEFFREY PASSEL—Director, Program for Research Policy, Urban Institute, Washington, D.C.

JOHN RAISIAN—Director and Senior Fellow, Hoover Institution, Stanford University

JULIAN SIMON—Professor, College of Business Administration, University of Maryland; Senior Fellow, Cato Institute, Washington, D.C.

PETER SKERRY—Professor, Political Science and Public Policy, Claremont McKenna College; Visiting Fellow, Brookings Institution, Washington, D.C.

RON UNZ—Cofounder, Wall St. Analytics, Palo Alto, California

GEORGES VERNEZ—Director, Center for Research on Immigration Policy, the RAND Corporation, Santa Monica, California

PHIL WHITE—Chairman and Chief Executive Officer, Informix Software, Inc., Menlo Park, California

INDEX

affirmative action programs: failures of, 49–50; public opposition to, 15–16; racial classifications and, 277; terminating, 284

Agrawal, Anant, 238

agricultural guest-worker programs, 15

Aid to Families with Dependent Children (AFDC), 43–44, 122, 138, 139. *See also* welfare system

Aiyetty, George, 237

Alien Nation (Brimelow), 34, 36, 102, 103, 111

American Immigration Lawyers Association, 31

American Mathematical Society (AMS) survey, 234, 235

Americans for Family Values, 18

amnesty law (1986), 17, 43, 259, 264

Anderson, Stuart, 224, 258

Arizona Republic, 163

Asian immigrants: coming to California, 58; described, 4–5; diversity of, 7; earnings of native-born vs., 229; economic achievements of, 24; English as second language programs for, 278–79; intermarriage rate of, 276; national origin classifications for, 284; as newcomer majority, 4; rising number of, 33, 114; using SSI, 74–75; welfare system and, 126, 136

Aspen Institute Quarterly, 148

assimilation: English language role in, 281; melting pot through, 37; new immigrant rejection of, 37–38; use of welfare system and, 129–30, 141–42

asylum law (1997), 272

asylum seekers, 116–17, 128, 270, 273, 275

Aztlán (mythical nation), 42

Baird, Zoe, 172

Barjas, George, 110

304

voter fraud, 41–42
Voting Rights Act of 1965, 15
voucher programs, 134, 138

wages: of California immigrants, 62–63; cheap labor supply and low, 46, 152–54; of foreign-born skilled employees, 225–28; issues of U.S. agriculture, 80–81; of raisin grape agriculture, 95–97; ratio of immigrant to native-born, 64; of skilled immigrant vs. native born, 226–31. *See also* income
Wall Street Analytics, 258
Wall Street Journal, 234
Walt Disney, 242
Warren, Robert, 194
Washington Post, 152, 153
welfare reform, 156–58, 209
welfare system: assimilation and use of, 129–30; average monthly probability of receiving, 136–37; California executive order (1996) on, 21; elderly immigrants and, 10, 44, 47, 74, 269; immigrant costs related to, 29–30, 42–44, 135–41; immigrant households on, 122–31; immigrant restriction from, 20, 268–69, 284; legalization to maintain access to,

269; national origin groups and, 125–27; native-born households and, 123–25; percentage of dollar benefits to immigrants by, 138; Personal Responsibility Act restrictions on, 76; political refugees and, 275; refugee households and, 44, 127–28, 130–31; restoration of immigrant benefits (1997) from, 266–67; survey of income and, 131–35; used by foreign workers, 147–48
Wells, Amy Stuart, 213–15
Wilks, Gertrude, 40
Williamson, Jeffrey, 153, 154
Wilson, Pete, 21, 41, 88, 209
Wisse, Ruth, 281
"Without Braceros, Tomato Growers Will Slash Acreage" (*California Farmer*), 99
Wong, Gil, 11
Wood, Kimba, 172
worker wage advocates, 80–81
Workforce, 2000, 19

Yardley, Jonathan, 160
Yuhjtman, Ehud, 230–31

Zero Population Growth activists, 9, 23